Emotional Intelligence in Schools

This text presents a methodical, organized approach to counseling students in emotional intelligence (EI) by detailing how to understand and direct emotions, while also keying counselors directly to the underlying emotional motivations behind the behaviors. Divided into four units, the book starts with an overview of emotions and continues to explore the nature of anger, fear, grief, and guilt. Chapters present both explanatory narratives and teen-centered activities to show how these challenging, uncomfortable feelings when unregulated may negate resiliency and lead to anxiety, bullying, depression, and teen suicide. Counselors and educators alike will benefit from the light, unexacting tone that encourages humor and levity and discusses how to handle difficult emotions without harsh and heavy overtones.

Katherine Krefft, M.Ed., Ph.D. began her study of emotions as a classroom teacher. In four decades as a clinical psychologist she subsequently evolved a positive view of our most challenging emotions of anger, fear, grief, and guilt. Sharing those understandings with counselors, teachers, and administrators, she offers systematized instruction for adolescents designed to develop emotional resiliency and widespread emotional literacy. She continues to embrace the education that private practice as a psychologist affords.

Emotional Intelligence in Schools

A Comprehensive Approach to
Developing Emotional Literacy

Katherine Krefft

Routledge
Taylor & Francis Group

NEW YORK AND LONDON

First published 2020
by Routledge
52 Vanderbilt Avenue, New York, NY 10017

and by Routledge
2 Park Square, Milton Park, Abingdon, Oxon, OX14 4RN

Routledge is an imprint of the Taylor & Francis Group, an informa business

Library of Congress Cataloging-in-Publication Data
A catalog record for this title has been requested

ISBN: 978-0-367-17549-8 (hbk)
ISBN: 978-0-367-17552-8 (pbk)
ISBN: 978-0-429-05739-7 (ebk)

Typeset in Bembo
by Swales & Willis, Exeter, Devon, UK

The learned will shine
As brightly as the vault of heaven,
And those who have instructed many in virtue
As brightly as stars for all eternity.

Daniel 12:3[1]

1 *The Book of Daniel, The Jerusalem Bible*. A. Jones (Ed). Garden City, NY: Doubleday; Darton, Longman & Todd, 1966.

To Faith, who lives her name

Contents

Tips

Preface

Emotional intelligence is emotional truth. Whether you just want to understand the teenage years better or simply embolden your work with teens, this book is for you. *Emotional Intelligence in Schools* is for all educators, from counselors and school psychologists to superintendents, principals, and vice-principals. Health teachers charged with incorporating mental health into the overall health curriculum will find content that illuminates the hearts of teens. The framework of this book mirrors the adolescent developmental tasks of individuation and community through the prism of emotions. Every teacher may use this book as a handbook to interacting with emotive, temperamental, moody teens.

This is a guide book for educators to learn how to develop emotional intelligence, EI, in high school students. With adaptation *Emotional Intelligence in Schools* may be used in any group or class setting. These include prisons, residential treatment and foster homes, substance abuse rehab centers, parenting education, and all 12-step groups. The concepts may be taught by a school system master teacher to large groups of teachers or counselors who will then bring the material to their schools.

First as a teacher and for 40 years now as a clinical psychologist, I have listened to hurting human beings. This book is an introduction to all they have taught me about what it means to be human. Listening to similar stories over and over has educated me about how mind and emotions work together to create behavior. My schooling started when teaching primary, elementary, and high school. When I reached the central office of a school system, ever escalating teen deaths by overdose and suicide propelled me to search for the mechanisms within ourselves that generate such behavior. I believe you will see as you read, I am now what I was then: a teacher at heart.

Decades as a clinical psychologist have led me to see emotions as the pivotal missing link. Emotions are difficult. Those of us born in the twentieth century have often experienced an area of life that is naturally difficult, our emotions, as woefully painful. Those born in the twenty-first century have the opportunity to experience emotions constructively and authentically. Challenging emotions will always bring some heartache and discomfort. But they do not have to be experienced as the overwhelming, seemingly uncontrollable drivers of behaviors such as addiction, suicide, and mass shootings.

Emotive intelligence is not intelligent if it does not lead us to being comfortable in our emotional skin. We have gone the route of pretending we are purely mental creatures, all cognition and reason. We have presumed that we were purely behavioral, all stimulus and response. There is one area left, the one we know but fear to know: emotions.

In the late 1980s a door began to open. This followed the work on multiple intelligences by Howard Gardner, who had presented emotional skills as one of the intelligences.[1] It also followed the foundational work of Albert Ellis,[2] whose model of A, B, Cs presented the *what* to do in order to initiate mental-emotional transformation in cognitive therapy. *Emotional Intelligence in Schools* in a further A, B, C model presents *how* to inculcate these principles in the young.

When that new door opened fully in the 1980s, anger management was defined. At last keen zeroing in on the unmentionable topic, emotions, had begun. Brave pioneers like Daniel Goleman and John Mayer offered the concept named EI, emotional intelligence, to the world in the 1990s.[3] Of the three aspects of our humanity—thinking, emotions, and behavior —we saved emotions until last. Sociologists may long debate why we did so, but we did. When we began, we went right for the hard one, anger. But there is more than one challenging emotion, and all require more than mere managing.

Acts of violence are acts of anger. Strong emotion drives suicide and substance abuse no less than mass shooting. But let us not now imagine that well-developed EI will absolve society from correcting its ills or substitute for values education. If a teen is being sexually assaulted at home, no set of lesson plans on emotion is the answer. The solution is to stop the abuse. Then lessons to develop emotional intelligence will greatly aid in healing. Hunger and lack of nurturance at home unaddressed will yield only empty eyes and steely stares as you attempt to impart knowledge about anger and fear and grief. Even so, such instruction may inspire the youngster to reveal how bad it is so that tangible help may be given.

Although this is not a values education curriculum, EI development does include teaching what is okay to do when you're emotional and what is not okay to do. Public schools may concurrently teach a values curriculum that centers on teaching kindness, helpfulness, and patience as well as honesty, truthfulness, and non-violence. Private schools may teach EI material concurrently with religion classes, Bible school, and lessons on the Ten Commandments.

Knowledge about comfortably directing emotions was missing from the upbringing of many adults. Ignorance led us to deny, repress, and reject emotions. In selecting this text for guidance you are choosing to reject the ignorance of the past. The concept of EI came at the end of a century of spinning a vast array of theories of mind and behavior. All the while we have seen one certain fact made plain to us—denying our human emotions is not the way. Denial has not helped. Perhaps it is largely responsible for bringing us to where we are. With hope we move forward with education that integrates the rational, thinking creature with the vulnerable, emotional being we all live with every day.

Notes

1 See Gardner's *The Development and Education of the Mind*, particularly Chapters 8 and 9 on multiple intelligences. New York, NY: Routledge, 2005.
2 There are many books by Albert Ellis (1913–2007) that explicate his A, B, C school of Rational Emotive Behavior Therapy. Developing emotional intelligence in the young follows Ellis's concepts in order to assure that no matter the activating event (A), the consequence (C) will follow an emotionally intelligent belief (B). For Ellis's own explanation of his therapy see his *Better, Deeper, and More Enduring Brief Therapy: The Rational Emotive Behavior Therapy Approach*. New York, NY: Routledge, 2013.
3 Daniel Goleman's pioneering 1995 *Emotional Intelligence* (New York, NY: Bantam) is available in multiple languages worldwide. His 2011 *The Brain and Emotional Intelligence* is a convenient eBook (Kindle Books, Amazon Digital Services). For Mayer's groundbreaking contributions see John D. Mayer and Joseph Ciarrochi (Eds.), *Applying Emotional Intelligence, A Practitioner's Guide* (New York, NY: Routledge, 2007) for a research-based exposition on developing, nurturing, and measuring EI.

Introduction

Emotional intelligence is not born into us. It is learned. What is learned may be systematically taught. Pure, physiological emotion is born into us. Our human emotions constitute a body of information that may be examined, systematized, and taught like any other school subject. Methodical, organized instruction into the nature of emotion and how to constructively develop and direct emotions is affective education, the purpose of this book.

Emotional Intelligence in Schools aligns with modern cognitive science. Experienced teachers have long known what neuroscience now demonstrates about the neuroplasticity of the brain. Actual images of the learning brain show that structured, practice-driven, repetition-based methods drive neurons to fire together and thereby to wire together. Such permanent wiring is called learning.

Purchases of *Emotional Intelligence in Schools: A Comprehensive Approach to Developing Emotional Literacy* may meet Title I and Title IV guidelines. Using it in your school will assist in compliance with emerging state laws that mandate explicit instruction addressing behavioral health issues and the ever escalating rate of teen suicide.

Collaborative Teaching

Many teachers may participate. One lead teacher may study the material and then enlist others. The lead teacher, who may be the health teacher, school counselor, school psychologist, or any designated instructor, presents the core concepts to teens. Other teachers integrate that material into their content areas.

A collaborative approach sends the message to students that all of the adults care about them as emotional beings. In both chapter narratives and the activities at the end of each chapter, multiple suggestions are offered to include language arts, social studies, science, art and music teachers as well as coaches into a school-wide strategy to develop EI. A full interdisciplinary, collaborative approach interweaves the topics between and among academic areas.

For example, the social studies teacher may teach the entire Mind Tricks segment in Chapter 11 with expansive use of examples from history, as in the

Reason and Emotion in History activity. At the same time the language arts teacher may assign activities that involve writing stories, poems, short essays, journaling, and, additionally, apply the lessons learned to analysis of the great works of literature already being taught. The music teacher may share songs about sadness and great classical music that throbs with anger, such as some movements of Wagner's symphonies. The art teacher has a palette of choices —pictures, paintings, and sculpture that all express the rainbow that is our emotions. Van Gogh's works alone are a stunningly comprehensive treatise on the soaring range of our emotions.

Science teachers may embrace the role of critical change agents in moving the next generation away from history's collective myths and misunderstandings about emotion to science-based facts. The brain is our largest and most critical organ of emotion. The science teacher is superbly placed to teach the biology of emotion. A vision of the future is a youngster turning to a teacher to cry, "Adrenaline and cortisol are flooding me!" rather than "I can't take it anymore!" Constructive action may be imposed on adrenaline and cortisol, namely, intense exercise. But what is the solution to "I can't take it"? What, indeed, does that even mean?

School coaches and resource officers may be enlisted as pivotal facilitators to teach pouring strong emotion into intense physical activity. Students who fight who are made to sit still in chairs outside the principal's office may simply be stewing in anger. Punishment and suspension may allow anger to continue, perhaps to mount to rage.

Rather, consider giving angry students the option to go immediately, well supervised, to the gym to work off their adrenaline and cortisol through intense physical exercise. Not to fight each other whether in boxing or wrestling—ah! so twentieth century. Rather to learn from respected adults that a real man, a real woman expels fiery emotion in simple but direct and powerful *solo* physical exercise. Such exercise is not punishment. It is the solution, one that expels the visceral rush of the emotion. Discussion of anger's reasons and remedies is pursued only after muscle fatigue quenches the flow of hormones.

If your school or community is impacted by a tragedy like suicide, fatal accident, overdose, or shooting, a collaborative approach with at least the unit on grief is strongly recommended. When all the adults actively participate in helping youngsters process the emotions stimulated by the event, that in and of itself communicates, "We're all in this together. We will all help one another. We will get through this together." When adults not only speak consoling words but demonstrate pulling together in their actions, that teaches "This is the way to handle such unspeakable tragedy." The tragedy is horrific enough. Going through it alone or in silence compounds the heartbreak and fosters the possibility that the underlying emotions will be buried in denial.

I hear the groans of teachers, "Ay! Another thing they want us to teach!" These grumbles may lessen when we consider that we all have emotions and deal with them, in ourselves and in our students, every day. Is it not better to learn to constructively handle those emotions than to continue in the denial of our ancestors? The content and activities herein are designed with constant mindfulness that teachers do indeed already have enough to do. Thus the activities are replete with ideas on how to integrate content on emotions into what is already being taught. Activities are simple enough for students who serve as teachers' helpers to assemble and organize any materials needed. Indeed, pulling teens into such tasks imparts, "I myself must take action to learn about my emotions."

It used to be said, "Every teacher is an English teacher." Whether or not your school still adheres to that principle, it is now and always will be true that every educator models human emotions. The twenty-first century offers the opportunity to teach how to recognize emotions and constructively express them. It is our privilege as twenty-first-century adults to assert, "Denial ends with us!" and consciously choose not to pass myths and errors about emotion down to the next generation.

Overview and Method

The four units are designed for maximum flexibility. Units present the core challenging emotions, called in the twentieth century negative emotions. But since the potential for anger, fear, grief, and guilt is built into us, continuing to call them negative is to continue the myth that our emotions are intrinsically negative, even bad. Emotions are not negative or bad. They just are. These emotions are difficult and challenging for us, yes. But not negative. EI requires us to reorient such thinking about emotion. All emotion is okay. Some behaviors are not okay.

Because the first four chapters present the fundamentals, their material should be taught initially. Then the units may be taught in the order given or in the order deemed fit. The lead teacher is encouraged to make ample use of the division of the chapters into segments. Teach what feels best to you in the time limits you have, whether in health class, counseling small groups, or individual sessions. This book is an idea farm. Harvest what you like.

The unit on anger includes a format for a comprehensive anger management plan, the AMP, which means both Affect Management Plan and Anger Management Plan. This format may be pulled from each chapter and be used as a separate entity for work with angry or otherwise emotional teens. Be aware you will still find you have many new understandings to impart. Attempting to use some of the activity sheets without reference to the chapter content would be challenging and perhaps confusing. The activity sheets support, extend, and instill the content.

Similarly, a conflict resolution protocol that highlights the emotions inherent in conflict is offered. What is sometimes called problem solving often ignores emotion in an attempt to arrive at rational solutions. *Emotional Intelligence in Schools* presents the framing of the issue as the first challenge to be met. Emotions, correctly named and expressed, are intrinsic to truly more rational solutions.

Novel structures to develop emotional fluency are offered. These tools for organizing knowledge about emotions include the A, B, Cs of emotion, diagrams and charts of the emotive process, categorizing emotions by intensity, and the division of emotion into the categories of valid and invalid. Invalid emotion is real but proceeds from erroneous thinking. When the self-talk behind the emotion is reframed and transformed, the emotion modulates. All bodies of knowledge have structures and tools. When it comes to emotions, these constructs and formulations are still evolving. Nothing in these chapters is meant to be definitive or final. Your own teens may brilliantly evolve the structures herein.

Each chapter is divided into content, activities, and suggestions for bulletin boards. That students keep journals is strongly recommended, as journaling is a powerful tool for discerning and expressing emotions. If your school already uses journaling every day to teach writing, you need only slant what is already being written onto the emotions that may be penned therein anyway.

Content presents the central material to be taught. It would be enormously helpful for all teachers to read through this content. The art teacher must be familiar with the unit on fear before giving a directive to "make a picture that shows fear." Similarly, the social studies teacher with the complete narrative of the unit on anger will quickly see how the material translates to the affairs of nations. Coaches, too, indeed all the school's teachers, must see the value of directing an angry youngster to "Work it out" and "Walk or run it off."

It is recommended that there be no tests or exams on the material. Life is the exam. If taught in health class and a grade absolutely must be given, grade for participation, A, B, C only, meaning highly engaged, moderately engaged, and everyone else. It is precisely the point of your lessons that no one shall fail emotions.

Content is followed by activities. These exercises are the heart of the learning because material is not absorbed until it is applied. If there is to be no carryover to other classes or homework for doing the activities, time for expressive activities must still be found. Better to teach less content and have youngsters pour their emotions into meaningful activities than to have them parrot back the content but never apply it. There is ample enough information about emotions herein to devote each year of high school to its teaching.

Each chapter ends with ideas for bulletin boards. Whether that board is in the health classroom, counselor's office, or hallway outside the cafeteria, these suggestions are meant for more than decoration. Succinct, powerful words are quickly memorized and internalized. They then serve as aids in times of emotional distress. When highly charged with emotions, the mind needs a short, simple directive that is easily repeated over and over.

As we examine self-talk, we shall see that managing emotions requires we learn how to "Give yourself a good talking to."

Finally, for school psychologists, counselors, and others who work directly one on one or in small groups with teens, succinct tips are presented throughout the chapters in **bold** type. Teachers, too, who know they are teaching emerging persons, not just subject areas, may also welcome the tips.

The Power of Words

Embracing the twenty-first century, we toss into the dust bin of history old verbiage used to describe emotion like positive and negative. *Emotional Intelligence in Schools* is rooted in an emotional literacy that reorients use of language toward honesty about emotions. Indeed, language arts teachers may find herein an approach that echoes the foundations of all proficient language skills, starting with precise definitions, expansive use of synonyms, and powerful verbal tools like metaphors. Using our words to express our emotions is the modality through which emotional intelligence shines. Historically, missteps with words have trapped us in emotional confusion and pain.

Science itself teaches us that new discoveries and expanded concepts require fresh language, literally new words and novel usages of old words. So herein we contrast comfortable emotions such as joy, love, and surprise with the uncomfortable, challenging ones of anger, fear, grief, and guilt. New words like "upsetness" and "complexifying" are offered to elucidate twentieth-century strategies for avoiding the naming of emotions.

Similarly, we leave behind the phrase, "Control your emotions." We ditch "coping with emotion." To cope implies enduring and contending with something hard. "Cope with it!" implies, "Put up with the pain." With full honesty we must admit that "Cope with it!" as a command really meant "Shut up already."

We set aside sentences like "I'm stressed out," "I can't take the pressure," and "I'm upset" with direct words that honestly state the emotion. We clarify deceptive, double-meaning words like stress. Assigning multiple meanings to one word leads to the logical fallacy called equivocation. If there is an emergency and you work for 36 hours straight, you will be stressed from sheer physical exhaustion. This is not what is usually meant by stress and never what is meant by the verbal form, stressing. "I'm stressing" clearly means I am feeling emotion.

Our ingenuity in inventing words and phrases to avoid naming our precise emotions has been brilliant. Converting a noun, stress, to a verbal, stressing, came right from our lexicon of denial. The conversion demonstrates more than mere semantic drift but actual change of meaning. As commonly used stress, pressure, and upset are all code for "I'm feeling emotion but not only am I not going to tell you which emotions I'm feeling, I'm not going to tell myself either." And from there the twentieth century expected us to figure it all out.

In these chapters we see that constructive management of emotions moves beyond passively enduring pain or struggling to sort out a muddle of poorly named feelings. Rather, we move to an active mode of constructively handling the emotion. "Handle it!" bears the subtle message "I know you *can* handle it." Being a role model means modeling the words necessary to convey a healthy perspective on emotion.

Incorporating appropriate emotional expression into your daily inter-actions with teens is affective education as much as instruction on the nature of our uncomfortable emotions. A youngster's EI will develop as it reveals itself in the language echoed back to you. As adults, shifting our speech patterns away from the language we grew up with will be very hard. Let us start by accepting that we will slip back into old usages time and again. Yet we begin. For the sake of our children and grandchildren, we begin.

OLD LANGUAGE	NEW LANGUAGE
• For the third time, be quiet!	I feel angry when I have to ask you three times to be quiet.
• Stop that! Someone might get hurt.	It scares me to see you roughhousing because I've seen youngsters get hurt like that.
• Can't you *ever* follow the rules? You're punished!	You know the rules. I feel angry when you don't follow them. Maybe you're angry, too. Let's talk about it.
• What's the matter with you? We spent three classes on this! You all have extra homework tonight.	Now, class, I thought we worked so hard on this. I feel sad that so many of you still have not got it. Help me figure out a way to teach it so everyone is able to get it.
• Who do you think you are to treat someone like that?	I feel angry when I see you treat someone so unfairly.
• You guys let me down. I *told* you to study.	I'm really disappointed with how the class did on the test.
• Read your books. (Silence)	We're going to do some quiet work today. As you know, my father's funeral was yesterday and, frankly, I'm feeling sad and out of energy just now.

Words empower. To say "Class, I'm thrilled you did so well!" is easy. To be honest about one's own uncomfortable emotions is enormously more challenging. Not, of course, those emotions that are intensely personal. But in sharing honest emotional reactions to everyday events, the educator demonstrates allowing, admitting, and expressing emotion. So do we model what we teach.

Critical Role of Laughter and Modeling

Laughter diffuses emotion. Often a silly face is enough to wipe an angry glare off the face of an antagonist. Not always, certainly. But when classes are silly and fun, the laughter imprints the message a hundred times better than a droning monotone. Better than this, the silliness itself communicates, "We do not have to be afraid of this subject."

It is sadly true that in our age many adults are indeed afraid of emotions, of their own, of the emotions of others. In part this is because our emotional vocabulary is so poor. Adults today were taught to fear what they were told they could not name rather than naming what they feared. You will comprehend the meaning of all the words in the word lists herein. They are in your passive vocabulary. But are they in your active vocabulary? Using daily the rich variety of words which name four emotions moves understanding from passive to active. This not only develops but actively expresses emotional intelligence.

However, teaching about emotions with a serious demeanor will only reinforce the myth, "Emotions are hard, scary, painful, too difficult to even talk about." When you have them laughing at your silliness, you'll know they're getting the lesson. The intent is to develop emotional intelligence as the educator diffuses and detoxifies the topic of emotion itself.

Laughter will do this. Make the classes or small groups fun. Wear a red shirt and slacks to teach about anger. Turn the lights off when you teach about fear. If there have been no tragic incidents prior to sharing the content on grief, wear a mock sad clown face. If there has been such an incident, be yourself.

But ordinarily, be light, even silly. Own your own emotions, too. "Class, I'm still catching my breath. Someone cut me off on the way to school and I had to slam on the brakes. I was so scared! My heart is still pumping fast." "Are you mad?" a student asks. "Gosh, golly with fudge on top, I'm mad!" Laughter. In this interaction you have just taught, "We're all human. We all feel. We all may express fear and anger appropriately." Better this than walking into the classroom with a frown on your face, hands fumbling papers. Teens will notice and mistakenly fear they are somehow the source of your visible angst. Be the role model your learners need you to be.

A Goal for the Twenty-first Century

In the twentieth century the field of education took enormous leaps forward. In America we advanced from one out of four graduating high school in 1900 to 89.1 percent graduating in 2000. In 2015 the figure rose to 94.1 percent.[2] Superb curricula in a wide array of subjects, remarkable tech materials, and the best trained teachers of all time advanced education and uplifted the nation.

But issues our great-grandparents could not dream of beset us. School shootings, teen suicide, rampant substance abuse, and downright cruel meanness as shown in all forms of bullying, including cyber bullying, signal to us that something is wrong. Something is missing. What? Emotions. We have omitted directly instructing youngsters about our human emotions. Too many adults have failed themselves by failing to learn constructive emotional expression. We have done so because no one ever taught us to develop our own positive EI.

Working with thousands in psychotherapy over decades, I have repeated the core messages of this content a myriad of times. "I didn't know that" and "I haven't thought about it that way" are common responses to information about emotions. It is time to know. It is time to think about emotions in a new way. It is time for everyone to know their own emotions, to be comfortable with them, to express them consistently in a constructive, healthy manner. It is time to own responsibility for developing our collective emotional intelligence. An impossible dream? So, too, was universal high school education in 1900.

Notes

1 My A, B, Cs expand Albert Ellis's concepts and surely his intention in order to teach healthy emotional expression. The use of my A, B, Cs model I first presented in my 1993 book, *Affective Self-Esteem* (New York, NY: Taylor & Francis).

2 *Fast Facts.* National Center for Education Statistics, Department of Education, 2018. Retrieved from www.nces.ed.gov/fastfacts

Unit I

Emotions

1   Our Emotions

Emotions are as much a part of us as reason. The ability to think we embrace. Down through the ages we have elaborated thinking into a multitude of disciplines and subjects. Every subject taught in school is an area many thought about and used their thinking to systematize. The write-up of all that thinking we call textbooks. Educators have absolutely no issue about accepting the thinking self. College graduates are justly proud of having honed their thinking abilities. Educators prize using thinking reasonably. A broad view of education is that it is a process of teaching the brain to reason and reason well.

Emotions are equally a part of us. But teaching and learning about our emotions lags far, far behind the purposeful development of reason. We have thought that if we just all become reasonable, rational, intelligent beings, the emotions would fall in line. They have not. "But!" we cried, "Emotions are irrational. How may we be rational and emotional at the same time?" Precisely. We begin by using our power to think and synthesize to consider the emotions themselves. Imagine that Emotions is a required course. It is part of the curriculum and you cannot graduate without it. Once upon a time in academia Logic was a required course. No good Roman was considered educated without it.[1]

But a course called simply Emotions? No. No, we don't teach that. The college psychology department may have a course with a title like *Emotion and Motivation*. Even that intrinsically scholarly course may lead the bewildered student at the end of the semester to wonder, "What precisely did I just learn about *myself*?" For the most part high schools and elementary schools have opened the door to didactic learning about emotions through the health curriculum. Concerns about what is called mental health put learning about mental health into the high school health textbook.

But note that we call it mental health. We do not yet name it emotional health. This use of language we insist on even though much behavior deemed wrong and hostile comes from people with perfectly intact reasoning faculties. Depression is labeled a mental health issue even as the emotions involved are ignored in the "Take this pill and you'll be fine" approach. Our history and heritage of denying emotions reveals itself in the very words we use to describe our states of being. We would rather believe we have a mental health issue than believe we have an emotional health issue.

I have heard highly educated people deliver long lectures about subjects inherently about emotions without saying the word emotion once. We talk about being afraid without using the word fear. Anger is almost always named something else. We say we feel bad but almost never "I am grieving." We say we are upset, stressed out, under pressure, and over-whelmed without stopping to ask ourselves if we are sad or scared or angry.

In the twenty-first century developing emotional intelligence must partner with the development of our reasoning faculties. From the perspective of a little distance now we may see the twentieth century as an era when people with high IQs and EQs of zero brought mass pain and suffering into the world. The intelligence that comes from reason is not the full and total answer for peace on earth or for peace within the human heart.

Educators are experts at systematizing data and information, packaging it as a subject area, and inventing the teaching tools necessary to convey that body of knowledge to the young. Parents, even well-educated parents, may not know how to teach a subject area as well as a teacher trained in that area. Parents should certainly adjust their parenting to support emotionally open children. But society's vehicle for conveying a specific body of knowledge to the young is called a school. Schools teach. As with any field of study, we begin with the fundamentals.

Beginning: The Fundamentals

Begin by sharing information about emotions by taking the time to define your terms. This is crucial. Precisely because our youngsters have grown up in a world of denial, the words you use may not convey what you think you are conveying. Asking, "Why are you upset?" only reinforces the teen's existing learning about emotions. The teen's brain, lightning fast, flashes on:

> You, too. So you, too, don't really want to know if I'm angry or scared or sad. Okay, I'll play the game. You want me to talk about events and people and things outside of me. You want me to tell you who said what to whom when.

So they do. In a 20-minute discussion the emotions may not even be named.

Our culture muddies the water by loosely using the word feeling to sometimes mean an emotion, sometimes mean a bodily sensation, and just to be sure we are all befuddled, sometimes mean an opinion. The word stress as used makes no distinction between the body's response to physical and physiological exertion and its response to emotions. Perhaps we may evolve toward a culture wherein stress only names the former, never the latter.

Work toward discernment about emotions by defining the simplest terms. These are the words feeling, fact, and emotion. Focus on basic words that convey core concepts. We do not want teens to fear they may come up with the wrong answer. In an emotionally intelligent world, all know there is no such thing as a wrong emotion. We feel what we feel. What we do is what may be right or wrong.

A display that lists the words feeling, fact, and emotion may be helpful. In initially working with this topic, accept spontaneous answers even if they reveal only what the culture has taught. After teens have given their spontaneous answers, they may enjoy using their phones to look the words up. In a counseling session the counselor may display a tablet or computer screen with a dictionary engaged.

As we will see, teens are hard at work on their developmental task of individuation. In extreme form this means behavior adults label oppositional. The last time they were so heavily committed to rebellion was when they were two and three. Right at the introduction to teaching teens about emotions avoid ego battles. When you define a word and the teen snarls, "No, it doesn't mean that!" know that you have inadvertently stepped into that teen's whirlwind of individuation.

Step out. Better, don't step in at all. When adults insist on being right, the teen's individuation drive pushes them to assert their truth even when that truth is in error. When adults insist on making teens see the error of their ways, the individuation drive pushes them to rebel. Adults may think they have won that battle with the teen. But we have lost. We lose when we take any action that undermines what nature is driving.

We lose because we cannot defeat nature itself. Nor should we try. Flipping the issue in a way that respects the teen's individuality uses that same drive to individuation to assist the adult's goals for the teen. We are supposed to be smarter than our teens. We may fight their sneaking use of phones in class or tell them to get on their phones to find a dictionary.

The adult must choose first. Just as with a two-year-old, the adult structures the choices. Then the teen picks from those choices. Being on the phone to text an absent friend is not on the menu. But using a tool that came with their cradle does not mean the phone is smart. It means the adult is. Counselors who begin a session with "Take out your phone" immediately elicit a smile and build rapport. Its right use is assured if you ask the phone be put down on the desk in between use and not continuously held in the hand or hidden under a jacket in the lap.

So we have our first two tips for working with teens.

Sidestep ego battles.

Build rapport by using familiar tools.

After teens offer their first guesswork answers, revise the chart with the understanding learned from online dictionaries. Compare and contrast the before and after answers. Feelings include bodily sensations. Examples are tired, hungry, sleepy, hot, cold, and itchy.

Feeling	Emotion	Fact

The above display may read: itchy for a feeling, angry for an emotion, and "The sun rises in the east" for a fact. If the teen comes to the counselor straight from a class, ask for one fact learned in that class. "The play was written by Arthur Miller" is a fact.[2] "Algebra is stupid" is not. Ask, "What emotion goes with the idea that algebra is stupid?" Look for anger whenever the word stupid is used. Its use is one of those backward ways of saying "I'm angry" without saying I'm angry. Behind the anger may be the fear I do not have the intellectual capacity to comprehend algebra. "Algebra is stupid" is teen code for "I fear I am too stupid to get algebra, and I'm angry about that."

As you continue, point out that the word feeling is also used loosely to indicate emotions, opinions, and beliefs. Beliefs are omitted as a separate category from the chart, as delineating them may lead discussion too far from an introductory level. Beliefs are configured in the brain as learned self-talk.

"I feel sad" states an emotion. "I feel dictatorship is bad" states a belief as does "I don't feel like you're listening." Ask for other examples. Feelings explored with counselors are generally emotions, not beliefs or bodily sensations like hot and cold. In some circumstances it may indeed be appropriate to first ask, "Are you hungry?" Even well-fed teens are hungry right before lunch. Admit "I know we're both hungry" and offer water before you continue with the real business of your session.

Encourage critical thinking and quick online research to resolve disputes between "It's a feeling" and "No, it's a belief or opinion." The very existence of dispute over the meaning of the words feeling, emotion, fact, and belief reveals our collective mass confusion about our emotions.

Emotions Are Like Magic

Teens enjoy fantasy. Their devoted enjoyment of a range of fantasy themes reveals that superheroes and villains, wizards and vampires, and games with castles and thrones speak of a realm the real world denies, rejects, and disparages. The best literature, too, offers adults the same world, the world of emotions. Thus, it may at times be helpful to speak of emotions as we would of magic.

Emotions and magic are alike in the following ways:

- Both *transform* one thing into another.
- Both are *powerful* and *frightening*.
- Both may be *hidden* and not always be what they appear on the surface.
- Both produce effects by *unseen, invisible* means.
- Both give special ability to *control* events.
- We have many *misunderstandings* about both.
- Both are *mysterious, surprising, enchanting, puzzling*, and never cease to amaze and *fascinate* us.

It is up to the educator how much reference is made to magic as a teaching tool. But if a youngster expresses their fascination with a certain fantasy theme, the opportunity presents to compare and contrast the magical themes with the teen's real-world issues. Whether a theme of magic appeals to a youngster or not, before proceeding with learning about emotions, we must first confront a legion of misunderstandings.

Misunderstandings and Myths

In the discussion some teens may give responses that are myths about emotions. Generate further comments by inquiring, "What common misunderstandings do you think people have about emotions?" Asking what people believe instead of what the teen believes depersonalizes the subject. The request is for misunderstandings. No self-respecting teen wants to admit to misunderstanding anything. The adult conspicuously appears to blame society or the brain, anything but the teen, so that the teen may grow into new understanding, "Well, wait! I'm part of society, too. And believe it or not, I know I have a brain, too." To augment this approach, let's name the brain our Brainy Boo. This tactic develops understanding without engaging the teen rebel within.

Such misunderstandings and misinformation are the legacy of the twentieth century. Today's young people will appreciate with delight your calling the beliefs of the past "old-fashioned." Old-fashioned means the olden days before cell phones. Teens already think of the past as being hopelessly antique. A savvy health teacher or counselor may use this bias throughout their contact with teens to embrace new information and reject ancient ways of thinking as being as derelict as phones with cords and eight-track tapes.

Emotions Are Animalistic and Degrading

The belief that emotions are animalistic and degrading is Misunderstanding One. Humanity has held this opinion of itself from time immemorial. In this belief emotions are seen as making us uncool at best and nonhuman at the worst. Share examples of such disparaging remarks.

Stop being so emotional.
Don't lose your cool.
Don't give in to your lower self.
He's so strong, he never shows how he feels.
He was as mad as a bull.
She was whimpering like a wounded animal.
He was laughing like a hyena.
Poor scared lamb.
You scaredy cat, you're a wimp.
To a boy: You're a girl, you pussy.
A girl's lament: I'm too sensitive. I'm weak.
If I feel bad feelings, I'm bad.
I'm not strong like some people. I'm so emotional.
Emotions are humanity's basest instincts.

Emotions Are Irrational and Self-Destructive

Misunderstanding Two is that emotions are irrational, dangerous, and self-destructive. Nonrational is different, not bad. Emotions are a necessary counterbalance to cold reason. Emotions are neither positive nor negative. Emotions simply are. As Pascal said, "The heart has its reasons which reason does not know."[3] Some examples of this myth follow.

I was so upset I was going crazy.
He's insane when he's mad.
I was scared out of my mind.
I must be stupid to let this get to me.
Don't let your emotions get the better of you.
It breaks my heart.
I'm quite shaken.
I'm falling apart.
Emotions called negative emotions exist.

Emotions Are Just Tools for Control

Misunderstanding Three is a much favored myth. Believing that people who show emotions are merely manipulative is a form of denial. People who believe this are themselves afraid of emotion. Here are some examples of the myth.

> You're upsetting me.
> People stir up my emotions just to be mean.
> You really know how to push my buttons.
> You make me so mad.
> You're stressing me out.
> You're bringing me down.
> I can't help the way I feel.
> I need someone to make me happy.
> If I feel that way, I'll do something terrible.
> She makes me feel guilty.
> Stop putting so much pressure on me!
> Keep it up and I'll hit you.
> He scares me.
> She's a drama queen.
> Other people have emotions in order to control me or have impact on me.

- **Journaling—My Challenges**

Assign teens to write about items like these in their journals.

○   What emotions are my greatest challenges?
○   What misunderstandings might I have had about emotions?
○   What myths about emotions do people in my family have?
○   What emotions do I most prefer?

If there is strong collaboration between the counselor and the language arts teacher, all such writing exercises throughout the school year may carry over to language arts. Whether the writing is paragraphs, essays, stories, or poems, all express our drive to convert emotion into words. If the writing is done for a language arts class, then, yes, spelling does count as do all principles of good writing. If done only for the counselor, responses that reveal a grasp of the concepts are primary.

By this exercise you are beginning the shift away from stating what not to do with emotions to "Here's what *to* do." Language is one of humanity's primary modes of constructive emotional expression. The other primary mode is the nonverbal. For example, turning raw emotion into a touching poem takes intelligent thought. Thus, the act of writing itself marries emotion to reason. Renowned poets are great not because they used iambic pentameter but because they beautifully expressed emotion.

If some of the teens you are counseling like to write, they are handing you a magnificent tool to help them. Your directive to them is "Write it out. Don't act it out." Unless, of course, the drama club is their thing. Then, of course, the emotional saga may be acted out. As we will see in Chapter 10, if sports are the teen's thing, it is imperative to teach that working out the emotion means working out. The development of emotional intelligence requires that each teen discovers what is going to be their primary, lifelong mode of positive emotional expression.

- **Small Group—Knowing My Emotions: Activity 1.1**

When working with a small group, have each member complete Activity 1.1 individually. Then the group may elect a leader to report on the results by summarizing what has been written. Alternatively, the activity may be completed as a group, assigned as homework, or completed when the youngster comes early for a session. Be mindful that at this point nothing has yet been shared specifically about anger, fear, grief, and guilt, so accept a wide range of responses.

- **Sleepwalking Through Life: A Fable**

Knowing little or nothing about our emotions and about why we do what we do, we may sleepwalk our way through life. This activity is designed to develop an awareness of why a study of emotion is constructive. Have a student Google the word fable and explain the fable as a literary form. Display what is discovered.

Then divide the class into two groups. Instruct each group, "Work together to invent a fable about a character who lived his or her whole life asleep! That's right. Every morning this person seemed to wake up, but actually the whole day was spent sleepwalking."

Groups work independently of each other. However, members of a group work together to compose their fables. As you circulate to supervise the groups, share prompts like "How did she show anger while sleepwalking? Was he afraid? Happy? What happens to emotion when you're sleepwalking?" At this initial point it is okay if answers widely vary. Have one member of each group read or tell the fable to the class.

Compare and contrast the results. Conclude by asking, "Know anyone who is sleepwalking through life?" Without clear knowledge of our human emotions, we all are.

- **Once I Was Upset**

Upset describes many emotions including fear and grief. Often "I'm upset" is a backhanded way of saying "I'm angry." Let learners discover this on their own by writing a short essay of three to four paragraphs titled *Once I Was Upset*. Notice that here we are purposefully using the word upset.

Instruct teens to "Describe a specific incident when you were upset. What did you mean when you said you were upset? What emotions were you feeling when you felt upset?" Essays may be read aloud at the end of this class period or beginning of the next.

Ask what particular form of upsetness was felt. **Upsetness** is not in the dictionary, but it is a useful word to force focus on the failure of the word upset to name emotion.

If the majority of the essays describe anger first and fear second, the counselor sees which emotions that group most needs to be addressed. If eight out of ten essays described anger, the counselor has the opportunity to state, "So a lot of upsetness is anger. Looks like we are going to have to learn a lot about anger."

- **Doing versus Being Bad, "I'm Bad, I'm Bad, I'm Really Bad": Activity Sheet 1.2**

Assign the activity sheet titled with the name of the classic song by Michael Jackson. Google the song to play it as introduction. If the activity yields nothing but blank looks and blanker papers, shift to fantasy. "Write a fairy tale about someone who was bad using the activity sheet as a guide." Teens may also enjoy finding a current song that articulates lyrics about bad behavior.

Center focus on the emotions behind the bad behavior. It may surprise students to learn that some of their favorite rap songs express not only anger but fear. Challenge your teens to imagine what fears lie behind the rage of the lyrics. Songs loved by teens in any age sing out the emotions of that age. As such, popular songs are excellent teaching tools to demonstrate stripping away the cool façade to the fears, disappointments, and shame behind the rage.

Using the classic song also presents a focal point for understanding the word bad. No emotion is bad. Mad, scared, sad, and shameful teens do sometimes act out in bad behavior. It is the educator's task to accept the emotion while always drawing the line at the behavior.

- **Universal Upsetness: Activity Sheet 1.3**

The counselor and the language arts teacher may both engage students with this activity. Given that "I'm upset" means "I'm feeling emotion but I'm not going to name which one it is," great literature is an excellent vehicle for developing not only the usual literacy but emotional literacy as well. Your teens may choose the story, book, or poem, or you may simply use whatever work is currently being taught in language arts class.

The activity sheet may be used as a guide in two ways. For the counselor, short answers may be given on the sheet as it is. For the language arts teacher, the guide may first be used to develop an outline from which a coherent essay may be written as a longer-term assignment.

For example, have students Google "Why was King Lear upset?" Probing the true emotions of the upset character in one coherent paragraph or essay teaches character delineation whether the character is King Lear or Ron Weasley. Start with the word upset and connect it with specific emotions.

Redefine the word upset with questions like "What was King Lear afraid of? Why was he mad? Was he sad? Was he guilty about anything?" For *The Merchant of Venice* you might comment, "This is a play about a great deal of upsetness." Break down that melee of emotions with questions like: Why is Shylock angry? What does Portia fear? What characters grieve? Who might feel guilty? Do they? How does fear of the different one become intolerance? Language arts instructors will immediately see how these questions will quickly help learners connect emotion to character delineation. Further insight comes from asking how each of these emotions drives the plot.

This exercise may be applied to whatever literature is being studied in the curriculum multiple times throughout the school year. It appears that our eminent authors were emotive beings acutely aware of the interplay and impact of emotion. Today's teens may discover a dormant love of Shakespeare when they realize his works are about emotion and, most specifically, about *their* emotions.

Throughout the year use the bulletin board to add pictures, stories, and sayings that relate to emotions.

BULLETIN BOARD MATERIAL

Emotions are neither good nor bad. They just are.

Emotions are our magic!

The heart has its reasons which reason does not know.

Pascal[3]

Notes

1 For a review of classical Logic see Susanne Bobzien's insightful synopsis, *Ancient Logic, Stanford Encyclopedia of Philosophy*, 2016. Online at www.plato. stanford.edu/entries/logic/ancient/ Note how Logic insists on an analytical and highly precise use of words. So does the field of study, Emotions.

2 Miller, A. (1915–2005). *Death of a Salesman*. (Harmondsworth: Penguin Books, 1996). This masterwork (1949) explores deep emotions like anger.

Its drama makes stunningly clear the connection between anger and suicide. As such, it may be used as a vehicle to teach teens how to handle suicidal thinking. What other steps might Willy have taken to *Handle It*? See my chapters on grief.

3 Blaise Pascal, 1623–1662, said, *Le coeur a ses raisons, que la raison ne connait point.* In *Pensees, Edition de Port Royal XXVIII* (1670), p. 263. Retrieved from https://fr.wikisource.org/wiki/Pens

Name: _____   Date: _____

Activity Sheet 1.1
KNOWING MY EMOTIONS

Complete the following sentences. If necessary, you may continue a long sentence on the back of this sheet.

1. I feel happy when_____

2. I feel afraid when_____

3. I get mad at_____

4. I feel good about_____

5. I feel sad about_____

6. I am surprised when_____

7. I feel delighted when_____

8. I feel excited about_____

9. I feel guilty when_____

10. I feel self-satisfaction when_____

11. When I'm happy, I_____

12. When I'm mad, I_____

13. When I'm in love, I_____

14. When I feel sad, I_____

15. When I'm contented, I_____

16. When I feel guilty, I_____

17. When I'm excited and elated, I_____

18. When I'm afraid, I_____

19. When I'm surprised, I_____

20. When I'm content, I_____

21. Right now I feel_____

Name: _____ Date: _____

Activity Sheet 1.2
"I'M BAD, I'M BAD, I'M REALLY BAD"

People are *not* bad, but they sometimes do unacceptable things. Think about something you once did that later made you feel very bad about yourself. Describe what you did.

_____

_____

Now think carefully. What were you feeling *before* this incident occurred? Angry? Scared? Hurt? Jealous? Sad? Circle your answer and tell about any other emotion you felt.

_____

_____

What was your self-talk *before* the incident? The quotation marks show that the self-talk is what you say to yourself in your head. Self-talk is your thinking word by word.

" _____

_____ "

Was some of your self-talk coming from a wounded ego? Hurt feelings? Or because you felt put down? If so, write the self-talk here.

" _____

_____ "

Was some self-talk coming from a belief you had been treated unfairly? Write it here.

" _____

_____ "

What were your emotions *after* the incident? Your self-talk?

" _____

_____ "

Think of a more constructive plan for handling the emotions and self-talk that led up to the incident. If you like, ask for input from a friend. Describe that plan on the back of this sheet.

Activity Sheet 1.3
EXPLORING UNIVERSAL UPSETNESS

Answer these questions about a story, fairy tale, novel, or poem, or about a song or movie showing strong emotions. Consider all the emotions, not just those on the surface.

What emotion or emotions predominate in the story? How do these emotions develop? What emotions drive the plot?

Does the lead character resolve these emotions? How? What is the outcome?

Imagine you know the thoughts, the self-talk, of the lead character(s). What were they saying to themselves *before* they felt the emotion?

What was their self-talk *after* they felt the emotion?

Were any emotions transformed or changed in the story?

Suggest a better ending to the story.

2 Emotions and Reason

A simple model for youngsters to understand the different qualities and aspects of reason and emotion is The Head and The Heart. Old language goes out the window in emphasizing the dichotomy of comfortable and uncomfortable emotions, which in the past have been called positive and negative emotions. Emotions are not negative or bad or base. They are simply human. As humans we have the power to choose feelings. We do not snap. We make choices. The natural, water-like flow of emotions provides opportunity for teens to be expressive by collecting pictures of water, whether print or digital, and by telling, writing, and illustrating stories related to the pictures.

In talking about key misunderstandings about emotions, focus on that student's own particular misunderstandings. Normalize their responses by commenting, "Sure. Many people believe that. But we're in the twenty-first century now so we have to get past those old myths." Teens often fear they are not normal, not like everyone else, somehow abnormal, out of step. It is normal for teens to feel not normal. This yields a tip.

Normalize the teen's feelings.

All feelings are okay. Some behaviors are not okay. Thinking one is not normal is actually an example of thinking one's fear instead of feeling the fear. Fear is felt first and then converted into the self-talk (the thought), "I must not be normal." Much maladaptive emotion that is converted into unacceptable behavior comes from thinking one's feelings in order not to feel the raw emotion. With teens, who have only had the capacity to employ logic and reason for seven or so years, this brings many false conclusions and errors in thinking. If you smiled because of the implication your students have been rational for seven years, well, then, all the more reason the culprit is the thinking.

In modern psychology the prominence of cognitive behavioral psychology stems from the critical link between behavior and thinking. Behavior is overt. We see it. Thinking is invisible inside the head. We do not see another's thinking. Centering almost solely on behavior in child rearing and in discipline, we literally announce to youngsters "I don't care what you are thinking. Nor do I care what you feel. Just behave." In the past this approach has been seen as simple and straightforward. Its advocates would maintain, "Well, we do want them to behave, don't we?"

Decades of this approach have not eliminated substance abuse on or off campus or violence in schools. An approach not yet widely tried is to make the invisible visible. The thinking invisible in the head and the emotions invisible in the heart propel behavior. Some may say they cause behavior. But while understanding the process, I believe it is truer to say thinking and emotions drive behavior. The car does not cause itself to drive. The driver does that. But without the structure of the vehicle and gas in the tank, you are just sitting in the driveway.

While holding the line on behavior, we move in the twenty-first century into directly and overtly caring about the invisible **self-talk** and challenging, unseen inner emotions. We do so not because, as some may accuse, we want the whole world to be touchy-feely, but because getting to the thinking and emotion behind the behavior is the equivalent of not only taking the keys away but also of simultaneously draining the gas tank. With a group of friends the car might still be moved. But at that point walking would be faster.[1]

Emotions drive behavior. Self-talk directs behavior. With our self-talk we create our emotions. The linkage between self-talk and emotion is so acute that it often feels to us that the emotion just arises spontaneously. We must stop ourselves and think. We must ponder questions like "What was I thinking that, when he said that to me, I got so mad?" We must look within and search for our inner fear-based thinking. "What is it about that matter that scares me so much?" If not raised as children to value and share emotions, such questions may initially feel very difficult to answer.

So, making clear the difference between reasonable thinking and emotion-driven self-talk is critical for helping youngsters change their behavior. Behind that behavior is always emotion and behind the emotion is the self-talk that creates the emotion. When you are addressing one of those teens who loves to "play dumb" as a defense against engaging with you, remind them we are talking about 3 steps—not 30 or 300. If it did indeed take 30 steps for us to understand ourselves, yes, we would be in trouble. But we need grasp three and only three things: self-talk, emotions, behavior.

A useful tool is a whiteboard or chalkboard in your office. Whether on a board or tablet or computer screen, display the following.

The Head	The Heart
Reason	Emotion
Thinking	Feeling
Logic	Intuition
Facts	Imagination
Judgment	Inspiration
Reflecting	Sensing
Detachment	Passion
Science	Art
Mathematics	Music
Grammar	Poetry

Engage in a dialog about the various ways we demonstrate this polarity in life and in ourselves. A completed chart may look something like the one above. Alternatively, share a printed copy of the chart.

Conclude by pointing out that only a combination of both The Head and The Heart in balance generates the fullness of human potential. When working with a group, demonstrate this graphically by drawing circles that connect each pair.

Use the pairs to invite teens to personalize the chart. "How do you show the thinking side of you? The feeling side? What subject or activity speaks loudest to your thinking self? To your feeling self?"

Comfortable and Uncomfortable Emotions

When initially working with a teen, share that some emotions we call *comfortable* because they feel good. Those that do not, we call **uncomfortable**. Admit that in the olden days of the twentieth century we called these positive and negative emotions. But a new century calls for new understanding.

Engage with your teens about which emotions are comfortable and which most uncomfortable in particular. Some comfortable emotions are love, happiness, excitement, pride, surprise, joy, delight, and satisfaction. However, since teens are beginning a lifelong journey to experience and comprehend what it is to be an emotional being, these emotions, though usually affirmative, may not always be comfortable. Love may be confusing and scary. For those who have been abused, happiness comes with fearful caution as the person wonders when the other shoe is going to drop and the joy evaporate.

Yet in general the main uncomfortable emotions are the ones that are the focus of our learning: anger, fear, grief, and guilt.

The Power of Choice

After engaging teens in considering comfortable vs. uncomfortable emotions, point out that both you and the student chose whether to list or center attention on a comfortable or an uncomfortable emotion. Stress that each of us has the same power, the power of choice, but our decisions and self-talk, our choices, may differ. Our emotions differ accordingly.

In both individual and group sessions accept all discussion uncritically. You are only at the beginning of helping your charges to develop discerning judgment about emotions. Students cannot be expected to possess refined judgment about emotions yet. So we begin with this tip.

All emotions are okay. Some behaviors are not okay.

Be clear about what these words mean. Before emotional intelligence is well developed, it may seem to the individual that emotions are spontaneous, powerful, and swiftly propel action. Thus, the cry, "I couldn't help myself." But this is an illusion and, indeed, a lie. Rational beings *can* help themselves. They may also make a choice not to do so.

In a century when our heads were filled with misunderstandings and errors about emotion, a time when we were taught no useful tools to handle and direct our emotions, it often did feel like, "I just couldn't control myself." Knowledge about emotions is power to positively embrace and direct emotion. We don't expect students to know what photosynthesis is until they are taught what it is. But many adults today, though never taught what to do with emotions, were nonetheless expected to possess that knowledge.

So all emotion, while it remains emotion only, is indeed okay. It is when the emotion propels action, inappropriate action, that we enter the realm of not okay. Anger is a prime example. Share with your angry student that feeling angry, being angry, even being very, very angry is okay. "You shouldn't be angry" is often meant to be helpful. But if you stubbed your toe and are really angry about it, well, then you're just mad. It's just emotion. But if you then forcefully kick the offending object, you have crossed over from the realm of pure feeling to the realm of action. Volatile young men have been known to punch telephone poles when mad. And end up in the emergency room with broken digits. Not okay.

A more extreme example is anger at someone. Share with your students that it is okay to be so angry at someone you find yourself fantasizing about hurting them. However, no matter how angry you are, it is not ever okay to actually hurt them. Explain to angry students that such fantasies and self-talk like "I wish she was *dead*!" are signs your inner anger is intense. The pot is about to boil over.

Such fantasies and self-talk are cues that it's time to engage our reason. "I must be a bad person that I'm thinking like this." No, but thinking like that means you are overdue with expressing your anger in a safe way. "Come see me whenever you're that angry and we'll talk about it," a counselor might advise. Thus, a person may learn to see even what are called horrible thoughts as signs that they must sooner rather than later expel the emotion in a safe, constructive manner.

Understanding how to safely and constructively express emotion and consistently applying that knowledge develops emotional intelligence. School counselors and health teachers are critical change agents in helping each youngster find, develop, and invent their personal toolkit of lifelong modes of constructive emotional expression.

The Natural Flow of Emotions

The downside of counseling is that it and all talking engages only half the brain. Teens, being at the beginning of developing their rational selves, often respond better and more quickly to The Heart, that part of us that naturally gravitates toward imagination and passion and the expressive arts. A picture does indeed speak more than a thousand words.

If you have the capacity to work with the school art teacher, images of water may be found, drawn, and painted. In any case, as a visual, water is fundamental to our understanding of emotion. Adults of the twentieth century are often afraid of emotion, their own and that of others, because they do not know that the fluidity of emotion means it comes with peaks and valleys. Commonly, these adults may think, "If I let myself cry, I won't be able to stop," and "If I let myself be really mad, I don't know what I'll do." This nonsense about emotion does not belong in the twenty-first century. Rather, seeing emotion like the waves of the ocean helps us understand that there is a crest of the emotion, a peak of the wave. But always and inevitably that peak is followed by a trough, a more quiet smooth flow. Yet, then again will come another crest.

Misunderstanding this natural, wave-like flux led twentieth-century people to conduct emotional lives in which they built dams against the crests. Also, when another crest followed the quiet trough, the complaints wailed, "Not again! How can I still feel this way? She died last week!" and "I can't believe I'm still so mad about that. That happened years ago." Tragically, too many twentieth-century people mistook the crest for the whole ocean. Believing the lull between the waves would never come or believing there was something drastically wrong because the tide kept coming back led many twentieth-century people to despair.

There is nothing intrinsically wrong when painful emotions arise again and again. The surfers have it right. Ride the wave. Hence this counseling tip.

Talk emotions first. Then problem solve.

Show a variety of pictures of water in its many aspects: turbulent (angry), stormy (fearful, angry), empty and vast (lonely, fearful, sad, awesome), calm (peaceful), underwater depths (awesome, fearful). Such visuals help silent teens share their emotions. With each picture ask, "Of what emotion does this picture remind you?" Expect a wide range of responses.

With these images explain that the natural flow of emotions is wavelike. Illustrate by using a picture of gentle waves or a digital video of waves on a shoreline. "We experience one wave of emotion, then a lull like the trough between waves, then another wave followed by another trough. It is a process of peaks and valleys."

Emphasize to those you counsel that to experience currents of emotion in an on-off, on-off fashion is usual and normal. The tide goes in. The tide goes out. When it comes to emotions, the flow comes and goes until by constant and consistent expression of the emotion, we reduce it to a lapping low tide and sometimes even to a trickle. Grasping this understanding while yet a teen will go a long way toward solid and lifelong emotional intelligence.

Building Dams versus Going with the Flow

But frequently we do not go with the flow. Rather than allowing ourselves to experience the ups and downs, we build dams. Images on the internet make it easy to find photographs of actual dams like the Hoover Dam to make the point.

All kindergarten teachers know Show and Tell elicits more sharing than Sit and Speak. So, too, teens may respond better to visuals and interactive sessions. Sitting and being expected to talk and talk may be inherently distasteful to teens who have been lectured and lectured. Additionally, not yet having the vocabulary of emotion, they may struggle to find the precise words to name their feelings. In either case silence may result.

Thus, proceed to engage the teen with visuals. Ostensibly, you are talking about pictures. "What effect does a dam have on the flow of water?" Continue,

> Where is the water the deepest, in front or in back of the dam? What would happen if water built up behind the dam with no release? But what happens when a steady flow of water is channeled through the mechanisms of the dam?

A channeled flow produces what is good and productive, like hydroelectricity, the power to make things happen. But too much undirected water in one place at one time is destructive, a flood.

Then share:

> It's the same with emotions. When we let them build and build with
> no release, they flood out suddenly. That makes us feel out of control.
> But when we go with the flow and allow ourselves to feel the feeling
> wave by wave, we may direct and channel our emotions ourselves.
> We feel in control.

The reservoir of emotions is like a powerhouse that makes life electric.
Emotions are the electricity that motivates us to get things done.
Emotions are the currents that make life exciting instead of boring.
Since today's teens are fast leaving the legacy of the twentieth century
behind, they will more quickly than their adults grasp and embrace the
concept that the wavelike flow of emotion is natural, normal, and the
only way to be.

At this point your students may be ready for personal examples. "Tell
me about a time you let your emotions build up until they erupted like
a flood." Examples of anger will be easy, but prompt understanding that
fear, sadness, and even guilt may be buried and ignored until they burst
out in a seemingly overwhelming flood.

Continue, "And what did you do then? Did you get drunk? Or high?
How did that change what you had been feeling? But how did you feel
when you sobered up?" If you know or even just suspect that drug use or
alcohol abuse are issues, connect these escapist behaviors right back to the
emotions they are meant to bury. "Do they? Do they really make the
emotion go away?" When sober, we have to admit that while substances
may swamp the emotion temporarily, they do nothing to the self-talk
behind the emotion. Nor does substance use do anything to constructively
express the painful emotion. Hence, a cycle may begin that may lead all
the way to overdose or suicide.

Ordinarily, we dam up only uncomfortable emotions. Since comfortable emotions like joy and love are pleasant, we readily express them.
We reject uncomfortable emotions because they are hard, painful, and
challenging—a process of pain avoidance. Thus, another term for
uncomfortable emotions is *challenging emotions*. Denying painful emotions is sometimes labeled as bad. Putting a moral judgment on denial of
an emotion is no better than putting a moral judgment on having that
emotion in the first place. While pushing away uncomfortable emotions
is not bad but only human, we may all learn more emotionally intelligent
modes of handling emotion.

Silence in Sessions

Silence communicates. The challenge is to discern just what it is communicating. Teens, enmeshed as they are in their task of becoming individuals,

often rebel mightily to prodding to speak, speak. My words are private, personal, even magic. Precisely because they reveal my thoughts, I prize them. They are *my* thoughts. Mine. A silent person is a powerful person. The silent one claims individuality and independence by refusing to engage.

Silence may also be anger. The eyes and face will tell you. Silence in a scowling face with glaring eyes is angry silence. This is relatively easy to address with the comment, "So I see that you are really mad." The student will either agree and tell you why or bark out, "I'm not mad!" which gives you the opening to remark, "So, then, just what *are* you feeling?"

If the eyes continue angry, intense is that anger. If the eyes soften, anger is giving way to the deeper emotion. Offer to help. "I know it is sometimes very hard to say how we feel. I'd like to name some emotions and you pick one, okay?" Mention fear, sadness, guilt, and yet again anger. Share that you know there are more than four emotions but you want to start with those that give most people the most trouble most of the time.

If silence yet continues, the teen is claiming the mountaintop, planting his flag and daring you to come take it. Don't play. You're bigger, older. You will win. And you will lose because you win. It never serves in the long run to deprive teens of their individuality. Do so, even just try to do so, and they will be just itching to ambush you. They will not cooperate. By winning you have declared yourself to be fully separate and apart from them, a power over them. This they already knew but secretly hoped was not the total truth of the matter. By winning you have squelched the hidden hope that the teen might ally with you as one human being with another. As far as the teen's developmental task of community goes, you have just announced that you are not part of his community group.

This silence is not resistance or stubbornness. It certainly does not mean the teen is at risk. Rather, silence may arise as a function of the tasks of individuation and community. These drives are innate. You cannot derail them. Fight them and you are fighting human nature. You will lose. All adults may do is direct them. And that is everything. Direct, foster, support, and enhance what nature insists upon. Gently direct the teen's developmental tasks by stepping lightly and even playfully.

Teens are old enough to know when a social situation requires speech. The teen is struggling or would not be silent, mute, struck dumb. Lighten the mood. Recognize the teen's independence and unique individuality. You have more of a chance that teens will come down the hill and lay down their flags if you validate what they are doing instead of fighting it. Remember if you choose to fight by insisting on speech, you are at odds not with that teen but with human nature.

Validate silence. "You don't have to talk. We can just sit together quietly for a few moments." In a few moments shift to a nurturing mode. "Oh, while we're sitting quietly we can eat some candy. I have some in my desk." This is not snack time in your office. This is purposely casting the teen's mind back to the time he was a child and candy from an adult was a sign of affection and nurturance. It is your own silent invitation, "Come down off your little mountain. Lay down your flag and let's just be two human beings together." You are communicating that you accept his individuality and yet are indeed part of his community group.

Another technique is to have a Talking Stick or Magic Wand on your desk. The one who holds the stick or wand is the one who talks. This is a useful tool when you are counseling a teen who rolls the other way and is a motor mouth. When you hold the wand, the student's role is to listen. When the teen holds it, their role is to speak. Reign in the motor mouth by silently holding out your hand for the wand. Communicate your expectation for speech by handing the teen the wand or gently pushing it toward the student.

If silence yet follows, that is your cue to say, "I guess you don't want to use your power to speak today. I'm sorry you're hurting so much." The talking stick or wand is a real, tangible symbol for the fact that we each possess sole authority over our thoughts, feelings, and actions. If all talking strategies fail, shift to expressive communication like art and music. Subsequent chapters offer ideas, like The Red Crayon activity in Chapter 8.

- **Journaling—The Tale of the Time of the Flood**

At the beginning of journaling early entries must contain factual information about emotions. Journals are usually thought of as tools to write about one's feelings and life. But without specific, factual information informing the writing, words may ramble. This may be useful for preliminary expression of feelings. However, without movement toward understanding emotions, journaling may go on well beyond high school with only rudimentary insight gained.

The particular type of journaling suggested here includes note-taking just as the student takes notes in class. Those notes are then applied. "Write down the information we discuss. Then write how it applies to you. Don't worry. I'll help you with all that. That's my job. That's why we're going to be meeting together." Just talking generally about emotions helps the teen in the moment. But the goal is to develop emotionally intelligent beings who will soon, by the knowledge you share, be able to help themselves with their emotions, not just now in high school but for life.

Teens write a short *Tale of the Time of the Flood*. The tale tells of someone who let emotions build up until they flooded out in a torrent. Display the four uncomfortable emotions (anger, fear, grief, and guilt) as you give the assignment. Stress clear identification of the emotions that caused the flood. Tales like the pictures may be posted or otherwise shared.

- **Small Group—Fairy Tale of the Magic Water: Activity Sheet 2.1**

When working with small groups use the collection of pictures of water to have the group compose a Fairy Tale of the Magic Water, Activity Sheet 2.1. The tale may be told orally or written like a book with a short paragraph accompanying each illustration. Explain that the narrative should relate feelings to the movement of the water. In the fairy tale water may be like a magic mirror. For example, "When the prince became angry, the waves pounded the boat."

Like all fairy tales this one begins, "Once upon a time there was a_____of Magic Water." Using the illustrations, teens decide which of the following words or synonyms fills in the blank: ocean, lake, pond, river, brook, creek, stream, pool, lagoon, drop, dribble, trickle, drip, torrent, wave, current, flood, bead, teardrop, etc.

First, display these words and students' ideas. Then add names of the major characters, prince, princess, witches, wizards, and so on. As the teens compose the story, repeatedly ask, "What was the character feeling at that point? How did the water reflect that emotion?"

- **Small Group—Our Cheating Hearts: Activity Sheet 2.2**

Assign the activity sheet at any point while instructing about emotions. Throughout the school year the sheet may be used as a format for connecting behavior back to emotion. Share feedback in small groups.

- **Displaying the Head versus the Heart Artwork**

Students who enjoy artwork and choose to exhibit it publicly may either alone or in groups of three or four design and craft posters or displays illustrating the difference between The Head and The Heart. A large heart may represent The Heart while a profile or outline of a head may represent The Head. List the appropriate qualities on each.

- **The Quest for Your Magic Water**

Direct your students in between sessions to search for their own unique picture of Magic Water, a photograph or drawing of a scene of water that has special, personal appeal. Instruct them:

You are not going to choose the picture. The picture is going to choose you! For this to happen you must *listen* with your inner ear for the picture that whispers, "Take me. I'm the one. I'm your picture of Magic Water."

If your student loves drawing or any mode of artistic expression, they will apprehend that the picture must just flow out of them.

Suggest a menu of approaches. Frame the picture. Draw or construct a special, magic frame. Or write a dialogue with the water speaking in first person and the writer speaking in third person. The story might begin, "I am Water. I am magic for [name of student] because ... ."

Another approach is to suggest that the student take the name Seeker and ask questions like, "Water, why am I so sad so often? What do I do when I feel like a hurricane? Will my little boat sink in the storm?" Elicit similar questions from the student. Or perhaps, the student would prefer to draw or paint the picture.

A group of students' expressive productions may be posted on hallway bulletin boards anonymously. But some may be so proud of their creations they want to put their names on the work. A title for the bulletin board might be *Emotions Are Like Water.* If some students are happy to share their creations, collectively this will broadcast to every student who sees them, "We all have emotions. And that's okay. Emotions flow like water. We're learning how to constructively channel them." The very act of finding or making a picture or creative expression is itself a constructive channeling of the underlying emotion. In requiring this Show and Tell approach, you are communicating, "See. You *can* express your emotions in a positive way."

BULLETIN BOARD MATERIAL

All emotions are okay. Some behaviors are not okay.

You have power over your mind—not outside events.
Realize this, and you will find strength.
Marcus Aurelius[2]

Notes

1 For a classic on self-talk, see the 1986 *What To Say When You Talk To Your Self* by Shad Helmstetter, Ph.D. The 2017 version updates the original (New York, NY: Gallery Books). His integration of cognitive science with neuroscience is *The Power of Neuroplasticity* (Charleston, SC: Create Space Independent Publishing, 2014). Both are exemplars of many books available to science and health teachers who choose to root knowledge of emotions in the science of the brain and human physiology.

2 The quote retrieved from section five, *Your Rational Mind is Your Greatest Asset,* online at https://dailystoic.com/meditations-marcus-aurelius/ Marcus Aurelius was a second-century general, emperor, and author of *Meditations.* An eternal prototype for self-improvement books, this work espoused cognitive behavioral science long before our behavior evolved to dissecting our cognitions. For a general explication, see Rachana Kamtekar's enlightening *Marcus Aurelius,* revised December 22, 2017, in *Stanford Encyclopedia of Philosophy* (*The Metaphysics Research Lab,* Center for the Study of Language and Information. Stanford, CA: Stanford University, 2016). Online at https://plato.stanford.edu/entries/marcus-aurelius/

Name: _____   Date: _____

Activity Sheet 2.1
FAIRY TALE OF THE MAGIC WATER

Write a fairy tale about Magic Water. These questions may help.

- What kind of Magic Water is it? Where is it?
- Why is it magic? Who uses its magic?
- What does Magic Water look like? Sound like?
- How does it feel? Does it have a taste, texture, or smell?
- How is it used? Who made it into Magic Water?
- Why is it important? Why is it important *to you*?

You do not *have* to use these questions, but you may if you like.

Once upon a time there was a _____ of Magic Water._____

_____

_____

_____

_____

_____

_____

_____

_____

_____

_____

_____

_____

Name: _____ Date: _____

Activity Sheet 2.2
OUR CHEATING HEARTS

We lie, cheat, and steal for many reasons. But often we use dishonesty as a way to express a strong emotion. Complete this sheet with ruthless inner honesty!

1 Tell about a time you were afraid and lied.

_____

_____

2 Tell about a time you were mad and lied or stole.

_____

_____

3 Tell about a time you were afraid or mad and cheated.

_____

_____

4 Tell about a time you were sad or despondent and lied or stole.

_____

_____

5 Tell about a time you felt guilty and lied.

_____

_____

6 Tell about a time your feelings were hurt and you did something that later made you ashamed.

_____

_____

Face your feelings. Then, the impulse to lie, cheat, or steal will not be as strong as it was before.

3 The A, B, Cs of Emotion Management

A systematized understanding of emotions calls for a structured protocol that is intuitive and easy to remember. We learn to read by first learning the alphabet. From this foundation we progress in stages to learning as much knowledge as we dare to embrace. In the same way our emotions are a field of knowledge, an area of information that calls for our understanding through simple structures.

When it comes to emotions, we all have some level of intuitive understanding. It is overlaid, however, with the veneers of cultural mores and beliefs that constitute the major misunderstandings we have seen. Intuition notwithstanding, many adults today learned about emotions through bitter trial and error. This is otherwise known as learning the hard way. When a fury you create brings your world down around you, that is learning the hard way. When anger turned fixedly inward smothers you in depression, that is learning the hard way. When not knowing how to grieve traps you in grief for years, that is learning the hard way. When fear of fear drives you to avoid your best path, that, too, is learning the hard way.

Enough. Do you agree? The twenty-first century beckons rational beings to a more thoughtful response. Let us begin to study emotions the same way we study literature and science, systematically with definitions and charts and well-ordered information. We begin with the simple and basic and then proceed to the more complex. Hence a simple and direct approach is the A, B, Cs of emotion recognition, feeling, and expression.

> A. ALLOW. ACCEPT.
>
> B. BE WITH. BREATHE.
>
> C. CHOOSE. CHANNEL.

When initiating work with a youngster, display the A, B, Cs on a whiteboard in your office, on a poster, or by digital display. An approach to engage teens is to display the words, but do not rush to explain. Ask teens what they think is meant. Thus initiate discussion of each step. This approach conveys you view the teen as a thinking individual who is able to read simple words and share ideas.

The Role of Expectations

Expecting the teen to have an idea of what the words mean conveys permission and expectation that the teen does so. When educators launch quickly into explanations that may progress to monologues, the message sent is "I know you have no knowledge about this matter. So I expect you to say nothing." If the monologue proceeds to a lecture, the message may deepen to "I have all the knowledge. You have none."

For this reason intuitively excellent teachers from Socrates to this day lecture, pause, ask questions, lecture, pause, invite discussion, lecture, pause, and invite more questions. We may call it interactive learning and detail fine educational reasons for it, but what the method says emotionally to the student is "I respect you as a thinking being. Yes, I have more knowledge than you, but I recognize our essential sameness. We both have emotions. So I value your thinking and want to hear it." This approach validates the teen's adolescent quest for independence and individuation. To be an individual, we first and foremost need to hear permission to be one.

Permission to be an individual is easily understood by the consequences suffered by those who never got that permission. They live as an impoverished personality enmeshed in a constricted, fear-driven life, too terrified to speak out loud one's personal desires and wishes, too afraid, perhaps, to even admit to oneself what those desires are. Anger in such an individual may be explosive or self-destructive. Being a self flourishes on permission to be a self. Educators value expectations.

Expect much. Constantly convey those expectations.

If you do not expect and do not convey those expectations, you are not giving permission. Saying, "I expect you will follow the guidelines we've discussed for studying" conveys "I have faith in you that you are able to learn how to study." Similarly, saying, "I expect you will practice the steps for healthy assertiveness like we've practiced them in my office" conveys "I give you permission to practice assertiveness and expect you to do so." Teens internalize explicit expectations. Chapter 19 on guilt explores this dynamic further.

Simply put, if we expect it of them, they are able to expect it of themselves. If we give them permission, they are able to give themselves permission. Thus, when we convey the expectation that they embrace healthy emotionality, they internalize "I have emotions. And that's okay. I know what to do, how to recognize them, what to do with them, how to express them." Then there is nothing to fear, deny, repress, displace, project, rationalize, or intellectualize away.

Educators are shapers of selves. They shape with the collective message, "We expect you to be a self, an individual. We also expect you to be a good community member." School staff continue the shaping with ongoing validation of the student's healthy choices. Progressing through the four years of high school, the teen moves from the freshman year's tentative, "I think I'm somebody but really I don't know," to the sophomore, "I think I'm somebody but I'm scared I might not be." Juniors wonder, "I'm somebody but I fear no one else cares." Seniors juggle, "Me and my pals are somebody, deal with it," and, "Oh, heavens! My somebody has to deal with all my somebodies bursting apart into the wider world!" In college or post high school the process begins again. Our hope is it is with less fear and more tangible confidence.

Into this mix of shape-shifting self comes emotion. It must. For the quest for self is alternately terrifying and anger-provoking. Sometimes it brings sadness and disappointment. When mistakes are made, it may elicit guilt or regret. All these emotions are intrinsic to self-growth.

Allow and Accept

To allow an emotion is to honestly recognize it for what it is. To allow is to take ownership for emotions. It is to forthrightly label the emotion instead of pretending it is something else. It is to accurately identify the emotion. To allow is to "Let it be" and accede to the felt experience of the emotion.

Most especially, allowing is distinguishing which of the four uncomfortable emotions is being felt during times of "stress." We consciously shift away from the concept of stress that detours us from acknowledging what we are feeling. Even stress management classes often switch participants from the actual feeling experience to the process of thinking about feeling matters without naming the emotions.

Stress is the physical and mental tension created by uncomfortable emotions. Anger and fear are usually the chief culprits. Stress, sometimes called pressure, is often thought of as something "out there" that we must "deal with." In reality, our emotional response to that which is out there is the true challenge. Thus, the A, B, Cs are a stress management plan that gets to and stays with the root of stress, emotions.

We begin by allowing the felt experience of the emotion to emerge and naming it. My strongest recommendation in starting this process to those that have not done it before is to keep the recognition abundantly simple. Thus, the four emotions that give most people the most trouble most of the time, namely, fear, anger, grief, and guilt, are the first emotions to consider. Allow and accept means recognizing and naming the emotion. This process is the opposite of denial.

The lists of synonyms for these four emotions in the chapters that follow show the richness of shades of these emotions. But we do not begin with lists. We help ourselves by keeping our choices limited. In sessions with teens inquire, "Which of the four challenging emotions are you feeling?" We sabotage ourselves if in the beginning we pretend there are so many emotions we just cannot name them. This is just denial by sophisticated strategy. Begin simply.

Always ask how someone feels. Don't tell them.

Yet if our aim is emotional intelligence, we cannot remain in emotional kindergarten our whole lives. Thus, by systematic steps, these chapters develop fuller and fuller discernment of the rich variety of our challenging emotions.

Be With and Breathe

To be with an emotion is to experience it, to feel it. To be with is to encounter and, if necessary, endure the emotion. It is to face the emotion bravely instead of running away. Those raised in a world of denial of emotions fear this step. They have been taught that emotions are hard, too hard. Indeed, some have internalized the notion that feeling strong emotion will kill.

Certainly, we owe it to the future to correct this misunderstanding. We have long done a better job of teaching women to endure the pain of childbirth and at times teaching men to endure the pain of battle than of teaching ourselves how to embrace our emotions. If the pain of childbirth and of fighting wars is not too much for us, how may our emotions be? Our emotions will not kill us, but, tragically, burying them, numbing them, and misunderstanding them might lead to a decision (not an emotion) to kill another or kill oneself.

Reminding oneself to breathe is as important for step two as it is for a woman in childbirth and for a soldier facing an enemy. We don't realize it, but when experiencing strong emotion, our breathing pattern shifts. We breathe in short, shallow breaths. The pattern is closer to panting than to the slow, long breaths of sleep. The brain knows this. The brain reads the activation pattern and shifts neurotransmitters into full-blown fight or flight mode. From being initially distressed the mode may progress to full panic attack.

But, graciously, we may trick our brains. Our brains are marvelous in that they play the games we dictate so very well. Breathe like you are scared to death and your Brainy Boo goes, "Fear? You want fear? I'll show you fear!" Think furious thoughts and your brain screams, "Angry? Oh, you don't know anger until I'm angry."

We begin to reverse the process by working with what our brains expect. The brain associates slow, long, easy breaths with relaxation and sleep. This is the opposite of fight and flight. Long, slow breaths that expand the lungs into the diaphragm trick the brain into responding as if the body were relaxed. This is known as **diaphragmatic breathing**. For teens just instruct, "Pooch out your stomach when you breathe. Hold it, hold it, hold it. Exhale." Such breaths bring more oxygen into the body. Well-oxygenated blood then rushes to the brain. The brain backs off fight or flight and comments dryly, "Why, silly human, make up your mind. Are you scared and mad or relaxed? Pick!" Keep up the deep breathing and the brain has its answer.[1]

Being with an emotion has a thinking part as well. The cognitive component is to actively practice self-talk like "I'll be okay. I'm just feeling strong emotion. I can take it. I just have to breathe. I'm going to find someone with whom I can talk this out." When such **Help Talk** is not used, the inner voice may wail "I'm dying. I'm going crazy. I can't take this." Hostile, unacceptable behaviors frequently follow. The next chapter presents more on self-talk.

Choose. Channel the Emotion.

To channel an emotion is to express it, to act on it constructively. To constructively channel emotion is to express it directly. It is to feel honestly and share the emotion but not in a way that is harmful to self or others. Destructive expressions of emotion are not acceptable. Elicit from teens you work with a brief list of the myriad unacceptable ways we express emotions. Emphasize that anyone may choose to act out emotions negatively.

Common expressions continue to deceive us. We act in anger and cry, "I lost my temper." Untrue. You did not lose your temper. You gave it away. "Something came over me, and I lost control." Untrue. You felt emotion and chose not to take control. Emotions may influence our choices, but they do not rob us of the power to choose. Given the enormous array of excuses we give ourselves as we claim "I couldn't help it," instructing the young that they have a choice is foundational to healthy emotionality. If we fail to expect generations of young to accept that expression of emotions involves *choice*, we will simply pass the errors of the twentieth century down to the twenty-second.

Continue by explaining that mature channeling of emotion falls into two broad categories of choice, verbal and nonverbal. Add to the chart or post the following.

A. ALLOW. ACCEPT.

B. BE WITH. BREATHE.

C. CHOOSE. CHANNEL.

  1. Verbally

  2. Nonverbally

Verbal Channeling of Emotion

The chief verbal way to channel emotions is Talk It Out. The very act of talking about what one is feeling uses up some of the energy of the emotion. **Talk It Out** is not just ordinary talking. It is a process of feeling the emotion and affectively expressing it with words.

Verbally sharing an emotion often relieves the emotion even as it builds friendship or emotional connection. A friend is a person with whom one shares honest feelings. Teens are intensely interested in making and having friends. Explain to your teens that learning how to verbally channel emotions is a key step in friendship-building. Disclosure about emotions is the glue that builds the bond of intimacy.

For the counselor, encouraging the verbal sharing of emotion creates and builds a bond of connection and nurturance. This is the opposite of alienation and isolation. Accepting a teen's emotions conveys acceptance of the essential self. Talking about a teen's feelings not only allows the teen to express those emotions, it affirms the bond of connection with that teen. As such, it is an affirmation of the community group of which you are both a part, the school.

Writing about emotions is another form of verbal expression. Explain to teens that writing about feelings is one of the most constructive ways to express them. Not only is the emotion expressed, but one may discover unexpected talent in creative writing. Thus, journaling and many written activities are offered at each chapter end.

Nonverbal Channeling of Emotion

Constructive nonverbal expression has three key forms: crying, art and music, and physical exercise or action. As you work with teens, involve them in a wide-ranging discussion of what they see as beneficial and helpful means of expressing emotions, other than talking them out. In Chapter 13 we see that crying is necessary and normal.

The world's greatest artistic expressions communicate powerful emotion. Nonverbal expression of emotion includes activities that involve art and music and any creative self-expression. If copies of great paintings are available, use them to invite discussion of the emotions they elicit. A similar exercise may be followed with passages of great music. Teens particularly enjoy playing a song meaningful to them. Though the music may not be to your taste, it may serve as a doorway to the sharing of critical emotional issues.

Finally, emotions are physiological. This means in the body. So, many times only physical exercise or appropriate action may relieve the emotion. Under strong emotion the immune system releases chemical messengers which stimulate the hypothalamus to release additional chemicals. These then stimulate first the pituitary and next the adrenal glands. The result is a host of physiological changes including altered heart rate, blood pressure, and breathing pattern. When you have "butterflies in the stomach" due to fear, it is not "all in your mind." It is, in equal part, also in your body. Chapter 10 explores how various sports correlate with how emotions are felt in the body.[2]

- **Journaling—My Story**

Display the following titles. Ask the teen to tell or write a story with one of these titles. Stories may be written in journals.

A Day I Felt Very Sad
The Maddest I Ever Got
Once I Was Afraid
Sometimes I Feel Guilty
I Cry Because
Something Sad Happened
I Get Mad When
Me and My Worries

- **Small Group–Our Story**

Break the group into small groups of three or four. Each group makes up one story as in the journaling activity, My Story. Teens may illustrate the story in booklet or storyboard format. As an added challenge, invite teens to relate the story in pictures only. The remainder of the group tells the story in words as the pictures are held up one by one. Encourage laughter and silliness. We will not teach the next generation not to fear their emotions if our teaching and coaching about emotions is ponderous, severe, and tedious.

- **Applying the A, B, Cs: Activity Sheet 3.1**

Assign the exercise. Giving examples, explain the meaning of metaphor and simile. "I felt like I was in a black hole" and "I was as mad as a pit bull" are examples of dramatic teenage emotions. Results may be shared in individual session or in small groups. This sheet may be used again and again throughout the course of a series of sessions with a student as well as in small groups.

- **Self-talk Analysis for Upsets: Activity Sheet 3.2**

This exercise is designed to give teens practice in identifying the overt or hidden self-talk that precipitates emotional states. As with Activity Sheet 3.1, this sheet may be used again and again, especially for real-life challenges.

Stress that quotation marks must be used to make it clear that self-talk is the actual words used. For example, teens should not write "It was a situation that was unfair," but "This is unfair! I always get the raw end of the deal. No one cares how I feel." A statement of apparent fact is already removed from emotion. But the word-for-word self-talk itself carries the emotion. Talking about is not the same thing as the emotion talking from the *inside*.

Step four on Activity Sheet 3.2 is crucial to learning. Students may work together on constructive alternatives. If at this point teens appear befuddled about what self-talk is, normalize the confusion. "Yes, well adults many years older than you are puzzled by what self-talk means even though it just means your actual, word-for-word thinking." We begin with clear definitions. We grow into more refined understandings. Further understanding of self-talk continues in the next chapter.

- **A, B, Cs in Great Literature**

Instruct teens:

> Find and read a story, either a novel or a short story, from the world's great literature that is mostly about one or more of the following: anger, fear, grief, or guilt. Write two paragraphs that show how the story does or doesn't move through the A, B, Cs of that emotion.

Applying the A, B, Cs may be used to elucidate literary plots as well as characters. Alternatively, assign a specific story with the instructions, "Tell what emotions this story is about. What character allowed which emotion when? Did a character breathe and just be with emotion? What choices revealed how emotion was channeled?"

If possible to collaborate with the language arts teacher, this activity may be repeated several times throughout the school year. The A, B, Cs provide a fascinating format for assessing the overt and hidden motivations of the likes of Captain Ahab. The peace of sea captains, it would appear, depends on self-acceptance, deeply inhaling the sea air, and purposely choosing to leave whales alone.

BULLETIN BOARD MATERIAL

When in doubt, talk it out.

A, B, Cs of Emotions

A. Allow. Accept.

B. Be with. Breathe.

C. Choose. Channel.

What can be expressed in words can be expressed in life.

H.D. Thoreau[3]

Notes

1 There are a myriad of online entries for relaxation and breathing. For a brief overview see *Relaxation Techniques: Breath Control Helps Quell Errant Stress Response* (Harvard Health Publishing, 2018). Online at www.health.harvard. edu/./relaxation-techniques-breath-control-help-quell-errant-stress-response
2 Nancy Philipott's *The Physiology of Emotions* at www.selfgrowth.com/articles gives an introductory, short synopsis.
3 Thoreau, H.D. (1906). *The Writings of Henry David Thoreau, Familiar Letters, Vol. 06*, F.B. Sanborn (Ed.). (Boston, MA: Houghton Mifflin & Co.). See Thoreau's (1817–1862) *Letter to Harrison Blake, March 27, 1848*, in section II, *Golden Age of Achievement*, p. 163. Retrieved from www.gutenberg.org/files/43523/43523-h/43523-h.htm#Page_120

Name: _____ Date: _____

Activity Sheet 3.1
APPLYING THE A, B, Cs

Describe a time you were emotional. What happened? Who did what? Who said what?

_____

_____

_____

ALLOW & ACCEPT

Allow your mind to dwell on the emotions you felt. Name them.

_____

_____

BE WITH & BREATHE

Be with what you felt. Using a metaphor or simile, describe what you felt.

_____

_____

Think carefully and recall the self-talk you used. Write what you were saying to yourself in your head about the incident and your emotions.

" _____

_____ "

CHOOSE. CHANNEL

Tell what you did with the emotion. Describe your actions.

_____

_____

_____

Describe a better way to handle such an incident. Describe a more constructive way to express the emotion you felt.

_____

_____

Name: _____ Date: _____

Activity Sheet 3.2
SELF-TALK ANALYSIS FOR UPSETS

1. Describe an upsetting incident.
2. Describe your self-talk during the incident. Fill in as many of the following as apply. Don't forget quotation marks. If necessary, you may write on the back of this sheet.

   a. List self-talk that suggests you were frightened.
   " _____
   _____ "

   b. List self-talk that suggests you were angry or frustrated.
   " _____
   _____ "

   c. List self-talk that suggests you were sad or despondent.
   " _____
   _____ "

   d. List self-talk that suggests you were feeling guilty or regretful.
   " _____
   _____ "

   e. List self-talk that suggests you were feeling another emotion. Name the emotion.
   " _____
   _____ "

3. Circle the self-talk above that most makes you feel disappointed in yourself. This particular self-talk may be followed by the self-talk, "I shouldn't feel this way" or "I wish I didn't feel this way" or "It's terrible of me to feel this way."

4. List some positive, constructive self-talk that may best help you to **Handle It!** If you like, ask for help with this step.
   " _____
   _____
   _____
   _____ "

4 Self-talk and Emotions

No model in modern psychology is as pertinent and essential for confidently managing emotions than a full understanding of and use of self-talk. Self-talk is thinking. Emotion generating self-talk is the thinking part of emotion. It precedes and accompanies the feeling part of emotion, which comprises physical sensations and physiological changes in the body. No self-talk is more destructive to the emotive life than cognitive distortions, which may best be explained to teens as garbage thinking.

A grasp of self-talk is critical to constructive channeling of emotions and true self-possession. In your sessions and small groups, use the term self-talk as often as possible. Some examples are:

> And what self-talk were you using when you felt that way? Just before you hit him, what was your self-talk? What was your self-talk when you began to get drunk last weekend? You just slammed your books down. What self-talk goes with that?

When teens spontaneously refer to "my self-talk," you will know they are on their way to building their permanent approach to productive emotional regulation.

Self-talk is thoughts. But the word thoughts is too passive a term to allow for active management of emotions. We know quite well that we think our own thoughts, but often we like to believe thoughts happen *to* us. We say, "The thought just went through my head," "The thought came to me," and "A troublesome thought keeps going through my mind." Each statement disowns the thought.

Using the word self-talk stresses that we are responsible for our own thoughts. Self-talk that is emotionally charged does, at times, feel as if it is happening to us. By claiming our thoughts, even those accompanying powerful emotion, we admit that we are in charge of both thinking and feeling.

Explain the core definition to your teens. "Self-talk is what you say to yourself in your head about yourself and your world. When we say 'self-talk' instead of 'thoughts,' we remind ourselves that we are the ones responsible for what goes on in our own heads." Self-talk does not float around in the air until it "goes through" someone's mind. It is *my* self-talk. I put it there. I have control. I may change it. Changing the self-talk changes the emotion.

Although a simple idea, grasping the full meaning of self-talk is very difficult. Try it yourself. You will find old, well-ingrained thinking patterns come to you again and again. This happens even when you silently comment to yourself, "Well, I know that's not really true." Self-talk is learned behavior. As with any well-established learned behavior, it takes work to change it.

Our young people have the advantage over us because whatever their maladaptive thinking, they have only been practicing it for 12-plus years. This puts the advantage in the educator's hands. Think of it this way. If you had the task to clean an attic out of 12 or so years of accumulation, you'd have a big task on your hands. But imagine the job if the attic had collected 30 or 40 years of stuff. Tackling the clean-out job when in high school is much more readily done.

The Feeling Part: In the Body

Explain simply, "Each emotion has two parts, the **feeling part** and the **thinking part**." It may be helpful to display the words in bold type as you invite discussion.

The feeling part of emotions is physiological, in the body. The sensations we experience in an emotion are the result of complex physical changes. When we feel an emotion, hormones are released that alter the biochemistry of the body. Then, neurotransmitters in the brain change, too. If collaborating in a school-wide approach, science teachers may provide lessons that detail the biochemistry of emotion.

One way to get a grip on powerful emotions is to use self-talk like "I'll be okay. It's only the body's natural chemicals in my brain and body. I will be okay." This is an example of the specific type of purposely chosen self-talk that is readily named Help Talk. While no one absolutely must learn the body's biochemistry to use such self-talk, it is easier to accept a technique we know is backed by science.

Moreover, teaching young people in science class takes the whole dimension of emotions out of the realm of mental health. Human anatomy is part of biology. The endocrine system is taught in biology class. But do science teachers make a direct and solid connection between the emotions we all feel and the biology of those emotions? Do your chemistry teachers teach the physiological chemistry of emotions? If acting system-wide, invite your school's science teachers to teach such lessons.

Doing so, you will be able to comment to a visibly distressed student "I see the hormones have really got you on this one. We're going to calm them down right away. Breathe. Breathe with me. Breathe." Consider how much more useful this approach is than "What's upsetting you?" Not only is this approach more useful in helping the young person regain calm, it is more scientifically accurate.

Using up the hormones may take more than deep, diaphragmatic breathing when the student is intensely emotional. Once emotion-connected hormones are released into the bloodstream, they cannot be willed away. Hormones are real. Once an emotion happens, it must be expressed. Emotions do not evaporate because hormones do not do so.

Rather, hormones must be used. Expressing emotions in the ways already described, by talking it out and in physical activity, uses up the hormonal discharge. Even more, the constructive activity itself begins to alter the body's chemistry as when talking to a supportive friend settles us down.

A demonstratively emotional student, one we have commonly called "really upset," if still not meaningfully calm after breathing with the counselor may be invited to work off the hormonal discharge in the gym. Intense anger produces a huge flux of adrenaline and cortisol. Just talking at that point is not what the brain and body have evolved to do. Intense emotion, in fear as well as anger, wants the legs to run and the arms to strike, pound, punch.

So especially when it was hitting someone that got the young person to your office, it is beneficial to consider the option of intense physical activity. Granted, this will take coordination with a coach or the school resource officer. Nonetheless, working out the emotion by working out is the best way to help the body use up its adrenaline and cortisol.

Signs a student needs intense physical activity are a rhythmically shaking foot, constant fidgeting, very frequent shifting of position, refusal to sit down, and jumping up and running out of your office. We may force ourselves to make our bodies appear still. Few can muster absolute mastery over facial expression and eyes. No teen can. They have not been on the planet long enough to learn to do so. So, watch the face. Watch the eyes. If facial muscles twitch, emotion is hiding within. If the lips smile but the eyes do not, intensify your quest for the emotion lurking within.

We may lie with our words. But the brain's neurotransmitters and the body's adrenaline and cortisol *cannot* lie. When the brain registers high concentration of adrenaline and cortisol and detects anger-provoking self-talk, screaming "I'm not angry!" will not fool it. Investigate whether your school system is ready to embrace the science of the matter and create protocols for school staff to work together to support angry, hostile students by teaching them that they, yes, even they may learn to channel their most intense, uncomfortable emotions into meaningful physical activity. Think of the colossal boost to self-esteem when their self-talk evolves to "I can be angry and show it in a way that harms no one."

The Thinking Part: In the Brain

The cognitive part of emotion is mental. The tendency for many is to treat the emotionally distressed as if they were rational. "Why did you hit him?" suggests there must be a rational explanation. "Why" in general asks for reasons, explanations, description, for "who did what to whom when." But emotion does not exist to answer the question why. Emotion does not have to be irrational, but it is certainly nonrational. Reason and emotion coexist as two qualitatively different, intrinsic dimensions of our humanity.

So in your counseling avoid moving too quickly to problem solving. Though problem solving is a necessary skill that may be taught separately, it may never substitute for productive manifestation of emotion. Trying to bypass our emotional selves to go right to our rational selves backfires. We just produce emotion-laden thinking. We try to substitute thinking our emotions for feeling our emotions. Fiery emotions turned into self-talk may rage, "How dare he! I hate him. I could kill him!" As pure emotional drive, that same emotion might push the angry person to run the track 20 times.

The thinking part of self is best accessed when the emotions are calm. That thinking part is self-talk. We do not really know what we are feeling until we talk to ourselves about the experience. Physiological arousal is greatly defined by the context and setting at the time of the arousal. A calmer self may reappraise the emotion-generating situation and thoughtfully consider the inner dialog that contributed to the emotional experience.

Discuss self-talk after validating emotions.

Advance to problem solving after emotions are accepted and expressed in a setting of compassionate empathy. Allow intense emotions to be safely expressed intensely. Then proceed to building the self-talk portion of all AMPs. Doing so means distinguishing two types of self-talk: self-talk before the feeling and self-talk after the feeling.

The Before Self-talk

Before self-talk often flashes through the mind so rapidly that we are not consciously aware of it. We say "I can't help how I feel" because emotions seem spontaneous to us. This is because ordinarily we are not aware of the self-talk that comes before the emotion. For example, two students walk down the hall between classes. A third hustles along and steps on the toes of first one, then the other.

The first student lets out a stream of obscenity and then shrieks, "Who do you think you are?" The second one yelps, "Owww!" and nothing more. Why the difference? The difference is the unconscious self-talk of the two wounded students. The first has inner self-talk along the lines of "Anyone who moves into my personal space does so on purpose just to attack or offend me. No one has the right to do that!"

Thus the shout, "Who do you think you are?" The question really means "You are not someone who has a right to enter my personal space." The anger results from a belief that one's rights have been maliciously abrogated. Some might say the offending student *dissed* them. This particular garbage thinking is guaranteed to produce anger every time.

The second wounded student does not possess the same inner self-talk. This student has self-talk such as "Accidents happen. In a crowded hallway toes sometimes get stepped on. It's no big deal." "Owww!" means "It hurts!" and nothing more.

The second student's self-talk accurately reflects reality. Garbage thinking does not. **Garbage self-talk** is thinking replete with highly personalized exaggerations and errors in reasoning. A key purpose of talking with a counselor is to make the unspoken garbage thinking conscious, to hear oneself say it out loud. Just turning the unspoken but real self-talk into spoken words uses up some of the emotional discharge.

Primary school teachers instruct, "Use your indoor voice." We need a version of this for teens.

Say your emotions with words.

That would be using our inside voice. Give your teens permission to speak passionately while in your office. Help them expand their vocabulary of emotions. "You say you're mad. Does aggravated and quite frustrated fit what you're feeling?" You'll see the process of change when later a student who had not previously had the word in her active vocabulary comes into your office crying, "I'm so exasperated today!"

Most especially, insist on such vocabulary expansion when the inclination is to use the same four letter words repeatedly. Adults are not modeling positive emotional communication if allowing young people to curse and use foul language. Four-letter words are easy expressions of an impoverished vocabulary. Correct students who slip into such language by inviting them to pick just precisely which words from the list of anger words best describe the color and intensity of their anger.

If every language arts teacher gave extra credit for a 200-word essay that communicates "I'm angry" using 20 different synonyms for anger, the school's reservoir of words for positive expression of anger would sky rocket.

The After Self-talk

The self-talk that comes after is critical to either ending or continuing the emotional experience. The student who believes "Accidents happen, no big deal" will quickly get over the incident. No additional emotions generate.

But Mr. Mad At The World cannot let it go. The "How dare you!" garbage self-talk repeats and renews the experience. This is nursing a hurt or working up a good mad. To each fresh wave of anger, the response is another variation of, "I've been attacked, my rights violated." We talk ourselves into a good mad.

We talk ourselves into being scared to death. We talk ourselves into being "so guilty I can't stand it." We talk ourselves into depression by internalizing anger and dwelling on sadness, guilt, and rage. We talk ourselves into alcohol abuse and drug use. We may talk ourselves all the way to suicide if we just keep talking long enough.

But by the same token we may talk ourselves out of suicide and other inappropriate expressions of emotion. A strong emotion keeps the podcast of garbage self-talk playing over and over. To stop it, we must first relieve the emotions. We must follow the A, B, Cs.

The After Self-talk is also the conscious self-talk we choose. As such it is critical to the development of teen identity. All self-talk along the lines of "I can't figure out my feelings. I can't control my emotions" causes self-esteem to plummet. How we recognize and handle emotions is part of self-image. Intelligent, successful people may be abysmally unhappy inside because they do not know their emotions, do not know why they feel what they feel, are not comfortable with saying "I'm an emotional person."

A fully positive self-image must include knowing our emotions, being comfortable in our own emotional skin, and feeling pride and joy as we exclaim, "I'm an emotional person." As an educator today, you have the privilege of seeing your role as more than helping your teens with the formation of their identity by steering them into compatible careers and occupations. Rather help your teens establish their strong, healthy identity by working with them to establish a solid emotional foundation. Being educated and externally successful is not enough for human happiness. If we are not happy in our emotions, we are not happy period.

In your teens' lifetime technology will change. New careers that do not exist today will emerge. If a teen struggles with a career path, consider that the best job that young person will ever have may not exist yet. You cannot validate a teen's inclination to pursue an occupation that does not exist. Stress to ambivalent teens that for the 105 years they are going to live, they need now only choose their *first* career. If you or someone you know are in your second or third career, share that personal example.

But what will endure is the emotional foundation. From career to career feeling comfortable in one's emotional skin serves us well. The modes of emotional expression chosen in high school may be consistent throughout the lifetime. Or, they, too, may just be the beginning of an emotive evolution.

Mental Rehearsal

After an angry episode, mindful visualization is a useful technique. The brain learns by action in the physical world but also by the images we place in our heads. Mental rehearsal introduces the brain to actions to be actually put into place in the real world. Sports psychologists make use of mental rehearsal when they teach basketball players "See it, then shoot it." First making a picture in your mind of what you want the ball to do advises the brain to tell the hands to move just precisely so that Swish! the ball sinks net and only net.

In the same way counselors may use mindful visualization to rehearse what the teen is going to do the next time anger arises. First, go over a time that has already happened. Go through the event again and redo it as with the teen you fashion more constructive responses. Make the internal response different. Change the self-talk. Also make the tangible response different, a different action taken. Just as in sports practice, practice, practice tells the brain what actions to direct the body to routinely perform.[1]

Too often adults appear to believe that telling a teen one time what to do and what not to do with their anger is sufficient. No coach thinks telling teens one time how to shoot a basket or block on the football field is going to create division champs. Similarly, practice with mindful visualization of constructive anger expression aids emotional intelligence in action.

Humor and Other Expressions

If teens are resistant or resort to joking about how anger feels, share that these responses are defenses. "Yes, it's scary to talk about how anger feels. It's a lot easier to make jokes about it. In fact, humor is an excellent way to dissolve anger, to lighten up, and not take our anger so seriously."

Humor is one way to use up the hormonal discharges connected with anger as long as we truly dissolve the anger and do not just cover it up. After a hearty laugh ask, "Is the anger really gone?" If not, have the teen talk about it directly by saying, "I'm angry that ... " and name the anger, specifically, clearly.

Explore with the teen how else, besides humor, might they use up the physical discharge anger creates. Some acceptable expressions are to run around the block, punch a pillow, clean out a closet, play a vigorous sport, talk it out, paint an angry picture, and play music. Inquire, "What music do you listen to that is angry music?" Elicit comments on lyrics and rhythms of songs popular with teens.

More physical expressions of strong emotion, for example in sports, are presented in Chapter 10.

Acceptance of Emotions in All

Many teens express their identity concerns by intense desire to fit in and not be or be seen as being different. In a culture that prides itself on individuality, we cannot escape the pull of the tribe. Teens want to be different and unique and fit in and not be different all at the same time. Teen emotions are often blamed on hormones. Consider that hormones are generated because the emotions fly in response to the teen years' developmental tasks of individuality, identity, and social development.

Thus all students will benefit from developing emotional intelligence. But your young people who are somehow challenged will benefit enormously. Nowhere is this seen more strongly than where self-image development is fixedly tied to body image. Support your young people as they wrestle with being different in body shape, skin color, shape of face, sexual identity, being too smart, being not smart enough, having the wrong labels or no labels on their clothes, and any exceptionality.

Support them by stressing what we all have in common. We are all emotional beings. Assist your exceptional students in taking pride in one area in which they may excel, namely, a solid emotive life, a high EQ. High IQs do not guarantee high EQs, **emotional quotients**. In fact, history reveals that those with high IQs and vastly deficient EQs have led the world to deep sorrow.

Validate your exceptional teens growing self-esteem as they learn to take pride in the fruitful emotive habits they are forming. This means more than just a glib "You're beautiful inside." It means helping the young person value their emotive gifts and skills as their unique identity and contribution to life around them. "I'm comfortable with my emotions because I know how to beneficially direct them" and "I have strong emotions and that's okay" are statements of inner self-talk that are foundational to good self-image.

Before Self-talk is the secret inner self-talk, our words that initiate the feeling of the emotion. The After Self-talk determines whether we will stop the emotion or continue it. Even though we cannot instantly obliterate hormones, we may learn to use natural approaches such as slow breathing, mindfulness, and visualization to alter body chemistry. Use of drugs like alcohol avoids the uncomfortable physiological feelings that accompany challenging emotions by numbing the sensations. The cause, the self-talk, remains.

Journaling—Mindfully Finding My Self-talk

Invite the teen you are counseling to go back over the story already written in their journal. Direct them to find their self-talk and underline it. If it's not there in so many words, they are to write it out. The next session they will share that self-talk with you. In this way you will discern any errors or exaggerations or just simply unhelpful self-talk. From there you may assist the teen in **reframing** the self-talk to words more appropriate, helpful, and factual.

When you first engage in this activity, you may have to do it line by line. That we at first may struggle with identifying self-talk is itself a sign of how deeply our culture teaches us to not know emotion-laden think-ing. Denial is not just denial of the raw emotion. Denial is also refusal to honestly look at and critically evaluate the thinking inside that is generat-ing the emotion. Always remember the youngster sitting before you was raised in a culture of denial. In early sessions or classes work line by line, self-statement by self-statement, emotion by emotion *with* the young person. As you do, they will get it.

Bypass any insistent "I don't know what I'm thinking" by encouraging a mindful approach to thinking about thinking. "Just sit with, be with that feeling for a while. Then notice what Brainy Boo is doing. What is it saying?" Interestingly, blaming our brains for what we don't want to take responsibility for often works to move us toward admitting and embracing the emotion. So invite your teens to blame Brainy Boo.

Being mindful of what your brain is doing is the opposite of "I don't know." Thus share this tip.

Give yourself permission to know.

•   Small Group —Find The Self-Talk

Using the story titles in Chapter 3, Journaling—My Story, have teens verbally make up a short tale. Others guess what unspoken self-talk generated the emotion. "What do you imagine was that character's self-talk?"

This is similar to the preceding activity, but this time the primary storyteller does not identify the self-talk. "Just tell the story. Don't worry about the self-talk." The others listen. When the storyteller is finished, the rest of the group says what they think might be the self-talk. This should generate as much laughter as insight.

As in all learning, developing the concept of self-talk begins with vocabulary. When teaching social studies and science, I often found that what are called poor students most often simply did not comprehend the meaning of three- and four-syllable words. When I made vocabulary lists for them, their understanding and performance soared. Learning about emotions is no different than other learning. Start with vocabulary. If students do not grasp what you are talking about when you say self-talk, you are stopped before you start.

• My Garbage Thinking: Activity 4.1

Like many of the activity sheets this one may be used over and over. To develop awareness of how self-talk generates emotion, have the teen complete the activity. This may be done before a session or in between sessions. Inserted in a journal that always comes to each session, it presents opportunity for your reinforcement. "Bringing your self-talk shows you are accepting that you and only you are responsible for your self-talk." Conversely, since scolding is interpreted by teens as punitive, not bringing the self-talk sheet merits a simple comment. "So I see you are making a choice to not be responsible for your self-talk." "No, I just forgot it." "Right. As I said, you are making a choice to not be responsible for your self-talk." Doing an exercise, not doing an exercise—it is all occasion for a teachable moment.

Awareness of self-talk is critical. Breathing changes emotional states in the moment. Much better is to learn how *not* to get to the place that you must engage diaphragmatic breathing. Excise the emotion before it happens. That kind of stopping of emotion only comes from identifying and changing self-talk. So, yes. Not wanting to identify self-talk is indeed making a choice to deny responsibility for that self-talk and the emotion it produces. In all written activities insist on the actual word for word self-talk enclosed in quotation marks to show that this is the explicit inner voice.

As an added touch when teens share their self-talk sheets, have them cut off the bottom of the sheet on happy self-talk and staple it in their journals. Then have them crumple the upper garbage portion and throw it in the garbage can. As they do so, they may say out loud the one item of garbage self-talk above all others that they want to be rid of. First candidates are extreme statements like "No one likes me!" and "I can't do anything right!" and exaggerations like "I can't get anything about algebra" and "All the teachers hate me." Expect misappraisals like "You just want to make me cry" and "The other kids are all so happy."

In your sessions continuously monitor the progress of the transformation of such self-talk. When the student leaves your office, retrieve the activity sheet and shred it. If our most negative thoughts from high school were filed in permanent records that followed us through life, none of us would advance past ninth grade.

BULLETIN BOARD MATERIAL

Give yourself a good talking to.

When you find you cannot change others, change your self-talk.

Garbage thinking is junky self-talk.

Men are not disturbed by things
But by the views which they take of things.
Epictetus[2]

Notes

1 Christopher Williard, Psy.D., psychologist and educator, is a leader in offering specific mindfulness activities for educators. With others, his *The Mindfulness Matters Program for Children and Adolescents* (New York, NY: Guilford Press, 2019) and *Teaching Mindfulness Skills to Kids and Teens* (New York, NY: Guilford Press, 2017) explain how to include mindfulness in education.
2 A Greek philosopher, Epictetus (55–135AD) was a cognitive psychologist before his time. He would scold us today for our pervasive imprecise use of words. His *The Enchiridion,* meaning *The Handbook* (T.W. Higginson, Trans. New York, NY: Liberal Arts Press, 1948) is in the public domain at www.gutenberg.org/files/45109/45109-h/45109-h.htm See section V for the quotation. I prefer a tighter, twenty-first-century rendering: People are not disturbed by events but by the view they take of them.

Name: _____   Date: _____

Activity Sheet 4.1
MY GARBAGE THINKING

List your self-talk in each area. Then, draw a garbage can around the top three lists.

Things I say to myself

That are guaranteed to make me angry:

"_____

_____

_____

_____ "

That are guaranteed to make me sad:

"_____

_____

_____

_____ "

That are guaranteed to make me scared:

"_____

_____

_____

_____ "

That are guaranteed to make me happy:

"_____

_____

_____

_____ "

Unit II

Anger

5   Our Powerhouse

In this unit we apply the A, B, Cs of emotions to anger. Taken together the chapters of Unit II provide a protocol for constructing a specific type of AMP, an anger management plan. Multiple options and approaches are given so that you may tailor the plan to each individual. Above all strive to make each student's plan pragmatic and doable. Running the track to expel anger energy probably won't work when weather is inclement. All anger management plans must be pragmatic with year-round, indoor, outdoor strategies.

Even as IEPs are periodically reviewed, it is helpful to review individual AMPs from time to time, certainly annually, with the goal of ascertaining if the plan is working or not. If not, the plan should be changed, perhaps augmented to include behavioral charts that track progress. When youngsters are tangibly rewarded for progress, sticking to the plan becomes much more meaningful.

The Powerhouse Emotion

Anger is misunderstood. If anger scares you or you wonder sometimes how to handle it in yourself and in your charges, it's not you. It's the age, the era we live in. Nowhere do we see the misunderstanding more vividly than in the labeling of anger "a negative emotion." The label reveals we miss the ego-protective function of anger. The best metaphor for ego, our sense of self, is to see it as our castle walls. They protect us, tell us where personal space ends, offer the comfort of home, and create the sense, "This is where I belong." When ego decisively crumbles, serious mental health issues arise.

The metaphor is not perfect. We humans are healthiest when our walls are moveable, sometimes transparent, and often with open gates. Walls protect but they also limit. Having ego is not a bad thing. It is just best when it is realistic, flexible, and open. We are capable of anger because we are built to protect our castle walls, to survive.

But in our age we not only miss the whys of our personal angers, we miss why anger exists at all. In the first four chapters we have seen how emotion is normal and built into our physiology. We don't get to say,

"Doc, I don't like uncomfortable emotions so take out my adrenals, please." Adrenaline and its partner cortisol support life. Dead in the ER, the patient is infused with adrenaline. With that and perhaps a shock to the chest, life returns.

Neither may we say, "I don't like anger. I can do without it." Anger is built into our psychology like the adrenals are built into our bodies. Life-giving and life-saving, the hormones of the adrenals are not looked upon as negative. Yet when we stimulate those hormones in what we name anger, we use the word negative. Certainly, intense emotion may be uncomfortable, even painful. That is not the same thing as negative.

Anger's critical role in human psychology is self-protection. So it is no surprise that for teens, anger has a key role in their developmental psychology. Specifically, anger comes both as a by-product of and aid to **individuation**, a central developmental task of adolescence. The task of identity may rise to crisis level when a teen's choices for individuality appear multiple, confusing, frightening, overwhelming. To grasp the level of pain and fear, imagine barbarians at the gate.

What will the castle inhabitants do? Fight. Fight or surrender. The expansive resiliency of our species is shown in the teenage preference to fight. Surrender, psychologically speaking, may lead ultimately to depression and suicide. Working with an angry teen is a matter of channeling that anger into healthy self-protection. But a suicidal person needs to first retrieve the anger they have pushed away. When anger is turned inward, depression may result. The two ills of depression and suicide that plague our world afflict our teens, too. They do so because as a culture we turn our faces away from healthy anger.[1]

In the teen years, as they work on figuring out who they are, the development of ego is often visible before our eyes as we observe teens struggling to learn what is me and what is not me. Have you ever heard a teen lament "I don't know who I am"? Just where to place those castle walls, how high to build them, and how thick are the daily stuff of teen life. You may see who's in their castle by looking at their social media pages.

When the me I think I am is threatened, anger erupts. Anger defends individuality. In this sense an angry teen has better mental health. At least he has some individuality he thinks is worth defending. But crushing one's anger, not knowing how to be justly angry, giving up one's anger for the sake of belonging, fearing one's anger, failing to learn assertiveness, if persisted in, leads to maladaptive emotionality and perhaps to poor mental health.

So when counseling an angry teen, silently ponder.

What is being defended?

Initially this may be a puzzle. But your knowledge of teens in general will help you narrow the possibilities. We commonly are impelled to protect our ego, our bodies, our self-respect, and our intimate community groups like family and friends. Since in adolescence ego is under construction and not yet a done deal, it is like that sore toe that just can't seem to avoid getting stepped on. In the worst of cases it is like having a body with no skin. Everything hurts. This is why it is so important for counselors to assist teens in their task of developing a meaningful identity. Identity is a skin, a castle wall.

A youngster who has no friends but joins the drama club quickly becomes one of the drama kids. Whether backstage or on stage, she literally has a role to play. She gets to join the other drama kids on the club's social media page and be applauded by the whole school. She has a skin and, if not a castle wall, at least a fence. She belongs. She is happy or happier than before.

Conversely, anger itself may become an identity. When a teen doesn't know who he is but knows he needs protection from more than figurative barbarians, he may join a gang. The gang serves the same purpose as the drama club. He, too, is struggling for identity, his role to play, his belonging place in the world. He is surviving but absence of pain is not happiness.

Thus the constructive purpose of anger is to drive us to protect our selfhood and our bodies. When the current definition of one's self-respect is insulted, anger explodes. The proper use of that anger is to stand up for ourselves assertively. "No," we must state quietly but firmly, "You may not come inside my castle." But too often the discourse is "What are you doing here? Get out!" Attacks, real or imagined, on self and on family and friends, elicit the anger to protect and to fight.

Be aware when working with angry teens that they may have more than an anger issue. They may have an identity issue. Or, the anger may stem from struggles with the other key developmental task of adolescence, **community**—one's place in a social group. For community as a developmental task, see Chapter 7. Since developmental tasks are most challenging, teens are frequently tested by the anger that may erupt as they toil with these tasks. It is not the anger in and of itself that is the issue. It's what to do with it.

The gang kid has the gang rules to tell him. The drama kid, too, learns what we do and what we don't do, as in, "No, we don't hang out there. All the jocks go there." It is learning to constructively manage and channel anger that transforms the confusion and misery.

From time to time structuring your words as a whispered secret may grab the teen's full attention and convey your belief that the teen is special and therefore worthy of special *secret* knowledge. Use this technique to share with your teens one such powerful secret. That secret is that anger is the powerhouse nature gave us to protect us and make us strong, resolute, and determined. Here's the secret.

The positive use of anger is determination.

Wanting to be powerful does not make teens at risk. Not knowing how to channel their anger into constructive determination just may. We all need to be powerful. If the teen you are working with enjoys fantasy, as many do, enter that world by shaping your words to reflect the fantasy. Characterize anger within as a dragon. Ask the teen to name that dragon. From earliest times naming has meant controlling and owning the power of the beast. Our sagas and legends, ancient and modern, reveal we humans don't mind dragons as long as we are able to direct them.

One such dragon name may be Determination. But let the teen choose. Explain that this magic dragon is there to help get what we want and need out of life. Well expressed, anger yields backbone, stamina, a fighting spirit, and healthy individualism. Many, many tales both ancient and modern have themes of the lead characters first fearing and then destroying or taming the dragon. The process is never depicted more perfectly than when a film depicts the magician–like protagonist transforming the dragon into a butterfly.

From time immemorial in myths and folktales, fire, too, has been used as an image for anger. It is an excellent image to help teens contrast the positive side with the unproductive side of anger. Fire under control may warm a home and cook food. Out of control it may burn down a house or forest. Like fire, anger is neither good nor bad. It depends on how it is used. It depends on the choices we make to express it.

The Two Paths of Anger

A display in your office or classroom of the following diagram may be helpful.

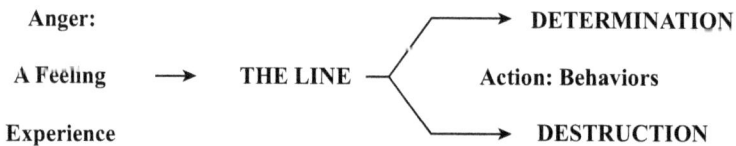

```
Anger:                                      ┌──────→ DETERMINATION
                                           ╱
A Feeling      ──→    THE LINE   ─<          Action: Behaviors
                                           ╲
Experience                                  └──────→ DESTRUCTION
```

From this diagram we see how anger begins as a purely feeling experience. It is then converted into action. The action may be the determination to act constructively. Or it may reveal the decision to act destructively. **THE LINE** is in the middle since common language offers the appraisal, "You've crossed the line." It is in the middle because there *is* a line, a decision point. It is illusion, in or out of the courtroom, to pretend the path of destruction just mysteriously happens. "It was not my fault, your honor. He just got himself killed by the knife in my hand."

Be sure your teens grasp that just as emotion has a thinking part and a feeling part and Before and After Self-talk, we may also contrast *experiencing* the emotion with *acting on* it. At some point in the total encounter with the emotion, we cross over the line between feeling and acting. Although common experience assures we know the difference between feeling and acting, the collective common culture too often propels us to pretend we have no earthly idea why we do what we do. Giving millions of people permission to *not know*, we should not be surprised when many cry, "I don't know!" as sufficient explanation for their destructive behavior. It is time to know.

Teens readily grasp that there is all the difference in the world between feeling angry and acting on that anger. Just feeling angry, even ragefully angry, is one thing. Destructively acting out that anger is another. It all depends on how one crosses the line. Feeling angry is okay. Acting with hostility is not.

Even while sitting in your office because of some hostile act, teens do readily grasp the difference between feeling and acting. They do because the wider world has not yet convinced them to not know. Let them get out of high school and college without converting not knowing to knowing and in another ten years the pull to be part of the wider culture may just trap them in the contagion of not knowing. This must change.

The destructive path of anger is **hostility**. Hostility is animosity actively expressed. Hostility is by definition immediately destructive. It is also remotely destructive in that it creates more hostility in a cycle that may be never ending. The difference between acceptably expressed anger and hostility must be taught. What is acceptable to do when angry is cultural and varies from culture to culture and age to age. As the culture evolves, previously accepted actions are deemed hostile and therefore unacceptable.

Teens today are caught in the flux of such cultural change. What, indeed, are today's teens supposed to do when they are angry? Currently, there are not enough adults actively helping them answer that question. Hence much teen anger gets poured into bullying, both in cyberbullying and in school corridors. A flat, implacable directive that bullying is crossing the line is an absolute prerequisite to stemming the tide. Bullies may think bullying is cute, smart, and gets them the spotlight. Educators as a whole and counselors in particular must clearly and repeatedly educate young people to the fact that fear and anger drive bullying. A proper response to a bully who is in the act of bullying is "You are angry." The proper response is not "You're being mean." Mean means angry, so let's just get right to the point. Let's get off the mean girls bandwagon and start saying angry girls.

But bullies without active AMPs will continue to bully. It's their way of convincing themselves that their castle walls are strong. Bullies are drunk on the power they feel from making another feel small. Bullies do not comprehend the difference between dumping their anger and harmlessly expressing it. It takes a counselor or compassionate educator's intervention to correct the errors in thinking, the maladaptive self-talk, that has them believing that they are strong when another is weak. The easiest thing to do with anger is to throw it at another. The easiest thing to do with fear is deny it and make someone else afraid.

When compassionate adults who understand the purpose behind bullying behavior intervene, the fear may be rehomed to its source, addressed, and relieved. The angry self-talk may be reframed as proof that the potential for firm determination hides within. Give former bullies goals to be fierce about. As they come to learn that they may build their castle walls without throwing some of the bricks at others, they may learn to channel their anger into fiercely determined positive action for the greater good. People lacking passion don't change the world. Bullies are leaders hiding from themselves.

The youngster who is on the receiving end of bullying also has an issue with anger and fear but in quite a different way. If that young person had known when the bullying began that it was acceptable to speak right up to the bully and state, "Stop! Don't talk to me that way. I don't like it," the bully may have moved off to an easier, non-assertive victim. The goal of assertiveness is not to change the behavior of the other, the bully. The goal is to stand up for yourself in full faith that doing so is the right thing to do. You don't get to dismantle someone else's castle walls as a fast track to building your own. Equally, you yourself lay the bricks of your wall or the wall does not get built and you are vulnerable.

Often victims keep quiet because they do not know they have a right to speak up for themselves or believe doing so "is not nice." Or, they attempt to do so when the bullying behavior is well established. Grasping the difference between a hostile act and an assertive act is crucial. Hostility harms. Assertiveness harms no one. When bullies respond to assertiveness as if that assertiveness is harming them, some inner self-talk along the lines of "You have to do what I say and be what I want you to be" must be addressed.

This is defining self by assuming the prerogative to define others. The actual words bullies use are key to comprehending the bully's issues. "You're ugly!" reflects the bully's self-concerns, as does, "You're stupid." Using negative words about another's race or country of origin is the bully's attempt to define self by visible differences. It shows his fear of his own inner contradictions. To stop bullying all educators involved must make it clear that bullying and any form of harming others is a flaw, an expression of the bully's own fear. If bullying is a meaningful issue in a school, fear is a consequential issue, too.

Conversely, appropriately standing up for oneself is strength. When bullying is extreme and pervasive, young people need adult intervention to co-partner with them in assertive responses. Bullies need to convert their anger back to the underlying fear. The bullied need to convert their fear to appropriate, assertive anger. Above all the bullied need to hear supportive adults say, "The bully's words are not about you. They are about him. They show *his* anger and fear." This must be spoken as soon as possible and repeatedly. Without these words as armor, too many teens assume such words are indeed about them. From there they blame self, tangibly feel ostracized from their community group, and tragically may decide to express their own fear and anger by committing suicide.

Both the bully and bullied have issues with anger. Both have issues with fear. Both require adult assistance in learning about these two emotions and integrating them into their emotional self with determination. **Determination** is resolute action of tenacious steadfastness. Determination is our external word for inner self-talk like "I can do it. I'm strong. I will keep going. Defeat is not in my vocabulary. I *will* do it."

But determination is not solely an attitude. It is action. It is positive action taken up with conviction and pursued come what may. Anger directed to create positive, just, and equitable outcomes is sometimes called *righteous anger*. The organization Mothers Against Drunk Driving with its poignant acronym, MADD, is a perfect example of the practical force of such anger.[2]

Verbal Hostility

Consider anger with your teens in light of what you have shared about emotions. Apply the key concepts learned in the first four lessons to anger exclusively. Invite teens you counsel to discuss the usual, familiar modes of verbal anger expression including cursing, swearing, and name-calling. These are common forms of *verbal hostility*. Lead teens in understanding that all hostility builds walls. Indeed, those with weak castle walls may show a penchant for convincing themselves they are strong by cursing and swearing. Verbal hostility does express the emotion, but it destroys communication, blocks logical thinking, stimulates more angry words, and could lead to physical aggression. Hostility is not okay.

Moreover, verbal hostility never gets to the core of the pain. Cursing is like flailing at flies at a picnic. They just keep coming back. Over time verbal hostility may become a habit pattern that deeply buries the original pain. More destructive behavior follows. Anger begins for a reason. It may continue simply out of habit. So cursing and using four-letter words is not simply impolite. Verbal hostility damages the person swearing by momentarily absolving them from absolute honesty about their anger. Flailing at flies never protects the potato salad for long.

Distinguish for your students the difference between talking about using four-letter words and actually using them to express anger. Ignoring the common use of the words does nothing to foster owning anger. When the teen lets a word slip, recognize they are handing you an opportunity to teach another way to express that emotion, a way that accepts the anger but not the hostility. Ignore for the moment the word and challenge them. "Say that again using words from this list of anger words." Hand them a copy of the List of Anger Words, Activity 5.1. If they are furious, they may just read the whole list to you.

Directly assert that cursing is just a substitute for not having the vocabulary to state just precisely how one feels. If that brings an "Everyone does it!" reply with a shrug, "Says a lot about our collective vocabulary level, doesn't it?" Accept the teen-speak of the day like salty, simping, and being in my feelings. Invite substitutions. Yuck, yuck, yuck or muck, muck, muck are acceptable. Insist on adding the one missing letter to that other favorite expletive and create instead s-h-i-f-t. For indeed, when we are full of mucking anger, we do certainly need to shift.

Accept the anger. Never accept the hostility. In correcting any form of hostility, collaborate with the teen on solutions.

Say more than what not to do. Say what to do.

Growing maturity is expressed by converting raw emotion and the acting out of that emotion into words. Contrast verbal expressions of anger with the non-verbal. If working with a bully, point out repeatedly the anger in their nasty words. For the bullied, encourage them to "find their voice" and speak up. Practice with them positive ways of doing so, explicitly give them permission to speak up, and take up your shield at their castle gate by advising, "And if that bully doesn't like you saying what we've practiced, just tell them, 'My counselor said I should tell you this and if you don't like it, you should go to the counselor's office.'" Some just may.

In the past, sadly, youngsters were often told "Just ignore them." Tragically, adults did not understand that this was the equivalent of saying to someone with a fire in their house, "Just ignore it. It'll stop." Youngsters intuitively grasp that ignoring emotions means ignoring the person. They have to be acculturated into not knowing, ignoring, denying, and displacing their emotions. "Just ignore them" may feel to the teen like the adult is saying, "I'm ignoring your emotions and want you to ignore them, too."

Ignoring a person's emotions deeply wounds as it feels to the ignored one like they are being told "Your emotions don't matter." And if my feelings don't matter, it is a very small step for a teen to conclude, "*I* don't matter." When this line of self-talk leads to suicide, the young person is saying, "I'm not going to live in a world where I don't matter." All teens need to know they have a right to be a self that feels reasonably secure. Living requires a fighting spirit. The bullied need counselors not only to fight for them but to coach them on how to fight for themselves.

Positive Verbal Expression

Ask your angry student, "What might be a more positive verbal means to express anger?" Lead teens to see that direct expression is best. However, most of us as children did not learn the language of positive, direct expression of anger. Constructive verbal expression of emotion is *learned* just as verbal hostility is a learned behavior.

Positive verbal expression of anger uses *I Language*. I language is a statement that uses the word I. It is the opposite of blaming, which uses the words you and your. A model statement of positive verbal anger expression is "I'm feeling very angry with you." "It's all your fault!" translates to "I'm angry and not only want you to take the blame for what I'm angry about, but I want you to be responsible for my anger, too." Impossible. No other human is inside my brain and body generating my neurotransmitters and hormones.

Using I Language is a simple technique much easier for young people to learn than for adults to embrace. Adults often want to cry, "But it really is her fault!" Emotions are not on trial in a court of law. A jury of 12 may adjudicate a matter and assign blame. However, anger is always *my* anger. Anger is inside the person. It is inside the brain and inside the body. Others may displease you but you decide how to respond. Give teens permission to say "I'm angry with you" and "I'm angry because" instead of cursing and bullying, and then stand aside while they say it a lot.

In small groups engage teens in a role play of past encounters with anger. Direct them to use I Language to express the anger as two or three role-play the incident. If one slips and uses you, be quick to point out how hard it is to be angry and not blame someone else.

Proceed from the verbal to brief mention of the physical expressions of anger. Just as antisocial behaviors express anger, constructive behaviors we choose may also express anger. Constructive physical expressions of anger are discussed in Chapter 10.

• Small Group—The Person Who Went Berserk

This exercise demonstrates the impact of laughter on anger. Discuss the difference between laughing at someone and laughing with someone. In general young people do not just automatically grasp the difference. If the other person is not wholeheartedly laughing, the likelihood is they are not finding the matter funny. When they say stop, the teasing should cease. But learning to laugh at our foibles is a valuable life skill all need for their lifelong toolkit. Like any skill, it must be taught in order to be learned.

Display the title. Define the word berserk. Let the group decide whether the berserker is to be male or female. Then instruct:

> Together we're going to tell a story about a person who went berserk because of anger. I'll begin. Each of you will add a line. Everyone will have two or three turns (depending on group size). Let's make it the angriest, silliest tale we may invent. Ready? Here we go. Once there was a very, *very* quiet person.

With each contribution encourage sillier, angrier depictions of anger. "The berserker was so angry he ate a bucket of nails." "She was so mad she typed so fast her social media page exploded."

Note that because the objective is to encourage perspective, healthy self-reflection, and laughter, the initial reason for the anger is irrelevant. Indeed, no matter the source of our anger, if we take the time to find a reason to laugh at ourselves, anger modulates.

After the group has had some good laughs, summarize. "Laughing at our own anger is the very *best* way to transform it into a powerhouse for good." When Brainy Boo is presented with anger and laughter, it must choose one or the other. It is most difficult to be angry and laughing yourself silly at the same time.

- **Journaling**

If learners have difficulty with spontaneous invention of the berserker story, have them first write a story in their journals. Then orally combine elements from the stories.

- **Social Studies Research**

The school's social studies teachers may also collaborate in developing emotional intelligence. The emotive history of the world is the record of who was mad about what when and what they did about it. Our collective emotive history is also about who was scared of what when and how they expressed that fear. Grief and guilt are in the history books, too.

Daily, human emotions play out on the world stage. Thus, it is relatively easy to integrate understandings about emotions into history lessons. In particular, wars of aggression versus wars of defense show how anger and fear work on a mass societal level. Biographies of famous leaders may illustrate how nations and persons expressed anger, e.g., compare and contrast Hitler and Churchill. How were they alike? Both were famous for great rages. How were they different?

If collaboration with social studies is not possible, your teens who share that they love social studies may yet embrace this activity. Ask the social studies teacher if they may get extra credit for the essay.

- **List of Anger Words: Activity Sheet 5.1**

Have your teens write a story, *One Day I Was a Little Mad,* using the List of Anger Words. In this first encounter with the list, direct that they use only words from the first column. In future they will use the other columns.

Instruct them to write a story about a time they were a little angry using at least ten words from the first column. If collaborating with language arts, all requirements for good English usage may be expected. If a class activity, stories may be shared. Hesitant students may simply make up a tale about someone who one day was a little mad. In this first chapter on anger, the point is not self-revelation of deeply held feelings but the expansion of students' knowledge base about anger as an emotion.

• **The A Word: Activity Sheet 5.2**

Instruct teens to complete the sheet. Discuss results in session or in small groups. The exercise may be expanded by making posters or PowerPoint presentations that detail statements in each area like "Our Class's Best Whining," "Our Class's Best Blaming," and "Our Class's Best Threats."

BULLETIN BOARD MATERIAL

When you get mad, get motivated.

Anger is a magic dragon named Determination.

Anger is okay. Hostility is not.

It's okay to speak up for yourself.

We live by our imaginations, by our admirations, by our sentiments.
R.W. Emerson[3]

Notes

1 Resources on suicide abound. A comprehensive text by a past president of the American Association of Suicidology, itself a fine resource, is Ronald W. Maris, Ph. D.'s, *Suicidology: A Comprehensive Biopsychosocial Perspective* (New York, NY: Guilford Press, 2019). *Helping the Suicidal Person* by Stacey Freedenthal, Ph.D. (New York, NY: Routledge, 2017) presents broad clinical understanding while offering pragmatic interventions. I particularly like her framing suicidality as a problem solving behavior, as that suggests the resolution is inherently: Find another solution. See my chapters on grief for additional key resources for high schools.

2 A mom began Mothers Against Drunk Driving at her kitchen table in 1980. MADD's efforts are largely responsible for cutting the number of drunk driving fatalities in half since 1980. Not only does the organization demonstrate positive social change fueled by righteous anger, it stands as a standard for infuriated teens outraged by school shootings and yearning for models of affirmative social engagement. Facts and details abound on their colorful and engaging website at www.madd.org

3 Emerson, R.W. (1871). The passage is in his *The Conduct of Life* (Boston, MA: James R. Osgood & Co., Late Ticknor & Fields, and Fields, Osgood & Co.) section IX, *Illusions*, paragraph five. Retrieved from www.gutenberg.org/files/39827/39827-h/39827-h.html#illusions Scholars still debate what Emerson (1803–1882) and his nineteenth-century cohorts meant by "sentiment." It does mean emotion, but the connotation then appears broader. June Howard's explication in *Key Words for American Cultural Studies* knocks at the door of what we mean today by emotional intelligence and its social function. Sensibility was nineteenth-century "emotion" without the twentieth-century pejorative coloring suggested in the accusation, "You're too emotional." Was emotion a good thing before the twentieth century happened? Howard's erudite synopsis is online at https://keywords.nyupress.org/american-cultural-studies/essay/sentiment/

Name: _____   Date: _____

Activity Sheet 5.1, p.1
LIST OF ANGER WORDS

MILD ANGER	MODERATE ANGER	INTENSE ANGER
aggravated	mad	inflamed
put out	irate	fuming
impatient	frustrated	infuriated
testy	petulant	surly
condescending	contemptuous	disdainful
contentious	belligerent	bellicose
cross	fractious	cantankerous
grouchy	peevish	crabby
annoyed	indignant	incensed
ticked off	irritated	bitter
offended	affronted	insulted
pushy	aggressive	pugnacious
piqued	inflamed	seething
irked	vexed	enraged
miffed	rankled	rant and rave
pestered	exasperated	deranged
smoldering	riled up	berserk
insolent	defiant	rebellious
pouting	sulking	grumbling
chafing	brooding	resentful

Name: _____   Date: _____

Activity Sheet 5.1, p.2
LIST OF ANGER WORDS

MILD ANGER	MODERATE ANGER	INTENSE ANGER
oversensitive	irritable	irascible
touchy	cranky	quarrelsome
crusty	crotchety	churlish
worked up	wrought up	furious
wrathful	hostile	warring
harsh	truculent	combative
biting	scathing	vitriolic
brutal	vicious	ferocious
abrupt	curt	brusque
mean	cruel	ruthless
sarcastic	mocking	scornful
sardonic	cynical	satirical
tart	acrimonious	caustic
acrid	astringent	virulent
smirk	sneer	scoff
deride	cutting	taunt
sharp	brutish	acerbic
beastly	vehement	vicious
fierce	violent	savage

Name: _____ Date: _____

Activity Sheet 5.2, p.1
THE A WORD

Are people *angry* at you more often than you like? If so, examining how you talk to others may help. Circle the items that are similar to the talk you use. Then add your own statements.

1. **DEMANDING AND WHINING**

   "I told you to do it *now!*"

   "Aw, why don't you buy me new jeans?"

   "You better not say another word."

   "She always gets more cookies than I do."

   My favorite demanding and whining statements:

   _____

   _____

   _____

   _____

   _____

2. **JUDGING AND BLAMING**

   "You should have known better."

   "You never know when to quit."

   "Now you've done it! You ought to be ashamed."

   "Well, what else should I have expected from you?"

   "It's all your fault!"

   My favorite judging and blaming statements:

   _____

   _____

   _____

   _____

   _____

Name: _____   Date: _____

Activity Sheet 5.2, p.2
THE A WORD

3. **NAME CALLING**

"You dingbat nerd."

"You clumsy fool."

"You stupid idiot."

My favorite name calling statements:

_____

_____

_____

_____

_____

_____

4. **THREATENING**

"If you do that again, I'll beat the #@*! out of you."

"Why don't you watch where you're going?"

"How'd you like it if I did that to you?"

"You're going to get it!"

My favorite threatening statements:

_____

_____

_____

_____

_____

_____

6   How Anger Feels and Thinks

Time to AMP it up. The most useful tool for reining in anger is an anger management plan, an AMP. Equally an AMP is an affect management plan. Individual Educational Plans are widely called IEPs. When a youngster with or without an IEP has anger issues, a formal, written AMP is appropriate. Each school system may create a format. The format is not as important as the principles behind the format and active, frequent reviewing of the plan. IEPs that are filed and forgotten cannot be effective in achieving educational goals. Similarly, AMPs that are devised but not regularly and consistently implemented are not helpful. Both IEPs and AMPs are tools. Results come only when tools are used.

Since anger is an emotion, all the principles presented in Chapters 1–5 are foundational to an AMP. Thus, the plan must address the feeling part of anger and also the thinking part. It is the self-talk that generates the anger in the first place that is often omitted or underestimated. We are thinking beings. We have the ability to refuse to know our own thinking, an ability sometimes called the subconscious mind. But whether we are aware of it or not, the thinking is there. Anger-provoking self-talk induces and maintains anger.

As with all emotion there is Before Self-talk and After Self-talk that comes before and after the felt experience of the emotion. Thus, searching out that self-talk is crucial. "I don't know why I got mad" is unacceptable in the twenty-first century. Know. To transform anger in the long run, the starting place is knowing the highly personal self-talk that repeatedly generates that anger. When anger continues, there is After Self-talk that maintains and, as is commonly said, "works up" the anger.

AMPs state word for word the self-talk that comes before and after. Omit this part and techniques like mindfulness and the ancient prescription to count to ten may modulate the immediate expression of the anger but do nothing to change self-talk. Only actively changing self-talk changes self-talk. From there we move to the use of I Language to reframe how we see both the situation and our emotions. As we advance we ponder anger's positive role, such as passionate play in a sport or activity and also in generating the determination to achieve some positive goal.

How Anger Feels in the Body: Teenage Temper Tantrums

There are two-year-old temper tantrums and teenage temper tantrums. Considering the display of the two-year-old assists in appreciating teenage tantrums. The underlying origin is the same. By two the child grasps the core concept, "I am a person." The brains of babies are not developed enough for full perception of the meaning of I am me and you are you. As the first year moves into the second, the galloping development of the brain propels accelerating word usage. The word I is learned. Fully self-reflexive individuality begins.

The child replaces the baby. It is a child that knows "I have my own mind." "No, I don't want to" enters the lexicon. When adults fail to understand that a free individual is developing and respond to "I don't want to" with "It's my way or the highway," the birth of the free person and the genesis of individuality is squashed before it may begin. Using the Give a Choice technique fosters healthy individuality while simultaneously educating the little rebel into the realization that they live in a world of rules and limits.

Preschoolers are the teenagers of childhood. For the teenager, too, is struggling with the concept of "I am a person." But now "I don't want to" may have enormous consequences. The issue is still individuality, freedom, and being myself. The preschooler's poor concept of time absolves them from the ticking of time. This is not so for teenagers. Fourteen-year-olds fully grasp that they will be 18 in four years, a young adult, a voting adult. Adults may empathize with the fear that results if they imagine the old image of the victim tied to the railroad tracks as the engine relentlessly approaches from the distance. When this fear is converted to anger, teens erupt.

Of course, this is not the only source of teen anger. But it is certainly an often ignored one. Whatever the source, teen anger is literally a gut-level response to perceived danger or threat. Anger's role in the human psyche is to protect and defend. Our brains do not make us angry just to torture us. Tell your brain the equivalent of "This is threatening to me" and the perceived threat clicks on the hormones and neurotransmitters that correlate with anger.

Having no anger management plan, not knowing what to do with their anger, not even, at times, understanding that what is happening to them is that they *are* angry, teens may act like two-year-olds. As with the young child, the hallmark of the tantrum is the moving of the arms and legs. Two-year-olds flail on the floor. Physical movement discharges the physical tension. More than that, the brain itself screams, "Act! Act! Act!" Adults who attempt to reason with a child in such a state are fighting not the child but the brain itself.

When teens pour their anger into their arms and legs, disaster may result. All behaviors that are called at-risk behaviors involve using the arms and hands and/or legs and feet inappropriately and often destructively. Rash, impulsive action follows the teen's initial perception of their brain's injunction to act. Addiction may begin when emotion and the inner command to act yields the action of hands picking up and using an addictive drug just to compel the brain to stop demanding "Act" and thereby to mellow the emotions.

Although obvious, the core expression that anger initiates, namely the moving of the arms and legs, is often overlooked. But the solution to anger expression is just precisely what nature drives us to do. All methods that fight nature will ultimately fail. These bodies of ours that have the built-in capacity to generate anger have been evolving in *hominin* form for millions of years. Just because we are well-educated modern people does not mean we stand a chance when we try to go up against 315,000 years of *homo sapiens* evolution.[1]

Teens know enough to know they live in a world where too many do not understand anger. Suppressing anger, being ashamed of anger, being angry about getting angry all come when teens never hear an adult say, "I understand your anger." This is true of everyone, but teen girls have the unique cultural challenge of knowing that angry women merit names like bitch. Tantrums suppressed do enormous damage and may propel the girl along a path that leads to cutting, to addiction, and possibly to suicide. Better dead than a bitch.

Transforming tantrums to constructive management of anger is an ability that is *learned*. As the two-year-old must be taught to get needs met by methods other than thrashing and screaming, so, too, must the teen. It is not a matter of teaching the teen to resist the natural impulse to move the limbs. but of teaching the transformation of the expression of that impulse.

Fighting and Other Teen Temper Tantrums

So growing up is a steady process of moving from inappropriate manifestations like tantrums to more acceptable expressions. Acceptable must incorporate accepting that the impulse to move the limbs is difficult to overcome. No matter one's age, the brain still wants the emotion-filled human to act. Only we, oh shall we say by 50, have learned to say to our bossy Brainy Boo, "Oh, be quiet already." And go for a fast walk.

Society is full of double messages about what is and what is not acceptable anger expression. While we pay lip service to the idea that fighting is unacceptable, movies and TV are replete with violent heroes that model fighting as manly and tough. Tantrums by any other name are still tantrums. Both murder and suicide, the ultimate tantrums, are glorified in pervasive media our teens cannot easily escape.

No wonder youngsters are confused and ambivalent about how to demonstrate that they are independent and strong. If fighting or any violent expression is an issue, all the emotional ramifications must be explored before the counselor will have enough information to assist the teen in writing an AMP. Since the anger in question is by definition the anger of the teen, that teen actively participates in crafting the plan. A plan made up by adults and imposed on the young person will not work. It will not work, not because you have a teenage rebel sitting before you, but because imposing solutions is just a version of "do what I say" and as such violates the teen's innate drive to individuality and freedom. Attempting something that tries to bypass the nature of the teen will not work.

This does not mean letting teens run the world. Adults underestimate the benefit of having ten, twenty, or more years on the teen. School counselors are called guidance counselors, not command counselors, for a reason. Long ago those working with teens saw that commanding does not work. But guiding is a form of teaching. Putting yourself in alliance on the side of the teen, you state facts and guide the teen. For example:

> I see you have an issue with anger. I've been angry, too, so I know anger doesn't feel good. We need to work together to come up with a strategy for anger that works better for you and better for everyone around you.

Probe the angry teen's view of the world with questions like the following:

- How do you feel when you get into a fight (or into whatever hostility)?
- How do you feel in your body while you are fighting?
- And after the fight is over?
- Whether you win or lose, how do you feel in your mind? How do you feel about yourself?
- What effect does drinking have on fighting?
- What does getting stoned do to anger?
- Do you like the idea that other people see you as the kind of person who starts or gets into fights?
- Do *you* want to be around a person like that?

Teens expect to be scolded for their angry acts and so may be slow to respond. Thus, it is imperative for the counselor to accept the anger while being abundantly clear about the limits of acceptable behavior. A high-school version of good cop, bad cop sometimes evolves with the vice principal playing bad cop scolding and punishing and the counselor cast in the role of empathetic good cop. I suggest both need to be both. We do need to clearly state, "You have stepped over the line," while in the next sentence stating, "I get that you are angry." We accept the anger, never the inappropriate behavior. If necessary, drive the point home with a strong statement like "You might feel so mad you think you want to kill someone. You just cannot actually kill them." We have no thought police. We do have real police.

The Angry Mind: Anger-provoking Self-Talk

As for all emotions, the cognitive part of anger is mental, the self-talk and images that precede and follow the physiological anger. Apply this knowledge specifically to the anger of a teen you are working with. Anger is both very individualistic, particular to that teen, and definable in categories that apply to all or nearly all teens. All are concerned about how they identify themselves and get mad when they fear that identity is threatened. All care about their social place, about whether they do or don't have friends, and whether people do or don't like them. So anger erupts both from what others do and from what they don't do.

Although social matters appear to be external and out of the teen's control, it is our internal self-talk, not the friends, that generates the anger. We talk ourselves into anger. We may learn to talk ourselves out of anger. Initially, expect resistance to this concept. Teens have been raised in a world that has taught them to say, "You hurt my feelings" and "You make me mad." It takes patience and careful but simple reasoning to shift such thinking.

> Someone may say something mean but you still have power over how you respond. You might say to yourself, "I know none of that is true. That's not me. Besides, saying mean things means that other person is angry. I'll tell them that."

Encourage a beneficial verbal response like "I hear your anger. Talking to the counselor might help you. It's helping me." Once such an assertive response is spoken, walking away is speaking by action. The action of walking away at that point states, "I have already spoken up for myself and have nothing further to say to a mean-spirited person." Walking away after assertively standing up for oneself further claims the high ground by bravely owning responsibility to de-escalate the situation. Those who unjustly initiate fights, verbal or otherwise, are not seen as heroes. Those who de-escalate the level of shared anger are courageous. Appeal to the teen's desire to be special, unique, and brave enough to cast their lot with the peacemakers. The approach is clear.

Support assertiveness. Invite peacemaking.

The individual's After Self-talk clearly demonstrates that each individual is in charge. Each of us is in full control. To continue to be angry or to release anger are our choices. If the teen laments, "I can't stop thinking about it," explain that strong feelings must be expressed more than once in order to release them. Teens bullied and teased must have multiple occasions to fully express and exorcise the depths of their pain. All the anger, fear, and hurt must be found, talked about, and brought to a resolution that, while not optimal, is at least acceptable to and possible for the teen. Adults often think that talking about a teen hurt once is sufficient. That works about as well as telling a two-year-old "no" one time.

I Am the Victim of My Anger

Whereas teens quickly see that negative expressions of anger generate negative consequences, they may be slow to see the destructive impact to themselves, to their own minds and bodies. Teens may be too well aware of how hostility disrupts relationships and leads to the failure of the family as our primary support system. But greatly underplayed in our society is how *my* hostility destroys *me*. Besides getting into trouble and other unpleasant social consequences, lead teens to see that I myself always suffer the worst from negative expressions of anger.

This suffering happens in more than one way. Intense hostility creates uncomfortable physiological sensations in the body. *My* hostility may physically harm someone else, but it also always harms *me*. Those who make revenge a way of life may end by destroying themselves—literally. Medical research has revealed that angry personalities have more coronary heart disease. Such individuals see an external person or object as a continuing anger-provoking source. Long-term anger, irritation, and perceived helplessness result.

Carefully done studies show that angry people have more heart attacks and strokes. Although research continues to investigate the underlying mechanisms, current statistics reveal coronary heart disease is nearly three times higher in depressed individuals and 60 percent higher in those with anxiety. The emotions at the core of depression are anger and fear, and often grief and guilt also. Thus, this research offers an intriguing metaphor. In attacking others, we attack our own hearts.[2]

Hostility lowers *my* self-esteem. It may or may not impact the self-esteem of another. Hostile people may justify their behavior. That does not mean they feel good about themselves. Generally, people do not want to see themselves as angry and hateful. This is so true that when the border is crossed between caring and not caring about one's own hatefulness we identify a different category of human, the sociopath. For the same reason, any teen that crosses your path who sets fires and harms animals and appears on the road to genuinely not caring must have immediate and maximum intervention.

Teens are at a crossroads. Those about to move down very negative paths may be turned around. The turning must begin with elucidation of the emotions inside. Hatred is crystallized anger. Hatred is anger shown in hostile and destructive actions. Teens are not yet so far away from the pain, the fear, the hurt, and loss behind the anger to not be able to retrieve that pain and redirect the emotion away from hatred.

However, their position at the crossroads drives teens to speak in their own teen code. The adult world does not mirror their experience. Neither does the world of childhood. Teens both know who they are and don't know who they are at the same time. It takes experience working with teens to decipher what they are saying in their teen code. For example, "I don't care" does not mean what it would mean if a sociopath said it. In fact, sociopaths are so far beyond caring they don't even bother to say they don't care.

For teens "I don't care" means one of two things, or both. One, "It hurts too much to care." Two, "I'm too mad to care." If you're hurting and mad about the caring, you are not a sociopath. You are a normal teenager. Smile slightly at "I don't care" and ask, "So what are you mad about?" If you have knowledge of or just an intuition about a hurt, gently ask, "So who hurt you?"

See when the hostile face is a mask. Consider that "I don't care" may translate to "No one cares about me" or "Someone I care about doesn't care about me" or "Someone who was supposed to care about me, a parent, didn't." And teen logic demands, "If they didn't care about me, why should I care?" To which the educator always responds, "I care." Anger that stems from lack of care is only assuaged by some adult caring. Educators nurture teens by making their caring tangible. That caring must inform every word written in an AMP or else there will be no anger management.

• Journaling—The Anger of Hostages and Prisoners

History offers enlightening examples of people using anger constructively. In conjunction with the social studies teacher or with your teens who love social studies, request a search for historical figures who used anger to survive. For example, the life of Senator John McCain may be explored as an inspiring example of converting the anger generated by unjust imprisonment into a force for good. His is a particularly good example because although those who knew him often felt the blasts of his anger, he never harmed others. His life as a whole demonstrates how anger over injustice may drive a lifetime of working for what he believed was the greater good.[3]

The story of Anne Frank equally shows positive use of trying emotions. In many high schools her diary is part of the language arts curriculum. It only takes a small shift in focus to use the assignment to educate about difficult emotions. Anne is a prime historic example of using a journal to express emotion and so to help oneself endure. A youngster who feels trapped in any way would benefit from reading her journal and then keeping one. Particularly, assist the young person in contrasting constructive versus destructive self-talk. Anne Frank's story is a beautiful record of positive self-talk expressed in the most frustrating of circumstances.[4]

Invite teens to research other examples of people who directed their anger into survival. If the exercise is done in social studies class, teens may trade journals and comment on what they feel is constructive versus destructive self-talk.

- **Small Group—The Self-talk of X**

Share pictures of great world leaders of today and yesterday who suffered some unfairness in life. Some examples are Abraham Lincoln, Mahatma Gandhi, Martin Luther King, Harriet Tubman, Helen Keller, Nelson Mandela, and all the founding presidents. For example, remind your teens that the revolutionary war lasted seven years. What got George Washington through? What might he have gotten mad about? What did he do with that anger?

Current-day well-known athletes and other celebrities may be included. The group may enjoy imagining the self-talk of celebrities caught on camera in temper tantrums. Group members may choose a person and bring that person's picture or angry episode, printed or digital, to the group. Alternatively, the choosing may be done, phones flashing, in the group.

Explore the self-talk of that person as the group imagines what it may have been. Ask first for the kind of self-talk the person might have used when feeling angry. Push for more possible self-talk by asking what the group thinks their chosen people might have said to make themselves even more miserable, more mad.

If there is laughter, point out that laughing lifts an angry mood. Then direct the group to suggest self-talk that their person might use to get themselves out of their anger. How could the celebrity have responded differently other than pitching a fit? This activity also counters the teen tendency to blindly admire the behavior of celebrities.

- **My Personal Anger Management Plan, Part I: Activity Sheet 6.1**

For those most needing it, begin to work on an individual, personalized anger management plan, an AMP. This may be quite formal and include the completion of a form that details all the components of an AMP. Or it may be less formal but still written. Because the anger is the student's anger, not the counselor's anger, it is imperative that the teen formulates the plan.

It would be faster if adults simply imposed a plan on angry youngsters, but that would mean teens would have no ownership of their plans. The likelihood of follow-through would be small. Moreover, working together with the teen creates an alliance between counselor and teen. The message is not "You control your behavior!" which puts the teen in a position of isolation. Rather the message is "*We* are going to work together on helping you to find better ways to be angry." As counselor works with teen, you are modeling the behavior you would like the teen to internalize.

If you ponder an emotional time in your life when you felt quite alone, you will appreciate the extent of isolation strong emotions create. No one likes to be alone with their own intense anger. No one. That's why we so quickly divert, displace, and deny anger. That's why sociopaths become *cold*-blooded killers. Just letting someone know they do not have to be alone with their intense emotions and supporting them with empathy and compassion already begins the dissipation of anger even before a plan is discussed.

AMPs like IEPs are written. Talking precedes writing but ending after only talking about anger management is like leaving the words floating in the air. Ideas are just ideas until they are written. Once written, the idea becomes a concrete, tangible plan. Meaningful plans have feedback loops built in. Reviewing the written plan periodically both advises the youngster that adults seriously expect a change in behavior and reminds adults involved about what the alliance with the teen is meant to achieve.

A simple approach is to have the teen choose a page in their journal and save several pages behind it. Ask them to write on the first page My Own Anger Management Plan. Other sheets will be for future use.

Begin by reviewing **The Line**. Without judgment, but quite matter-of-factly, describe the hostile behavior. Probe for the self-talk behind the behavior, the self-talk both before the behavior and after it. The young person enters My Angry Self-Talk and writes that self-talk down on the left side of the page. On the right the teen places What I May Say to Myself Instead. So if on the left is entered "He called me a name. He dissed me!" (and so I hit him), then on the right may be self-statements like "Names don't hurt me. I don't have to get angry back. Just breathe. Breathe and walk away." Assist the teen in understanding that name-calling means the name-caller is angry and probably scared as he is trying to make someone else feel small. Meanwhile, of course, the angry name-caller also needs an anger management plan.

Next help the teen formulate and then write helpful self-talk. So Help Talk is written as a subhead on the first sheet below the first entries of self-talk. Prompt the teen with examples of self-talk that help remind us that anger is physical, such as "I'll be okay. It's only the chemicals in my brain and body. I will be okay."

Anger management is the process of getting distance from anger. When anger feels like "this is just me," the result is fear that may be mild anxiety or abject terror. Until someone teaches us otherwise, we may just assume that our intense anger means "I am a bad person" or perhaps just wild and irrational. We believe we are "emotional" in the pejorative way that word is used. Anger is normal but when you reside in a culture that rejects anger and indeed declares it "negative," you may quickly conclude that your anger means you are not normal.

Here is where having the correct information about the biological basis of emotion as presented in the preceding chapters is most useful. Help the teen gain the distance needed to take the blame off the teen and place it where it belongs, on our hormones, our neurotransmitters, our bodies, and our Brainy Boo. As you coach the teen to write their own Help Talk to show that anger is a physical thing, invite them to give a *name* to the physical side of their anger, like Mr. Hormone or My Dragon or something similar. Take time to support and direct the teen as they ponder the name.

This is not a minor step. Inventing a name for the physical side of anger shifts the focus from the teen's behavior, which adults label bad, to the teen's humanity, which necessarily means hormones and neurotransmitters. No one is angry because they are bad. We are angry because we are human. If I have named my anger My Dragon, then my task is to tame the dragon. So as learners write their own Help Talk, they already have begun to address the physical side of anger and so to manage that anger.

At this stage of anger management it is most useful not to overly dwell on *why* the teen is angry. Often adults jump too swiftly to the whys. As soon as you are pondering the whys, you are getting into problem solving. Too quickly conveying the message "This positive thing is what you should do" may inadvertently suggest to the teen that you are ignoring their anger. This guideline yields a clear tip.

Help the teen express the anger first. Then problem solve.

When anger has risen to the level that it has driven inappropriate behavior, the first issue is not the why. The first issue is the anger. An extreme example puts this into focus. When a murderer kills someone, the crux of the matter is not "Why did you do it?" but that a person is dead. If the judge chooses to consider extenuating circumstances and listen to the whys, that comes after the primary consideration, "Did you kill, yes or no?" Society so well understands this that we declare that there are degrees of murder and deaths that are manslaughter, not murder. The issue is the death, and loved ones may not at all care about the whys.

Similarly, the issue is the anger. Address the anger first. Then process the whys. In actual discussion you and the teen will jump back and forth between focusing on the anger itself and the circumstances, the issues, the whys. While working on the AMP, initially keep the focus on the anger itself. If the teen keeps insisting "But he dissed me!" point out that not all people who feel disrespected punch the offender. Yes, all punching must stop. But that is easier to achieve when first anger itself is identified as the issue.

As you move forward in your sessions and examine specific incidents, ask the teen to add to their journal pages *The Day I* entries. For example, entries might be The Day I Punched Joe, The Day I Threw the Eraser at the Teacher, The Day I Called Emma Names, The Day I Cursed at the Cafeteria Lady, The Day I Cut Myself, The Day I Got Drunk, The Day I Told My Friend I Wanted to Kill Myself, and so on. The behavior is described simply, straightforwardly, no whys. Whatever the behavior, focus on the emotion itself and not the behavior, not yet. As you accept and empathize with the emotion, the youngster may jump ahead to the behavior by lamenting, "I know I shouldn't have." Agree, then invite the teen to work with you on better ways to be angry. This approach accepts the emotion while setting limits on the behavior.

Each *The Day I* entry follows the format My Angry Self-Talk, What I May Say to Myself Instead, and Help Talk. Always remind youngsters to include "Breathe, breathe" in their Help Talk. Help Talk may also include directives to Mr. Hormone or My Dragon such as "Quiet down! I'm the boss of me, not you."

If teens act like it is just impossible to say their self-talk, shift to game-playing, that is, to apparent game-playing. Ask the teen to imagine they are in a time machine. "Go back to that day again. All will be easy to see because everything is in slow motion. Now think. What were you saying to yourself in your head just before you erupted? What was your self-talk?" Teens may initially resist this step, as saying the words out loud makes motivations clear and real.

In the AMP all self-talk begins and ends with quotation marks to show it is our inner voice, what we actually say to ourselves, the specific words that carry the emotion. What we say, we are able to change. The next chapters continue to develop the role of self-talk in anger management.

- **List of Anger Words, Activity Two: Activity Sheet 5.1, pp. 1 and 2**

Ask the teen to write a story *When I Was Mad* using the List of Anger Words from the last chapter and selecting words from the second column. "Relate a story about a time you were *moderately* angry, more than a little angry but not furious. As you tell the story, use at least ten words from the second column of your List of Anger Words." As before, state your requirements for good English or coordinate with the language arts teacher.

As a variant instruct, "In your story use as many words from the second column, and only the second column, as you can." In small group or in the classroom if the language arts teacher participates, have a contest to see who uses the most words in good sentences that make sense. The teacher, counselor, whole class, or participants from another class may judge the contest. Those who desire and certainly the art students may illustrate the stories.

- **I Imagine**

Collect pictures of angry, aggressive acts, and hostile people. Teens write paragraphs or verbally describe the nature of the anger. If pictures from phones are used, your techies may assist in casting pics from individual phones to a large screen all may see. Most particularly, encourage photos of close-ups or selfies of angry faces. The paragraphs or descriptions begin "I imagine this person is [angry] because … ." In describing the anger teens use the List of Anger Words to fill in the brackets.

For example, "I imagine this person is peeved because," and "I imagine this person is irritated because," and so on. When teens slip into common slang words, shift their focus back to the List of Anger Words. The core message is clear: You get to be angry in an okay way. You do not get to be angry in a not-okay way. Foul language is not only not okay, but in a language rich with synonyms for angry it is also unnecessary.

Language arts teachers may apply this approach to each character in every literary work in the curriculum. Was King Lear peeved, irritable, furious, or all three? What did Romeo feel when he could not see Juliet? In *The Sound and the Fury*, what emotion was the sound and what emotion was the fury? Interpreting the emotions in characters elucidates the finer nuances of character development.

Expanding a young person's vocabulary about anger helps manage the emotion by verbalizing just precisely what degree of anger is felt. Turning raw emotion into words and images has been humanity's anger management plan since we first painted the cave walls.

BULLETIN BOARD MATERIAL

What's it all about?
When in doubt,
Talk it out!

The Rule About Anger
No matter how angry I ever get,
It's not okay to hurt someone.

The best plan is to reject straightway the first incentives
to anger, to resist its very beginnings ….
Seneca[5]

Notes

1 Brain evolution includes evolution of the parts of the brain mediating emotion. A graphic synopsis of brain evolution for both teacher and teen is Russell Tuttle's *Human Evolution* in *Encyclopaedia Britannica*, December 5, 2018. Online at www.britannica.com/science/human-evolution

2 The foundations of research on these connections go back to at least the 1980s. For early research see Grossarth-Maticek, R. and Eysenck, H.J., *Psychological Factors in the Prognosis, Prophylaxis, and Treatment of Cancer and Coronary Heart*

Disease in *Directions in Clinical Psychology, Volume 2*, pp. 2-1 to 2-17. New York, NY: The Hatherleigh Co., Ltd., 1992. For current research with statistics on anger as it relates to depression and anxiety, see Davidson, K. W. *et al. Selected comorbidities in coronary heart disease: challenges and grand opportunities.* Washington, D. C.: American Psychological Association, 2018. *American Psychologist*, Vol. 73, Number 8, 1019-1030.

3 Biographies include Elaine S. Povich's *John McCain: A Biography* (Santa Barbara, CA: Greenwood, 2009) and her picture-laden *American Maverick* (Edison, NJ: Sterling, 2018). Senator McCain's own books also detail his experiences.

4 There are many editions of Anne's diary such as *Anne Frank: The Diary of a Young Girl* (New York, NY: Bantam Books, reissue edition, 1993).

5 Retrieved from Lucius Annaeus Seneca's (4 BC–65 AD) *De Ira, Of Anger* (A. Stewart, Trans. London: George Bell & Sons, Bohn's Classical Library Edition, 1900) online at www.en.wikisource.org/wiki//Of_Anger/Book_I#VIII The philosopher's wisdom remains valid. Immediately changing self-talk clips off anger before it takes hold.

Name: _____   Date: _____

Activity Sheet 6.1
FORMAT OF ANGER MANAGEMENT PLAN

In their own hand, students write the following in their journals.

The Day I

Succinctly describe the hostile behavior. This is short, to the point, a sentence or two, not a paragraph.

My Angry Self-Talk   What I May Say to Myself Instead

Before the behavior

After the behavior

Help Talk

Pointers

1. All self-talk is enclosed in quotation marks to show it is the actual words you say in your head. Self-talk is usually short: noun, verb, object.
2. Emotion changes as self-talk changes. To change behavior, change the emotion. To change emotion, change the self-talk.

7 Three Sources of Anger

To thoroughly understand anger, we must recognize all its sources. Only then may a source be identified, specified in writing in the AMP, and so addressed with a meaningful plan. Key cognitive distortions, false or irrational self-talk, may stem from a failure to comprehend the meaning of threat, fact, belief, egotism, and ego. A simple but direct way to work with young people on these definitions is to name the three sources of anger. Teens then select their specific, unique source for the AMP.

A threat is an expression of intention to hurt or harm or something perceived as undesirable. It may come from a person or thing. A threat may be something *perceived* as harmful as well as that which is actually harmful. The distinction is important because we frequently do get angry about things that cannot really hurt us.

Especially when teens make sweeping, declarative statements, a failure to differentiate facts vs. beliefs may begin a process that ends in anger. Be certain your teen grasps the difference between a *fact* and a *belief*. If necessary, invite teens to look up the definitions on their phones. A teen may initially believe "They hate me," but that is only a belief, not a fact. Pretending to ascertain another's motivations often leads to error. The other may be angry, certainly, but if they are hurling that anger at you, they may also be scared or sad or full of other difficult emotions. Emphasize that a belief is essentially an opinion. When it comes to anger, our beliefs about what is and is not threatening are all important.

The Drive to Community and Adolescent Anger

The developmental tasks of adolescence inherently stimulate anger. But individuation is not the only task of adolescence. Parallel to and simultaneous with the task of individuation is the task of community. This task is presented in texts of adolescent psychology with much discussion of socio-emotional development, the role of family and friends, and the impact of peer pressure. All this may be subsumed in the overriding category known as community.

Community groups range from family to neighborhoods to friends to social groups like Girl Scouts, the soccer team, and social media. Community includes each individual classroom, the class or year, like freshmen or senior, the school itself, all the way up to each particular school system. Community is family, extended family, the town, the part of town lived in, the state, and the nation. The ultimate community is the earth-wide community of humanity.

Adolescence asks the teen to identify a place in each. That place must be identified with only the experience of 12 years to rely on. Figuring out who you are in the group is as frightening as figuring out your unique, personal identity. The drive to community is so enormously strong that the teen, though frightened, may exhibit more anger than fear. People are notoriously difficult to control. Whereas I myself may decide who I am and who I am not, when it comes to the group, any group, the same plan does not apply. In the group, cooperation, collaboration, and teamwork are required. Throughout adolescence teens move in and out of groups as they strive to balance the drive to individuation with the drive to community.

Progress in both is required for healthy adolescent development. A simple protocol a counselor may use for each teen worked with is to comment or chart in the teen's file two things. One, how is this teen coming along with developing a sense of self, with individuating? Two, how is this teen progressing with the development of a personal community? Isolated teens are not progressing well. Teens in gangs or rigid cliques are misunderstanding the constructive role of community. They may be using a rigid group identity to escape the task of individuation. When the group tells you who you are, you don't have to figure that out yourself.

This simple tracking may be a page with two columns divided down the middle. On one side is the title *Individuation*. On the other is the title *Community*. The counselor notes observations in each category. Again, this may be done simply under the framework of too much, too little, and balanced. If the teen shows a strong sense of self but is always coming into the office complaining about friends, the task they need to play catch-up with is community. If the teen has friends but sits in front of you dumbfounded when you ask what interests them in particular and what they want to be when they grow up, the task of individuation needs some remedial work. So constantly recall this tip.

Is this an issue of individuation? Or community? Or both?

Teens often attempt to use one task as a way of absolving themselves from the other. The dumbfounded teen may so identify with the peer group that the identity with the group is the primary identity. Unfortunately for this strategy, there is no such thing as a collective college degree. There are only individual degrees for individual persons. Moreover, it is highly unlikely that the entire high school peer group will go to the same college or trade school. Some teens make the attempt by choosing a post high school college or even career by what their friends choose.

There are many ways teens let the drive to individuation be sidetracked or hijacked by the drive to community. Traditionally, this is called peer pressure. Standing alone is apparently more terrifying than standing in a group with a poor sense of who *you* are. Groups may be used as cover, even masks. The social butterfly may be flitting around in a constant race to escape self. The negative impact of the group is seen when the group is removed. If independent self-development is progressing, the loss of the group is experienced as sad but not as devastating. The feeling is regret and perhaps nostalgia. But when individuation is off track, the feeling is desolation, even complete emptiness.

The same dynamic is seen in boyfriend-girlfriend matters. If the mutual choice is a normal adolescent pairing, the break-up leaves two young humans who have their own feet to stand on. But when the pairing may be imagined as two planks leaning together to form an inverted V, separation is going to mean something crashes to the ground. It is normal for teens to sometimes think, "If I don't know who I am, maybe this one special person will tell me." But the degree to which this is pursued is everything. If the belief "I can't live without you" is fixed and firm, suicidal attempts may result. Often alcohol and drugs are used to escape the emotional pain. The interpretation is commonly "His girlfriend broke up with him so he got drunk." But, more deeply, when individuation is weak, it is more like "Without her I don't know who I am and fear I'm nothing so I'll just get blotto." Blotto = nothing. When you feel like nothing, you make yourself nothing.

Whether in health class or individual sessions, teens must be taught that they are able to stand on their own feet. A teen does not just automatically know this. After a break-up, teens need to hear supportive adults affirm.

> You can stand on your own two feet. They're good feet, firm feet. I know this hurts now, but you're a great individual. I particularly love [name one: your ideas, your compassion, your smile, your friendliness, your generosity]. You're a super person. Maybe it's time for you to explore who *you* are.

Contrast this with the traditional adult words of wisdom, "You'll get over it." That statement ignores teens' emotions and says absolutely nothing about teen individuality and the ability to be a person in one's own right.

Community Is a Choice

The impact of what is conventionally called peer pressure is the playing out of a mass of quite unfinished, not yet completely cooked humans rubbing together, all vying to find their unique place while still being a part of some whole, some group. Peer pressure is not about the impact or influence of the group. Rather, it is a sign the individual has not yet developed a clear concept that they are not only able to stand alone, apart from the group, but that at times life blatantly demands we do so. Community is so much the fabric of being human that standing alone against the group may feel wrong, not permitted, and too terrifying to embrace. Courage, too, must be taught to youngsters. Chapter 15 is devoted exclusively to courage.

Social creatures that we are, we need to remind ourselves and teach our young people that at times our role in the group is to get out ahead of it, to be pioneer, innovator, scout, maverick. This may feel like isolation. But it is not the isolation of the sociopath but the temporary isolation that service to others sometimes requires.

Developing a sense of community means selectively choosing what group no longer fits. Social-emotional development advances as teens learn the skills of friendship-making, give and take, and come to understand it is okay to move from group to group as their own identity matures. All teens must have a belonging place. Counselors know it is a very bad sign when a teen is adamant that they have no friends, no group, no communal human place. Adults often excuse non-participation with "Well, you can't make them join if they don't want to." To the contrary, if the adults cannot structure the social world of the teen, who is going to do so? Community is not optional. If you are human, you are a primate. Primates are social creatures. Sadly it appears our cousins the chimps know what we at times pretend not to know. We need each other.

Certainly, it would not be useful to coerce teens even if we could. That other developmental task, individuation, would slam down on even the hint of coercion. Forcing teens to do something they don't want to do yields rebellion, sneakiness, and rage. Thankfully, there is no need to attempt to mold teens the hard way. Nature has given us a much easier way. Community. The drive to community is built in. All we need to do is find the entry point for that teen into a meaningful community. Harnessing the drive for community is the antidote to individuation run amuck in expressions of extreme isolation and dramatic countercultural manifestations.

Depending on the degree of alienation and woundedness, entry into a community, into any group, may take some time. If people have already deeply wounded the teen, isolation may feel safer than being part of a group. Trusting any group may feel like foolish self-destruction when the first community group, the family, was or is a source of great pain. If the teen is acting like a two-year-old, exhibiting either by pouting isolation or by trauma drama and teen tantrums, a technique useful with preschoolers may be scaled up to the teen age.

The Give a Choice technique means structuring choices for the child. So the choice is never "Do you want to brush your teeth (or not)?" because you, dear parent, are stuck if the toddler responds to the unspoken *or not* and affirmatively declares, "No!" A constant stream of no's from the child is two-year-old speak for "Look, adult! I'm a *person*. Get it? I decide for *myself*. So when you present just one choice, my *only* choice is No!" Careworn parents may regret the day they taught their baby to say "I."

Rather, savvy two-year-old tamers know to structure their words carefully. "Do you want to brush with the pink princess toothbrush or with the blue fairies toothbrush?" The child decides. The choice is never between brushing and not brushing. The so-called terrible twos dissolve in an endless set of choices. The challenge for the adult is to keep up with inventing the choices. "You made good choices today" is a wonderful way to close the day with preschoolers as it teaches the child to internalize "I have the ability to make choices and, by golly, I make good ones."

As for two-year-olds, so too for teens. Perhaps your teens did not have the opportunity to learn before kindergarten that they have the ability to make choices and to make good ones. Thus, the educator's challenge is to structure the choices for the teen when the teen refuses to do so. See the refusal as fear. Hear the unspoken "What if I make the wrong choice? Can I perform that skill? Accomplish that task in that group? But I have no talent. I have no skill. Besides, they won't like me." Get to know the teen's likes and dislikes. Tentatively offer a choice, "You could do this or that" to be part of a group. For primates the choice is never be part of a group or be part of nothing. When it feels like we are part of nothing, life is so dim the conclusion may be reached that it is not worth living. Deep is the woundedness that results. Suicide and homicide are the ultimate severing of community ties and response to the perception of isolation.

Three Causes of Anger, Threat One: Threats to Self

This threat includes the threat of physical danger, the threat, real or imagined, of actual physical harm, and the social-emotional damage of isolation, ostracism, and all the dynamics of the in-group vs. the out-group. Self includes our emotional self. So, by threat to self we mean all real and present dangers and those things potentially dangerous to both physical and emotional self.

This threat is always from the person's own perspective. Divorce does not cause the actual death of the child. But the emotional impact may have the young person nonetheless feeling like they're dying. They do grasp that the world, the very intimate world of the family, their most primary and immediate social group, is dead as they have known it. In that sense divorce may be experienced as a quite real threat to self.

Having to walk home in gang territory is a real danger. Not having food in the fridge is a real danger. Having to change clothes in a locker room that feels like a dungeon full of dragons since the teasing and bullying are merciless is a blatant threat.

In sessions explore with your teen any very real threats to self that apply. A hostile student in school may be acting out anger over not being safe in another environment. The school in contrast feels relatively safe. The actual unsafe environment may provoke intense fear along with the anger. So the anger is suppressed. If someone is hurting you, it's terrifying, but acting with hostility in the face of someone much more powerful may be the end of you.

Humans intuitively know this. So children scared and mad about their parents' divorce may flip into hellions in school while being good as gold at home. Despite the horrors of our day, school is still safe harbor for most young people. With hostile teens, always ponder for yourself whether the anger acted out in school is a text message in all caps that screams, "Would someone please notice I'm dying here!" This factor may drive teens' love of zombies. "I'm walking dead here, my dear adults, and you want me to *not* be horrifically hostile?"

With the teen make a list of physical and social-emotional threats to self. If the teen animatedly lingers on a subject, have them write down the issue in their journals on a page marked Threats to Self, Physical and Social. Those issues must be addressed in the AMP. Note the frequency of fear and anger as normal responses to tangible threats.

The very act of talking rationally about why we get angry *is* anger management. We talk instead of acting out. We talk first to learn our self-talk. Then we choose new self-talk that does not provoke anger.

The Second Threat: Threats to Ego

Most people do not experience extreme or unusual threats to their physical safety on a daily basis. With your teens, contrast this lack of daily physical danger with the frequency of threats to ego. Given the developmental task of individuation is working overtime, the threat to watch with teens is perceived threats to ego. In the journal the teen enters the next category, Threats to Ego.

Differentiate for your teens the meanings of ego and egotistical. Again we see that precision in vocabulary is an aid in grasping the source of our emotions. Dictionary definitions on phones may be consulted. Using a tool that for most teens is their third hand bridges the gap between adult and teen. It says, "I'm in your world, too."

Prompt extended and enriched definitions by sharing the visual of castle walls. Ego is like castle walls. It defines where the self that is you ends and the rest of the world begins. So by ego we also mean our self-esteem, self-worth, and self-efficacy. When working with teens, it is most useful to define **ego** as our *sense of who we are*. Ego is a function in our minds that tells us who we are and who we are not. It is a mental self. When sense of self is still in formation, ego-stimulated anger is frequent.

Fury comes over where my castle walls are and where they are not. In truth, castle walls still being erected are easily overrun. Piaget puts ages 11–12 as the age when we reach our full adult rational capacity.[1] Though high school educators may debate him, this means teens know they are vulnerable, comprehend their unfinished nature, are often fearful about where to lay a brick, and wonder endlessly if their castle is good enough. Just touching one of their precious bricks may set off a volcano.

Assaults to Ego

So just as our physical and emotional selves may be attacked and subjected to harm, the non-physical, mental self, the ego, may also be threatened. Assaults, real and imagined, to self-esteem, independence, and individuality constitute this threat. This includes humiliation, shaming, put-downs in general, and anything the teen believes a similar threat. Belittling name-calling is a favorite teen put-down.

When your castle walls are not yet high enough and strong enough, rocks and arrows easily pierce the inside. No cannon are necessary. Adults who historically have cried "Just ignore them" are adults who have forgotten how life with a fragile castle wall feels. Adults may imagine being in the open as ax-wielding, whooping barbarians encircle from all sides to comprehend the depths of fear and anger teens feel when ego is attacked. The intensity may evolve to the despair that leads some to suicide. In a school shooting, the despairing teen empties the full load of the accumulated terror and rage upon the school.

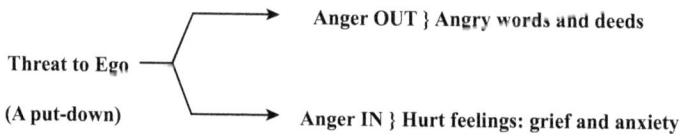

Threat to Ego

(A put-down)

Anger OUT } Angry words and deeds

Anger IN } Hurt feelings: grief and anxiety

Diagram the above for your teens.

The Third Threat: Threats to Fairness

Of all the threats that make citizens of a democracy angry, threats to fairness stand at the forefront. Welded to a long tradition of democracy and fair play, even a minor threat to fairness may be seen as the Terrible Threat. Teens who act in hostility often think they are just balancing the scales. The behavior says, "You treated me unfairly. So now I treat you unfairly." When this tit-for-tat thinking is not discovered and reframed, it may evolve to a more general "Society has treated me unfairly, so all humans are fair game." The flip side of the belief in liberty and equality is the rage that results when I believe I am being treated unequally and unfairly.

Have teens enter in their journals The Terrible Threat: Threats to Fairness. Most teens will need no more than that title to come up with a string of examples. Remind teens that terrible includes a range of strong emotions, from intensely horrific to mildly unpleasant. "It's terrible! She gave me an A minus. So unfair!"

Civil Rights versus Uncivil Fights

Collaboration with the social studies teacher is an extremely useful aid in expanding teen consciousness about what is and is not unfair. Teens may start from a position where they believe that not having a phone is unconstitutional. A teen once stated empathically that having to pay for a phone "wasn't right." Fairness to the phone company got all thumbs down on her social media page. Elicit other examples from teens' lives, such as "I got grounded for a whole week. That wasn't fair!" Add examples of inequality from society as a whole.

As with the other threats, we include actual, true deprivations of civil rights as well as intimidations and threats of potential deprivation. As long as a genuine social inequality exists, it constitutes a continuing threat to fairness. Go over examples of inequalities and unfairness and ask, "What emotion would you feel if this happened to you?" Putting "It's unfair!" into rational perspective reduces teen anger by assisting them in restructuring the self-talk behind the anger.

Thus discuss with your teens this principle.

Life is neither fair nor unfair. It just is.

Share that when we take things personally, we fall into the common misunderstanding that an oversupply of life's unfairness is intended just for us alone. Such a belief is prime garbage thinking, a cognitive distortion. This is not teen selfishness. The culprit is the innate drive to individuation. Bluntly put, nature drives teens to think of themselves first in order to complete the task of individuation. This is not the same thing as adult, well-calculated self-centered behavior.

• Journaling—Definitions

Instruct teens to write in their journals their understanding of threat, fact, belief, egotism, ego, Before Self-talk, After Self-talk, the two parts of anger, Help Talk, inequality, and the three threats. All may be entered or only what the teen sees as most personally relevant. What we write and reread and reread we master. In academics this is called studying. Anger management is studying and learning how to understand our anger and how to reframe it at its source.

• Book Report

Assign teens to search the library or internet for a biography of someone who was treated very unfairly. Have teens as individuals or in small groups give book reports. The reports should tell the person's story and detail the person's imaginary self-talk over the unfairness. Writing the self-talk in quotation marks designates the words as more than nebulous thinking about thinking. Quotation marks make it clear that the actual words that carry the emotion are being stated.

Such self-statements are generally short: noun, verb, object, or modifier. The story *about* the self-talk may go on for paragraphs. But the word-for-word dialogue or monologue within consists of strings of short, declarative, emotion-driven sentences. A prime example is "It's unfair." For self-referencing teens, learning of those treated unjustly provides an antidote to perceived unfairness. This aids in transforming one source of their anger.

• My Personal Anger Management Plan, Part II: Activity 7.1

At the top of the second sheet in the journal where the AMP is being written, teens add My Special Threat. The top of Activity Sheet 7.1 is for composing with the teen one or two descriptive paragraphs about which threat particularly applies. The activity continues with stating the anger-provoking self-talk (noun, verb, object) as described above. The format ends with the new Help Talk that the teen will use to reframe the original self-talk.

The whys of the matter may be included in a longer description. Ask for examples. If you are intervening after a hostile incident, the choice of threat should jump out at you. What did the teen see as the threat? Be always mindful this may not be what an adult might see as threatening.

Most teens will choose Threat Two or the Terrible Threat. Those who have experienced a real physical or social-emotional threat may choose to write about that experience. The goal is to personalize the learning by having each teen relate what they perceive as threats.

• List of Anger Words, Activity Three: Activity Sheet 5.1, pp. 1 and 2

Assign teens to write a story *The Day I Turned into a Tornado* or *The Time I Erupted like a Volcano*. Instruct teens to use the words from the *third* column of the List of Anger Words. Direct them to relate a story about a time when they were just furious. The story includes both at least ten words from the third column and the threat that applies. For example, if the fury was because the teen felt treatment was unfair, they are to bring the Terrible Threat into the tale. As before, the essay may be a language arts assignment. Teens may relate an actual incident or simply make up a fantasy tale.

BULLETIN BOARD MATERIAL

Life is neither fair nor unfair. It just *is*.

Community is family I choose.

When anger has breached our castle walls,
it changes the mind itself.
paraphrasing Seneca[2]

Notes

1 A concise summary of Jean Piaget's (1896–1980) four stages is online at *The Psychology Notes HQ* at www.psychologynoteshq.com/piaget-theory/
2 Sourced from Lucius Annaeus Seneca's (4BC–65AD) *De Ira, Of Anger, (op. cit.)* online at www.en.wikisource.org/wiki//Of_Anger/Book_I#VIII Teens may find the original wording a tad obtuse for their tastes. Seneca and his fellow stoics valued the image of building the castle walls of our interior castle. Now, as then, anger breaches those walls and distorts the mind.

Name: _____ Date: _____

Activity Sheet 7.1
FORMAT OF ANGER MANAGEMENT PLAN, p. 2

My unique threat is

_____

_____

This is my personal threat because

-
-
-
-

Examples of me demonstrating that this is my threat are

1.

2.

Specifically, I get myself angry because I tell myself

My Self-Talk

" _____ "

" _____ "

" _____ "

Help Talk

So I will stop telling myself this, and next time my threat attempts to rear its head, I'm going to tell myself instead

" _____ "

" _____ "

" _____ "

8   Empowerment and Anger

Working with teens to refine their understanding of common sources of our modern anger means exploring the differences and similarities between valid and invalid anger. Only then may teens add examples of their own invalid angers to their AMP. It is cognitive distortions, errors in thinking which create the invalidities. Chapter 9 will frame the use of valid vs. invalid angers for use in the AMP.

But first we must be aware of how the difference between valid and invalid anger lays the foundation for **empowerment**. Anger construc-tively used is empowerment. Authentic empowerment is both a thinking thing and an emotional thing. The thinking part is the self-empowering self-talk. The emotional part is raw, visceral anger chan-neled into persistent, resolute determination. It is better to name this kind of anger the emotive part of anger as the usage connects emotion to motivation. Both words are related. Both come from the Latin root *movare*, to move. This relationship reminds us of what our brains always recognize. Our brains know that the purpose of anger is to move us to act to protect ourselves. Thus, when we convert the emotive force of anger into motivation to act constructively, we are only doing what our brains want.

In the end the brain always wins out. Its eons of evolution *will not* be defeated. Either its imperative to act will drive the angry human to destructive, poorly chosen actions, or the thinking human will choose to direct the emotion. Directing the emotion used to be called controlling one's emotions. But, as widely interpreted, this kind of controlling really meant suppressing, denying, ignoring. "You're so emotional" was never considered a compliment.

What the old approach ignored is the fact that no one controls the end result of hundreds of thousands of years of evolution. The same brain is built to think, to ponder, to make choices. That is the brain in charge. Embracing that function of the brain means accepting responsibility to turn the emotive force of anger into driving motivation, into empowerment.

Empowerment in Individuation and Community

Perhaps nowhere in the high school world is the drama of empowerment vs. powerlessness played out than in the heartbreak of bullying. Vicious cyberbullying has tragically pushed teens to suicide. Gender-based sexual mores, too, embrace an ethos of the one with the power vs. the one without power. The rapist seizes all power. Victims are held powerless. Policies of national economies pit the powerful few against the marginalized. Clearly, early twenty-first-century people are toddlers when it comes to proactive empowerment.

Though humans have been violent throughout history, our twentieth-century misunderstandings about emotions in general and anger in particular have not aided us in transforming our seemingly never-ending violence. No one may say that education about emotions, affective education, will or will not stem the tide because humanity has never before attempted such education. Some of the ancient philosophers like Epictetus and Seneca came close to presenting such beneficial education, but who listens to ancient philosophers?[1]

What is clear is that human beings do not just automatically know how to channel their emotions. Many adults today have no earthly idea what to do with their anger and have no use for it. If we had been taught as children and teens what we now have the opportunity to teach our young people, this would not be so. Our teens have the chance to learn while they are young. We adults may have to go to remedial classes to learn what no one ever taught us in childhood.[2]

So be aware that your own empowerment may grow as you work to empower your teens. Do not flinch at sharing that you are learning, too. Teens, caught in the web of fiery emotions, are consoled when they hear an adult admit to sometimes feeling powerless in still working on the task of their own empowerment. What's not to admit? All humanity is working on this task.

The bully and the bullied have a central focus in common: Power. One claims all of it. One does not have enough. This is the drama on stage. Behind the stage the bully in some way feels powerless. The bullying acts are not so much to announce to others "I am powerful," but to convince self that one does indeed have power. Behind the overt anger is fear. The measure of the fear may be taken by the measure of the angry acts. Acts that are merely annoying and bothersome reflect a milder fear. Acts that are overtly harmful to another reflect fear that may approach terror and demonstrate as well complete distortions in thinking about how human relationships work.

Power is an aspect of individuation. We literally start life from a position of complete helplessness and grow in gradual stages more and more powerful. Around age 12 nature says, "Okay, you have all the basic tools now. Use them. Be powerful. Be a person." Thus we embark in adolescence on our lifelong journey to be somebody. Individuation is not about being a nobody. A nobody has no power and may feel invisible. The power of being a somebody goes by many names. Self-esteem, self-worth, self-actualization, competency, efficacy, and resiliency are a few.

The bullied teen, often seen as being low in self-esteem, is on the same stage as the bully. The face presented may be that of a competent, friendly, hard-working student. But backstage doubt rules. Many fears, all perfectly normal teen fears, mount to a crippling level. If cyberbullied, why does the teen not just simply disconnect? So adults often advise. Perhaps if we cast our minds back to our own high school years and imagine that as soon as we stepped into a corridor all the students there would disappear, we would begin to comprehend. Imagine high school corridors with no one there but teachers hurrying about their own tasks. In the classroom the other kids appear but you cannot talk to them. Imagine and consider how you would feel in that high school. So in working with teens, ponder thoughtfully.

Who has the power? Who has little power?
How may I intervene to create balance?

Blocking and unfriending may be part of a strategy to help the bullied. But much more important and potentially effective is developing that teen's own empowerment. Instead of an AMP, this teen needs an Empowerment Plan. Interestingly, by any name the plan for both the bully and the bullied is nearly the same. A bully without an AMP exhibits power as force and hostility. That is not empowerment. So their AMP might also be deemed an Empowerment Plan. The bullied are clearly not yet empowered and surely need help with their own positive anger expression, often completely internalized at first, so their Empowerment Plan could be called an AMP.

Whatever the rubric, start by having the teen name their emotions one by one. Have them write out their self-talk behind each emotion. Assist the bullied in reframing the words to use I Language to claim independence from the hurtful words. Assist both bully and bullied in clearly naming each anger, each fear one by one, not with "She makes me mad" language but with "I feel angry because" language.

The bullied hears others say, "You are this or that." If the teen believes what is said or even just worries that what is said may be true or that others may think so, fear, sadness, and anger result. Fear comes because the bully has power. Sadness comes from being cut off from part of the community group, from losing friends, and being on the outside. Anger comes because all that is unfair. But if the teen has not learned otherwise, those raw emotions may be held inside. Not only does the teen not talk to any adult about it, these painful emotions are not expressed in *any* positive way. Depression results.

Medicine cannot alleviate this kind of depression. If you were in that high school where your peers disappeared in your presence, how much medicine would you have to take to cheer up? Likely, if you took enough to impair your walking, you'd be merry. Okay, not even then. The solution is finding and directly addressing the teen's emotions, all of them. Fear must give way to courage, sadness to knowing someone stands with them, and anger to resolute empowerment. Counselors don't prescribe medicine. They *are* able to share courage, stand with their most isolated students, and practice empowerment coaching. Chapter 17 explores multiple aspects of depression.

When youngsters are most afraid, a compassionate adult must offer to share their own courage. **Courage** is being afraid but doing what you have to do anyway. Biological fear may be blinding. The adult not being similarly afraid is able to invite, "We'll be brave together. You and I together will practice being brave. We'll talk together about specifically how to do that." For those specifics see Unit III on fear.

For the bully the message is "We'll work together to figure out okay ways you may be angry. The school could use a powerful, assertive person like you. Wonder how we could use all the power that you like to show?" Sessions developing that teen's AMP also need to address the fears and perhaps other emotions like sadness behind the hostile behavior. Children of divorce, especially those enmeshed in a bitter divorce, may be angry at any handy peer who seems to be from a happy family.

Since bullying is a disruption in community, it distorts the developmental task of community as well as individuation. The pain of not being able to do what nature itself is driving you to do, namely to build a meaningful community for yourself and know your place in it, may be experienced by teens as excruciating. The bully may be attempting to solidify a place in their community group by using intimidation and force. The bullied fears loss of some community group with which they strongly identify.

Thus, standing with both bully and bullied is a must. Even as teens are compelled by their drive to individuation to rebel against adults, they will accept us as defenders of last resort. Give the bully permission to be a leader. Share insight on the difference between a leader and a bully. We follow a leader because we want to. We follow a bully because we have to. Or think we have to. Give the teen permission to act appropriately and offer help. Then watch.

Give the bullied permission to assertively stand up for themselves. If the bullied teen stands up for herself, your permission to do so was all she needed. If her pain continues, do not just offer help. Insist on it. If the bully embraces a leadership role and behavior modulates, you have assisted in a meaningful restructuring of self-concept. If not, insist on change.

Insist by using sessions for empowerment coaching for the bullied and anger management for the bully. Both are working on the same issues but from different directions. Practice what you expect the teen to do in the corridors and online. Your very expectation forcefully states, "I have faith in you that you *can* stand up for yourself" and "I have faith in you that you *can* use the power you have to be a constructive leader."

Often bullied teens simply need permission to stop being "nice" and start being assertive. The bully may not yet have developed a concept of self as a leader in any form. In any case, let us move away from considering standing up for yourself inappropriate. Assertiveness is not aggression. Both the bully and the bullied fail to grasp the difference. Coaching youngsters to be properly assertive is teaching a key life skill. Learn the skill in high school, and it is forever an advantageous tool in each teen's personal mode of lifelong constructive emotional expression. So to build individuation and community, follow this empowerment tip.

Share courage. Stand with the teen. Be an empowerment coach.

If educators in a school system have reason to think bullying or any aggressive behavior including sexual assault must be addressed, a system-wide approach is beneficial. If many think the need is there, it probably is. Schools sponsor clubs and groups as well as sports. A Guardians' Club may be formed. Similar peer support groups have been used since the 1990s in a variety of peer-on-peer contexts.

All in the club commit themselves to practice kindness and to stand up for anyone being bullied or needing help. Establishing such a group wherein adults are both monitors and mentors sends many positive messages. It builds community and thus supports and confirms the developmental task of community. It sends a powerful message to all teens, and not just to the bully and the bullied, that community is a prime value. It exhibits kindness and support of others, not just as platitudes but as real-world actions shown in standing up for those who are under siege.

Establishing a group of Guardians flips the power equation. Now the bully must stand alone with no support. The bullied is now the hero who stands up to aggression. All who support that heroic stance, the Guardians, are applauded in school assembly. The bully goes to counseling. The previously bullied student strides the corridors head held high.

Valid and Invalid Anger

Both bully and bullied and many, many other teens stockpile cognitive distortions that make them quick to anger. Forming self-talk that calls something a threat makes it a threat for that person's brain. In essence, then, a threat is internal self-talk along the line of "This is dangerous to me." The decision "This is dangerous to me" may be valid and real or invalid, not founded in reality, a phantom.

When considering anger, our beliefs are the all-important deciding factors. To discount a real danger is as damaging as to label as dangerous that which is harmless. In the first instance one sets oneself up to suffer real harm due to foolish disregard of the reality of danger. The second instance brings another type of foolishness. Unwarranted and disproportionate anger results from belief in the harmfulness of that which is not intrinsically harmful.

AMPs and Empowerment Plans may include simple entries that make this distinction clear. Writing forces the brain to think, to reconsider. Writing out our garbage thinking forces us to have it stare us in the face. This is so true that while people may enjoy talking endlessly about distortions in their self-talk, they resist writing it down. Vocalizing only, we may comment "But I know that's not really true." But when we write down that questionable self-talk, the image of the words on the page sighs, "But I really fear it might be."

Refocus attention on threats to self but build distinction between valid threats and imagined ones. A valid threat is one that is real, actual, true—a threat that would be one to any other human being in the same circumstances. In this case the self-talk "This is dangerous" reflects reality.

At other times we imagine that something is harmful or we uncritically accept an unfounded belief that something or someone or some group is harmful to us. This is an invalid threat. We may nonetheless respond with anger to that invalid threat.

Give concrete examples. An example teens may enjoy is the old belief that bathing frequently was not safe. Parallel with this was the firmly held belief that invisible bugs could not possibly cause disease. The nineteenth-century genius, Dr. Louis Pasteur, suffered untold ridicule from one Dr. Charbonnet and the learned physicians of the French Academy for continuing to insist over many years that what was invisible could and did harm us. The rage of those who were absolutely certain that the quack with a microscope was prattling nonsense literally drove Pasteur from Paris.[3]

Not to be detained out in the countryside, he saved some peasants by inventing the rabies shots protocol. Invite discussion by asking how teens think Pasteur might have felt. What did he do with his anger? Knowing that a hundred years before those out of step lost their heads, what did he do with his fear? Continue discussion on anything else that was believed to be harmful and was later found to be perfectly safe. Or something thought safe that was later found to be harmful.

If collaborating with the social studies teacher, a class on the topic would not only be enlightening but a fun-filled romp for your teens. "You used to think you had to wear a girdle?! You used to think you'd go blind if you …! Boy, you grown-ups were dorks." Or whatever today's slang of the moment equates to dork. Laughing now at our historic human foibles serves as a warning lest we weld our egos so fixedly to some belief that, when science or progress discover otherwise, we realize all our anger over the subject was for nothing. All paranoia and imaginary harms are examples of invalid threats to self.

Continue to process the invalid threats to ego and then finally those to fairness. Review with your teens that threats to ego are often at the heart of bullying. Bullies often imagine that the bullied teen has attacked them in some way. Perhaps they did but did not anticipate such a virulent response. Perhaps they did nothing but possess or appear like what the bully wants or fears. Perhaps the bullied did nothing but present as a handy target. Imagined threats to ego may generate as much anger as a slap in the face.

Imagined threats to ego are self-created, the put-downs we put on ourselves. This process is sometimes called being too hard on yourself. For some, being wrong about anything is a massive, entirely self-created put-down. The wounded ego syndrome is often a sign of invalid anger. A phantom put-down is based on self-talk that is real only as long as we believe it. It is real only *because* we believe it. It is real but invalid.

Though invalid, it creates real anger. A phantom may not be real, but if you think you see one, your fear is real enough. It is enough that the sojourn of life offers real humiliations to endure. We compound the challenge by inventing additional put-downs by our faulty beliefs. "Everyone should like me" is an example of a faulty belief that may yield anger when even one person dares to not like you. A world awash in perpetually clicking Like and Don't Like does nothing to correct such cognitive distortions.

Finally, those schooled in democracy and liberty view threats to fairness as the terrible threat. Whereas deprivations of civil rights are examples of valid threats, imagined threats to fairness stem from false appraisal of rights. Anger due to a supposed lack of fairness is invalid when it stems from a belief that one has been deprived of something that is a right that, in actuality, is not. The abject unconstitutionality of phone deprivation has already been discussed as an example.

• **Small Group—Phantom Rights**

Begin by distributing magazines and asking teens to find advertisements that appeal to them. Phones may also be used to search for pictures. Also provide a copy of the nation's constitution. It may easily be found online. Explain that a constitution is the proper source to consult for a listing of rights as understood in a democracy.

Initiate discussion on how often we confuse rights with privileges. Elicit from teens a list of phantom rights, those things that are believed to be rights but are not. For example, driving a car is a privilege, not a right.

As for "the right to be happy," a close reading of Jefferson reveals he was wise enough to promise only the *pursuit* of happiness, not its final achievement. Much modern anger derives from our collective fantasy that life is and by right ought to be pain-free and blissfully happy. Phantom rights create enormous anger.

Close scrutiny of advertisements and TV commercials reveals that many have the theme "You have a right to be happy, and so you deserve this product to make you happy." Elicit examples from the ads. In particular, point to ads and commercials for alcohol and over-the-counter drugs. Commercials that show smiling people drinking alcohol because the gusto of life is found in a can suggest that substances, too, are our right and so are necessary for happiness. Too many ads for medicines blatantly exhort, "If you have a pain, take a pill."

Our anger is real. But the self-talk behind it is not valid. The social studies teacher may find this an enlightening slant on the topic when the constitution and founding of the nation are taught. Asking today's teens to ponder what they think should be a right but is not yet today may yield prophecy of the world to come. Perhaps one day phones *will* be free. Our great grandparents certainly had no notion of the concept of a free school lunch.

Whether in social studies class, in small group, or individual session, invite teens to search the constitution. Ask, "Find where it says that happiness and freedom from pain are inalienable rights." When we choose to imagine happiness is our constitutionally guaranteed right, we only guarantee ourselves angry constitutions.

- **List of Anger Words: Activity Sheet 5.1, pp. 1 and 2**

Ask your teens to write *A Whopper*. Explain that before a whopper was a hamburger, it was a tall tale full of exaggeration, like the Paul Bunyan stories. Instruct teens to use as many synonyms for anger as possible. Direct them to:

> Make up a story, a whopper, a tall tale, about someone who showed all six kinds of anger. Use as many words in the List of Anger Words as you can. Be sure to bring in all three types of threats.

For kinds of threats categorized in a display, see Activity Sheet 9.1.

As before, state your requirements for good English or coordinate with the language arts teacher. The goal is to highlight the ridiculous extent of our invalid angers and how silly even our valid anger makes us when we destructively express that anger.

After multiple exercises with the List of Anger Words, teens will possess an extensive toolkit of words to precisely verbalize anger. Gaining facility with converting raw anger into words is central to anger management and therefore central to emotional intelligence.

• The Red Crayon Exercise

Give the teen a red crayon and paper. A sheet of paper may be used or the drawing made on a page in the journal. The same teen may make multiple drawings over time. At the end of the school year, line up the pictures so the teen may visually see where they began with their anger and how far they have come.

The initial instruction is to draw a picture that shows the maddest the teen ever got. This evolves to "Show me how mad you got since we last spoke." The picture may be whatever the teen wants. It may be pictorial and representational. It may be cartoon-like with stick figures. It may be as abstract as a Jackson Pollock. It may be a tangle of spaghetti or a collection of blobs.

Play with the activity with your teens. Who knows what anger looks like? Stress that your anger is *your* anger. No one else may tell you what it looks like. However, from time immemorial the color red has been associated with anger. We still say "I saw red" to mean "I got angry." Limiting the palette structures focus on the color of anger.

Everyone has old boxes of broken crayons at home. Ask teens to bring in the red ones. Your collection will build over time. Red markers, too, may be used but their ink dries out, whereas the smallest one-inch bit of red crayon may scrawl a message of anger. Moreover, using a crayon casts the teens' minds back to a time when scribbling on paper was a fun way to make the grown-ups babble praises. It is a subtle but powerful way to communicate to a teen "I know you are a big kid now, but we adults accept your raw anger now just as when you were a toddler."

Whether in group or individual session, take time for discussion. Be sure to resolve the anger to a comfortable level before finishing. A display of these drawings for the school to see would be a spectacular affirmation of anger beneficially and beautifully expressed.

• TV Homework

Direct teens to watch TV for two hours. The assignment is to write a summary of every commercial that has as its underlying message "This will make you happy" or "You have a right to or you should have this and what it will bring you." Teens add next to each entry whether they agree or disagree about whether the advertised product would make them happy. If they want the product but don't have it or can't get it, how do they feel?

• Self-Empowering Self-Talk

Activity Sheet 8.1 is offered as a format for cognitive restructuring. The format targets self-talk particularly emotion-provoking for a teen. It may be used as a handout sheet or simply as a guide sheet for entries into the AMP or Empowerment Plan written in the journal.

Although this chapter is primarily about anger, we have seen that it is almost impossible to talk about anger without quickly uncovering under-lying fears. The two emotions often go together. We get mad because we are afraid. Then we get scared because we're mad. Ah, to be human is a wondrous journey.

• **Who Are You? Activity Sheet 8.2**

Teens working hard on their identity may be stimulated by Emily Dickinson's inspirational work.

BULLETIN BOARD MATERIAL

Empowerment is self-mastery.

Fear drives bullying and the pretense of power over others.

Things do not change. We change.

Notes

1 Short biographies and key teachings of both Epictetus and Seneca are online at https://dailystoic.com/category/profiles/ Click on *Profiles* at the bottom.
2 Remedial classes for adults are called psychotherapy.
3 Scholastic has a lovely short biography, *Louis Pasteur*, by Allison Lassieur. London: Franklin Watts Publishing, 2005. His life, an exemplar of courage, might also be referenced in sharing the material on courage in Chapter 15.
4 Dickinson, E. (1891). *Poems, Series 2*. M.L. Todd & T.W. Higginson (Eds.). (Amherst, MA: No publisher cited). Retrieved at http://gutenberg.org/cache/epub/2679/pg2679-images.html.

Name: _____   Date: _____

Activity Sheet 8.1
SELF-EMPOWERING SELF-TALK

Everyone thinks. Everyone talks to themselves in their head. From thinking comes our emotions. To know where your emotions are coming from, listen carefully to what you say in your head.

What do you tell yourself which, when you say it, you find you feel afraid?

" _____ "

" _____ "

" _____ "

What do you say to yourself which, when you say it, you feel angry?

" _____ "

" _____ "

" _____ "

Now consider what you might tell yourself instead.

Instead of self-talk that produces fear, I'm going to say

" _____ "

" _____ "

" _____ "

Instead of self-talk that produces anger, I'm going to say

" _____ "

" _____ "

" _____ "

Activity Sheet 8.2
WHO AM I?

America's greatest woman poet, Emily Dickinson, struggled with understanding who she was. Read her poem and write about what her words mean to you. *Who* are you?

I'm nobody! Who are you?

Are you nobody, too?

Then there's a pair of us—don't tell!

They'd banish us, you know.

How dreary to be somebody!

How public, like a frog

To tell your name the livelong day

To an admiring bog![4]

First published 1891, five years after she died.

Do you ever feel like a nobody? How does that feel?

If you are or were a somebody, who is that? How does that feel?

What somebody do you want to be?

9 Distortions of Individuation and Community

As we advance our insight into the role of the developmental tasks of adolescence, new light is cast not only on teen emotions but on the most challenging teen behaviors. The twentieth century saw us target painful behaviors one by one. Labeling teens delinquents in the 1950s and 1960s gave way to the term at-risk youth. Both terms put the focus on behavior. Society said, "We don't care why you are stealing. We just want you to stop."

Fast after that came society's sweeping concern for substance use. Cigarettes, alcohol, and drugs, both legal and illegal, became the focus of national prevention efforts. Spearheaded by the Drug Free Schools Act, in 1986 monies flowed to schools to establish substance abuse prevention programs. The focus was on education about drugs. Society said, "If they just understand the dangers of these substances, they'll stop." Some enlightened school counselors and health teachers began to teach about the disordered emotions behind the behaviors. But the message from the top was "We don't care why you're using. Just say no."

In 1994 the Safe and Drug-Free Schools and Communities Act was included in ESEA, the Elementary and Secondary Education Act. Federal money for violence prevention as well as for substance abuse prevention flowed to schools. Skills-based programs to develop self-efficacy, resiliency, and life skills swept the schools as educators struggled to find "violence prevention programs" to use up all that federal money. Some programs helped, surely. But learning meditation, mindfulness, and detailed protocols of behaviors designated life skills does nothing to get to the root causes of anger. Society said, "Okay, so we are starting to care about your emotions, about your anger anyway. Just chill, meditate, and above all don't shoot."

What all these programs have in common is they are behavioral and mental. They are mental in that they rely on words, messages, instruction, and training that is mostly verbal. Early advocates of Drug Free Schools curricula really did think that if teens just had the right information, if we just educated them to the facts, they would change. "Ah yes!" teens were expected to cry. "We see the light. All your facts and statistics and detailed information have convinced us. We shall never touch drugs." Yet the legalization of marijuana continues and binge-drinking is rampant.

Past programs were behavioral in that they taught techniques and behaviors that were actions to be taken or not taken. Behavioral techniques are tremendously helpful. Life skills are by definition the string of behaviors or actions that are most conducive to a happy, healthy, drug-free, violence-free life. Did you teach life skills and puzzle over the empty eyes in some of the faces? Those were the teens crying, "Okay, so you want to help and to please you I'll try to behave the way you want. But inside I'm hurting so bad I sometimes cannot hear what you are saying."

Extreme Behaviors and the Developmental Tasks

The more extreme the behavior, the more disordered the emotions behind it. Alcohol and substance use may begin as a tangible way to numb the physiological side of emotion. But since any repetitive behavior may become a habit pattern, alcoholism and addiction may evolve. Indeed, depending on the individual's unique physiology, one usage may be enough to entrain the continuing response.

The age of first use of substances is generally 11–12.[1] This is no coincidence. Nor does it mean they have to be that old to figure out how to open the locked liquor cabinet. Many are the savvy eight-year-olds who can do that. But Piaget's last stage of mental development hits at just the time nature insists that the young preteen embark on the journey of individuation and community.

When you don't know who you are, one way you try to figure that out is to look around you and see what the grown-ups do. The classic reason given for teen drug use is peer pressure. They want to be part of the group. It is true that the drive to community does induce teens to do what their group does. But someone in that group has to be the first to steal the beer or get ahold of some drug. Neither beer nor drug just appear under their pillows to replace lost teeth. What is the origin of the original impulse?

Ideas about how to be human come to young people from the adult world in which they live and breathe and have their being. Young teens begin their path to individuation by observing the adult world. As much as teens appear to rebel against us, on a deeper level they believe just what we tell them. Present them with a world awash in alcohol and "You need to drink to be grown up" and "You need to drink to be a real person" just may be their conclusions. From there it is an easy road to "The more you drink, the bigger, badder dude you are" and "I can show everyone how great I am by drinking the most." On the surface the mechanism at play seems to be peer pressure. But below that is constant, unrelenting adult pressure.

Teens do not create their own world. We adults create their world. We display what we are creating in television commercials, printed advertisements, and online visuals. Why is age of first use 11–12? Because before that they hear and see our world but have brains not yet formed enough to fully comprehend and internalize what they are seeing and hearing. The six-year-old hears the cry, "I need a drink!" and offers, "Daddy, you can have some of my lemonade." The twelve-year-old hears and is mute.

From age 8–12 the child is daily seeing more and more. But the tasks of later childhood are all consuming. The roots of what will evolve into the full-blown tasks of individuation and community are growing and grabbing hold of the older child. They are busy practicing this self this month, that self another month, Cub Scouts today, no, no, make that soccer. They are laying the foundations for their adolescent tasks and are often visibly not yet ready to leave childhood. Playing with younger siblings is sometimes a pain and sometimes a delight. The adult world is far away.

Not so for teens. Whether we structure their world with seventh to ninth grade middle schools and then high school or with four-year high schools, the message is the same to the fourteen-year-old: You have four more years. Childhood is gone. Your adulthood officially begins in four years. Start acting like an adult. Now.

So they do. The easiest initial path of individuation is to copy the adults. Copy it, but twist it. Imagine the teen's thinking:

> They drink alcohol. I'll use drugs. They smoke cigarettes. I'll smoke, too, but not their nasty stuff. This tobaccoless stuff is slick. They pay at the checkout. I'll get what I want, too. I'll just take it. They sleep at night. I'll meet my friends at midnight at the park, and we'll play Commando Tag all over the neighborhood until 2:00. Oh, the fun things we'll do that they won't even know about.

We sleep and they return to childhood. Midnight tag aside, most of their fun things are some type of imitation of the adult world.

Movie images of adults having sex lead to shallow and poorly understood notions of the role of emotions in human sexuality. In the worst cases, total lack of empathy fuels the "I want what I want when I want it" sexual acts that constitute sexual assault. Observing the sex in many movies and in pornography does nothing to foster the conclusion that a sexual partner is first and foremost a human being and a separate individual, and that each individual's integrity may not be breeched. When it is, rape, even gang rape, may result.

There is no empathy in rape. Rape is a behavior, a crime, but behind it is abject failure to own one's own emotions and passions and absolute absence of emotional intelligence. It is true that someone may have hurt the rapist in his past, and he has internalized his fear, twisted his emotions into anger, and externalized that anger in rageful hostility. But many,

many of those who were deeply wounded as children bravely carry their woundedness and have never acted to harm another so grievously. These somewhere along the line learned something of empathy. They have at least a rudimentary grasp of emotions, their own and those of others. Hurting still with their emotional wounds, they nonetheless have chosen as a core element of their identity "Do no harm."

It may be that someone, a teacher, a counselor, a minister, a parent, taught them that there is power in empathy, in feeling with another. But before empathy may happen we must first know our own emotions. It is most particularly when one is in denial of one's own fear and anger that these emotions are projected outward in hostile action that may be acted out against self or another.

Hostility against self includes all self-destructive behaviors. It is shown in the cutting teenage girls do, the pounding the telephone pole or wall boys sometimes do, and the alcohol and drug use that too often leads to tragic outcome. The worst form of hostility against self is suicide. Acts of violence are acts of anger. Anger suppressed and converted into depression is nonetheless anger. Suicide is the final expression of a teen who was long angry and, sadly, never learned to retrieve the anger and hurl it outside.

Fostering Empathy

You cannot feel with another if you cannot first feel with yourself. You may intellectually comprehend what another feels. That is not the same as feeling with another. In full empathy our attunement to the other may lead us to cry because the other is crying. Another's fury, particularly when it is a just anger, enrages us too. We feel the rising of emotion within and have to swallow hard. This is manifest or overt empathy.

There is also quiescent empathy. Adults at times comment, "I must be getting hard-hearted. I used to frequently cry when I saw pictures on TV of people suffering. Now I don't." You are not hard-hearted. Neither is it simply systematic desensitization at work. Learning after years of practice to surmount the physiological signs of emotion does not mean that within we fail to deeply feel another's emotions. The hard-hearted do not notice the suffering of others. In the worst cases, noticing may draw a laugh. Quiescent empathy is more mental than physiological. If you notice and you care, a flash of physiological emotion may zip through you. We teach our brains to ignore this so that our entire focus may be on empathy in action. Precisely because we care about another's pain, we set aside our own.

Children are well known for being emotionally open and empathetic. Babies offer their rattles to crying adults. If young teens observe that empathy is not valued, they just may shove it aside. Empathy must not so much be taught as given permission to arise. Having emotions and being an emotional being is natural and as a process need only be guided and directed.

It is suppressing emotion that takes work. Rejecting, denying, displacing, projecting, and in general stuffing emotions is a lot of work. Nature does not want us to do that type of work, but our world has insisted that we do. Turning around what we have learned is initially difficult, not solely because some emotions are painful, but more so because we have worked very hard over the years learning to stuff, stuff, stuff. What we teach our brains, our brains learn.

Empathy as a function of our emotional selves is the same. It is natural. But if we work very hard at suppressing our empathetic inclinations, we shall succeed. Acting unempathetic, uncaring, and cruelly unkind are learned behaviors. While that learning begins in childhood, it is the teenage years when empathy vs. no empathy becomes a part of the teen's identity. Here is where high schools may make all the difference.

Like all matters we want to teach our youngsters, we must speak about, discuss, and tutor what we want them to learn. Ignoring a topic is a powerful kind of teaching, too. Ignoring the concept of empathy as an absolutely necessary component of everyone's individuality leads the teen to muse:

> This empathy business is not important. Do I even know what that word means? Something about feelings, I think. But I hide mine, so ... oh, never mind. Grown-ups never talk about it so why do I even have to think about it?

When the adult world does not talk about what it values, their young people do not know how to value what their elders value.

So fostering emotional intelligence necessarily means teaching about empathy. This includes being sure all students do indeed know the meaning of the word. Some schools have Be Kind weeks. Perhaps one of those days might be Empathy Day. If every teacher said one thing, just one, about the concept of empathy at the start of each class, by the end of the day the student body would know more about empathy than they did riding in on the school bus that morning.

The teacher with the bow tie known for joking might comment dryly, "I have great empathy for you about how you hate homework. I hated it, too. But I'm still giving you homework." The art teacher might hold up a picture of a Van Gogh painting and invite, "Look at this picture. Feel what Van Gogh was feeling when he painted this. Empathize with him. What was he feeling? Can you feel that, too? What does it feel like to you?"

When all adults participate, the message from first period to last is "We adults value empathy. We are empathetic. We expect you to be empathetic, too." Subsequently pointing out lack of empathy is easier when everyone, to use that old school metaphor, is on the same page. When empathy becomes a prized value of any given school system, the teenage drive to community grabs hold of empathy as a valued element of blossoming identity. "We're empathetic here at South High. That's us. E-M-P-A-T-H-Y. Empathy! It's what we do. That's us! Go South!"

Crystallized Anger

Consciously chosen anger is the opposite of empathy. In the choosing one says, "I don't care how the other feels. My anger is all important. Their feelings are nothing." Thus are revenge and hatred born. Both may be seen as forms of crystallized anger. Too many do not consciously connect acts of retribution with anger.

However, "Don't get mad, get even" is a classic piece of garbage thinking that clearly shows conversion of anger (a feeling) into revenge (an action). Revenge and hatred are expressions of anger that convert the initial anger into actions of vengeance and retaliation. When adults do this, it is genuinely juvenile. The real juveniles have authentic reason to try the tactic because their weak castle walls propel them to attempt to grab power, howsoever illusory, by striking out. Adults who use these tactics are just advertising "I have made a decision to be a juvenile forever." Perhaps you have known such a teenage grown-up.

Teens will stop using revengeful tactics when they understand that hatred and revenge are expressions of weakness. Such expressions say, "My castle walls are so ill-defined and my sense of power so weak that I have to invent power tricks to hurt someone to convince myself that I am powerful." Guidance in as many sessions as necessary will help refocus the teen onto the real issues. Those real issues are not "But she did such and such to me!" but rather "How did I get to be 15 and still not have a glimpse of an idea of who *I* am?" It is her perception of power-lessness that must be addressed. Hand the teen a mirror. Every time the teen's talk is about what the other did or did not do or about why revenge is justified, quietly ask her to look in the mirror. When one's own castle walls are strong, hatred, revenge, and retaliation are useless wastes of precious energy one chooses to better spend elsewhere.

However, to yell "I hate you" is not usually true hatred. It is a way of saying, "I am mad as can be with you." If we were more honest, we would directly state, "I'm furious!" I have found that with young people, exaggerated repetition both helps them get the anger out and helps them put their own anger into perspective. This twin-fold benefit helps them feel good about how they are expressing their anger.

My technique is to ask, "How many reallys are you mad?" or "How mad are you really, really?" This usually yields a response like, "I'm really, really, really, really, really, really, really, really, really, really mad!" The inflection and force rise with each repeated word.

Redirect curse words spoken in your office into reallys. Words from the List of Anger Words may also be chosen. But there is something about the word really that leads young people to really enjoy framing their anger in reallys. The R sound punches out the emotion in a burst and then ebbs in the L sound to the next crest. Teach teens to own their anger.

Own your anger. Do not let your anger own you.

Anger expands ego. People sometimes choose revenge and hatred because they make ego feel large and powerful. The actions taken allow us to move our limbs—as in the flailings of the two-year-old. These actions make us feel big and relieve the physical tension of the anger. "Revenge is sweet" because feeling powerful is sweet, that is, ego feels expansive and comfortable when acting with power, even illusory power. When the revenge-maker crows, "Guess I showed them!" they are exulting in that illusory power. Truth is, what they really showed is how powerless they feel.

Mature ego feels large enough without stealing power by hostility. Hatred and revenge are cheap ways to feel big. Infant egos feel bigger at the expense of others. Little egos step up by stepping on others. Mature egos are confident enough in their own power that they refuse to steal it. They reject harming others in order to make themselves feel bigger. They may get just as angry as revengeful persons, but the difference is how they cross The Line. The difference is in the choices made.

Taking hostile action due to anger is indeed hatred. True **hatred** is hostile action taken with malice aforethought. Revenge and hatred are teen temper tantrums best left behind in adolescence.

Forgiveness in Individuation and Community

To forgive is to release anger. It, like empathy, is another value intimately tied to beneficial emotionality. Forgiveness is not an emotion. It is a decision. However, it may be felt as relief from anger. Release and tranquil peace are felt experiences that follow a decision to forgive fully. Not forgiving, holding onto anger, has more to do with feeling powerful in the castle than with what another person does or does not deserve.

To say "I forgive, but I won't forget" really means "Mentally, I forgive for that's what I've been taught to do, but I'm holding onto my anger." It is emotion that makes us remember. "I won't forget" means "I choose to hold onto my anger because not to do so is to experience my ego's smallness." When I feel you hurt me, I am reminded my walls are vulnerable. I say I'm not forgetting but what I really am not forgetting is how I was hurt. Not forgiving, not forgetting I may be forever mending the same spot in the same wall over and over.

Such useless holding onto anger impoverishes the self. The task of individuation gets sidetracked into a mode of constant self-protection and a never-ending alert for the enemies that may yet come. Releasing anger frees all that side-tracked energy for healthy self-definition. The developmental task of community also gets side-tracked and twisted by unforgiveness. One's definition of community may shrink to the smallest group one feels safely possible. It may even shrink to total isolation.

True forgiveness comes only after feeling, expressing, and releasing the anger. Keeping hurts and angers as secrets maintains their emotional energy.

The secret is the sickness.

Talking it out with someone, whether with God or one of God's children, frees the emotions. Share with teens that releasing anger in forgiveness is not an altruistic act, a favor to the other person. Releasing anger heals one's own heart.

• **My Personal Anger Management Plan, Part III**

Our chapters on anger have been moving toward the exercise which is the heart of an AMP, a personal analysis of the teen's valid and invalid threats to self, ego, and fairness. The anger management matrix is an inventory of the teen's sources of anger and its expressions, valid and invalid. Make explicit with your teens that boxing in our angers uses thinking and judgment to redirect and fix our angers in a structure we create.

Even math teachers may participate in school-wide emotive education by explaining that a matrix is a chart that arranges information in rows and columns. Just as a matrix grabs ahold of and orders mathematical and scientific data, an anger management matrix structures and orders our angers. That structuring *is* anger management. Raw emotion is tamed in the rational boxes we create.

Activity Sheet 9.1 may be used. Completing one matrix as a group may serve to explicitly demonstrate the process. Each teen's own matrix may be as detailed as possible within the time limits allowed. Instruct teens, "Fill in each box in the matrix. For each threat you enter, state the nature of the threat and its expression. What are the threats? How do you react?" Valid threats are largely societal and external. Invalid threats tend to be internal and are often a wholly made up story in the head.

Share with teens several pointers for completing a good matrix. First, stress the importance of honesty. To be honest about invalid threats is especially important. Now that teens realize such a thing as invalid threats do exist, they may hesitate to admit to having had beliefs they now realize are inaccurate. When we uncritically accept an unfounded belief that something is harmful, that is an invalid, imaginary threat. "People hate me!" is such an invalid, imaginary threat.

Second, remind teens that imagined threats to ego are frequent. The daily ones are the self-created threats to self-esteem and self-worth, the put-downs we put on ourselves. Ask your teens to delve deeply into themselves to discover the ways in which they are too hard on themselves. "I'm stupid" is a common example.

Third, urge teens to think about the self-talk that limits and diminishes their sense of self, their individuality. Though this self-talk is in error, it creates real anger. Fearing one is wrong may be a key and crucial self-created put-down.

Fourth, urge teens to be especially honest about what they believe to be threats to fairness. Young people are particularly apt to lament the unfairness of life. "That teacher never calls on me. It's so unfair!" is an example. Imagined threats to fairness result from a false appraisal of rights.

• **Small Group—Anger Management Partners: Activity Sheet 9.1**

Encourage teens to find an anger management partner, a friend with whom they do not mind sharing their matrix, or pair up the members of the small group. The role of the partner is two-fold: to give honest feedback on the chart and to serve as a sounding board to whom the partner may vent anger.

• **The Sound of Anger**

Teens have long gravitated toward emotive music as it reflects and expresses their own emotions. In the first two to three years that you present information about emotions to your teens, ask them to bring in songs that reflect that emotion. As time goes on, you will acquire a collection expansive enough to play a song at the beginning or end of each class or small group, or indeed, at the start of a one-on-one session. Today, many songs may be "played" on computer. Your teens probably know all the sites.

Classic pieces from Mahler and Holst (*The Planets–Mars*) to the Beatles to today boom with anger. Listen to the Beatles *You Can't Do That* and *Run for Your Life*. For instruments and tone, look to drums and cymbals and soaring, crashing crescendos. Music, band, and choral teachers all may contribute to developing EI by continuously looking for and naming the emotion inherent in the music.

Any music teacher may initiate a music quest for their students. Ask your teens to pick a *My Song—Anger*. All emotions deserve "their song." The teen picks a piece of music or song (one free from foul language) that they intend to be their special anthem when they are feeling angry. Teens will listen to their music anyway. Let's help them get clear on the emotions they are hearing and feeling. Music and songs were suggested by a music teacher and a musicologist.

The Circle of Forgiveness Ceremony

To bond the group and foster community, some schools offer retreats for entire classes. Whether at a camp in the woods or in the school building, such group activities demonstrate that community is a value the school system prizes. This is a perfect opportunity to inculcate principles of emotional intelligence and focus on empathy and forgiveness as critical elements in any community group.

Distribute papers in the shape of a circle. Explain:

> In your hands is a forgiveness circle. On it write a brief description of something you've been very angry about. In particular name the person or persons at whom you are mad. Start writing around the outside of the circle. Move inward toward the middle, writing around and around. What you leave in the middle is yours to keep. So as you get close to the middle, claim forgiveness with words like "I forgive Person X and release (her or him) into the Light" or to their Higher Power or into God's hands. Choose the wording you prefer.

If community sensitivities preclude using the language of a higher power, advise, "In the middle claim forgiveness by writing 'I forgive. I release all anger. I release. I release. I release.'" Higher power by whatever name we claim or don't claim works through the forgiveness power we ourselves claim.

Conclude the ceremony by burning the circles. As teens take a turn dropping their circles into the fire, they may declare, "I release my anger and forgive." If lighting a fire is not possible, the circles may be torn to confetti-sized shreds. If done inside, that confetti with more added by moderators may be tossed up and thrown snowball style to celebrate the release of anger and the joy of forgiveness. Let music and dancing follow.

BULLETIN BOARD MATERIAL

Anger divides. Forgiveness heals.

Small people steal power. Big people share power.

Forgive and forget by releasing anger.

To avoid being angry with individuals,
you must pardon the whole mass,
you must grant forgiveness to the entire human race.

Seneca[2]

Notes

1 Surveys differ but the average age of first alcohol use is around 12, and 14–15 for other drugs. In March 2018, the American Academy of Child & Adolescent Psychiatry stated, "The average age of first marijuana use is 14, and alcohol use can start before age 12." Online at: www.aacap/families_and_youth/facts_for_families/fff-guide/Teens-Alcohol-And-Other-Drugs-003.aspx

2 Retrieved from Lucius Annaeus Seneca's *De Ira, Of Anger*, (*op. cit.*) online at www.en.wikisource.org/wiki//Of_Anger/Book_I#X In section IV Seneca advises that an emotion "is brought into existence and brought to an end by a deliberate mental act." The philosopher's apex emotional intelligence notwithstanding, our endeavors to make our mental acts deliberate continue. And continue. And continue.

Name: _____   Date: _____

Activity Sheet 9.1
AN ANGER MANAGEMENT MATRIX

Each box is a category of threat that generates anger. Fill in as many items as you can in each box. For each box ask these two questions: (1) What are the threats? (2) How do I react?

THREATS

	Valid	Invalid
Threats to Self		
Threats to Ego		
Threats to Fairness		

If necessary, use the back of the sheet, too.

10 Handling Emotions

With a solid foundation in the language of emotions, we are ready to advance our understanding. Life is not a problem to be coped with. Yet many use the phrase "to cope with emotions." This usage implies an ordeal and thus reinforces the twentieth-century belief that emotions are negative, injurious, and impossibly painful. Emotions are indeed a horrible plague to be struggled through and "coped" with when we fixedly believe they are so. When we lack skills with emotions, we battle ourselves when we battle our emotions.

This is particularly true of anger. The phrases "to handle an emotion" and "to deal with it" are an improvement, but not if handling it is construed as an enormous burden. "Handle it," "Deal with it," and "You can handle it" should imply "You have the inner resources to handle it, so do so." Handling it always means constructively addressing and expressing the emotion.

Inner words that are powerful enough to create rage are like magic. With inner words, our self-talk, we generate emotion. So, too, we use words to begin the process of handling emotion. Like a magician in the stories our teens love, we have within ourselves the amazing power to find the inner words that are the magic that will dispel the uncomfortable emotions our own words first created.

With our words, our faulty words, we trick ourselves into getting angry. So with our words we may trick ourselves out of the anger. In this sense we could say that the following steps are all word tricks, but most powerful word tricks.

The Four Steps of Handling It

Handling emotions consists of a thinking part and an action part. When adults instruct emotional youngsters to "Just stop it!" they are giving instruction about an action but no information at all about the thinking, the self-talk, behind either the emotion or the desired behavior. Thus it is helpful if initial counseling sessions or the initial portion of one session center on giving teens the tools to understand themselves and their emotions, anger in particular. So the first step in handling it is to understand it.

A display of the following is useful as a memory aid for teens.

```
┌─────────────────────────────────────────────┐
│              HANDLE IT!                       │
│  Step 1. Understand it.                       │
│  Step 2. Apply ruthless inner honesty.        │
│  Step 3. Change self-talk.                    │
│                                               │
│     • Eliminate self-judgments.               │
│     • Use Help Talk.                          │
│     • Pitch out garbage thinking.             │
│                                               │
│  Step 4. Handle It! by applying the A, B, Cs. │
└─────────────────────────────────────────────┘
```

Using the material presented in Chapters 1–9 helps teens to initiate, develop, and mature their comprehension of emotions. But understanding may be abstract and impersonal. Only a subjective approach yields the highly personal quality needed for truly handling it. That quality may be called ruthless inner honesty.

Such honesty, by definition, is a challenge. Share with your teens that you know inner honesty is hard. It is supposed to be hard. We do not gain the qualities of determination, courage, and endurance without hard work. But each simple act of ruthless honesty is like a walk on the moon: one small step and one giant leap.

The fruit of honesty and understanding is action, step three. If we understand and are honest but do nothing, we have only indulged in an academic exercise. Thus, this step is an actual, tangible, concrete *inner* change. Share the following principle.

The first change must be an inner change.

To reduce anger we begin, always, within. We shift focus from what is happening "out there" to "make us angry" to what is happening within ourselves that is allowing the out there to have so much impact. The power of this switch from the out there to the in here is shown in the intensity with which some resist the shift. We intuitively know that if we shift focus from the things and events and people out there who we say make us mad, we are left only with what is within. Hence, we resist the shift.

Shifting within, we learn there are many ways to change self-talk. One good way to start is to examine the judgments we make about ourselves. Frequently, these judgments are self-statements using the word "should." Other ways to modify self-talk are to use reminders and to eliminate garbage thinking.

A self-reminder is self-talk we choose to remind ourselves to change our thinking. It is easily remembered if we call it Help Talk. Some examples follow.

- This is only my emotion-stimulated imagination.
- That's my fear talking.
- I'm angry. That's why I'm thinking these things.
- Mr. Hormone's got me again.
- I'm not really going crazy. It just feels like I am! I *can* handle it.

Elicit other examples from your teens.

At this point in our strategy we are ready to act on the emotion. The first three steps—understanding, honesty, and changing self-talk—are mental steps. But words are not, and will never be, feelings. We handle emotions by using our full humanity, our thinking, and our feeling. Steps one through three use thinking skills. The next step directly uses the emotions.

Refer back to Chapter 3 to review the A, B, Cs. Focus on how they apply to anger. Most particularly, review step B, breathing. Then move to the last phase, channeling the emotion, which includes both the verbal channeling of the emotion and nonverbal expressions of the emotion.

Feelings in the Body

Before we may fully understand how to nonverbally express anger, we must see how anger feels in the body. One way to clarify what we are feeling in our bodies is to investigate how the emotion makes us feel physically. Display the following chart.

Makes Us Feel		
ANGER	→	big
FEAR	→	small
SADNESS & GUILT	→	lousy

The Hot Air Illusion

Assist teens in understanding that we choose anger over fear because, no matter how irrational the anger, it makes us feel bigger, more powerful. Anger puffs out the ego. Inflated egos feel stronger, and that's why we keep inflating them. Alas, the inflation is an illusion, no more substantial than the air in a balloon. When push comes to shove, the balloon bursts. The chief recourse of the egoist is more hot air.

Yet still we choose anger over fear, for fear makes us feel very small and helpless. When emotions are so strong that we crawl into bed and wither, crying, into the fetal position, we are feeling fear in all its painful purity. It is to avoid this indignity that some choose the numb stupor of alcohol, drugs, and any frenetic behavior like gambling to attempt to trick the brain into agreeing "See, I'm not scared." Our brains will not be so fooled. The fear is there when we sober up, crash, or pause for breath.

Fear makes us feel so small that we retreat, even pulling our limbs closer to the body. Since fear feels so uncomfortable, we convert it into anger. We do so because we much prefer the feeling of power, even illusory power. This strategy, innate in us all, is not totally without reason or purpose. It seems nature itself prefers us to be big and strong and abhors the retrograde motion that would drive us to perpetual childhood. Maturity demands ever more refined discernment between illusory, temporary, and even pointless power and solid emotional strength.

So it is true that anger may be a cover for fear. Anger is sometimes what it seems to be, anger, unalloyed rage. But frequently anger is a cop-out, a mask for fear or another uncomfortable emotion. Only ruthless inner honesty is able to sort out the difference between simple, honest anger and the stew of anger that is cooked up out of fear, sadness, and guilt.

Lousy Feelings

Sadness and guilt do not, so clearly, make us feel large or small. The word lousy seems to fit both. The lousy feeling of grief is an ache, a void, as expressed in the statement, "When I lost him, I felt like my heart was cut out." Grief is the pain of loss of an attachment.

Guilt also seems to invoke a lousy feeling, that of imagined nonexistence as when we say, "I feel so guilty, I could die." The guilty frequently engage in self-sabotaging, self-damaging behavior. Guilt is the rejection of an erroneous behavior by rejecting self. The fundamental error is to identify self with behavior. "I did bad. Therefore, I am bad." Chronic guilt, then, is self-punishment based on this misunderstanding. Unit III explores sadness and guilt.

As you work with teens on their emotions, stress that the lament "I don't know what I'm feeling!" is no longer acceptable. For it is always possible to reflect on whether we are feeling large (that is, inflated), small, or lousy. If inclined to fight, anger is on the surface. If we want to run, fear predominates. Teens may point out that fear and sometimes anger feel lousy, too. This is true. However, with just some practice most learn to identify that unique, ego-inflated, self-justifying, lousy feeling as anger and that particular, shrinking, lousy feeling as fear.

Locus Pocus

As a final aid in identifying and expressing anger, we look at how anger sits in the body. *Locus* is Latin for place. Display the following.

Physical Locus of Anger				
LOCUS		**IMPULSE**		**REMEDY**
Upper body	→	Fight	→	Swing arms.
Lower body	→	Flight	→	Move legs.
Upper and lower	→	Fight and flight	→	Move arms and legs.

By understanding this model we may move to the final means of constructive directing of anger, the nonverbal. It is imperative that teens know that emotions are physiological, in the body. This physical reaction consisting of hormones and neurotransmitters is real and truly physical, not just all in the mind.

Use It Up, Work It Out

For healthy emotional expression, the physical discharge must be used up. It does not just instantly disappear because we say to ourselves, "Calm down." Now, "Calm down" is an excellent piece of Help Talk. But when anger is intense, something more physical than speech is called for. Our brains gradually listen to calming Help Talk, but adrenaline and cortisol have no ears. They exist to be used.

With hostile students, initiate discussion about constructive physical expressions of anger. The clearest way to support positive expressions of anger is a simple directive.

All anger is okay. Some behaviors are not okay.

The not okay behavior is anything that does harm. This includes harm to self and harm to living things. If teens want to know if it is okay to break things, the answer is that depends.

Breaking something that belongs to another is not okay. It harms them by harming their property. Breaking your own property, items you purchased with your own money, is okay if you destroy the item in a way that does no harm, fully accept the consequence of no longer having the object, and clean up after yourself. If breaking is chosen to express strong anger, it is not helpful if either parents or grandparents replace the object. Such behavior stops when the consequence, the loss, is meaningful enough.

Schools, of course, may insist breaking anything on school property is unacceptable. Even if the object destroyed belongs to the student, such behavior frightens others and so harms them. Moreover, schools have no assurance that harm will not accidently be done as when breaking one's own glass or ceramic cup endangers the eyes of everyone around. But acceptable kinds of breaking exist.

Sitting on the floor and tearing up last year's notebooks uses up considerable adrenaline and cortisol when the attempt is to tear 20 to 30 pages in one rip. Sit on the floor with your angry student and see who can at one go rip through the most pages. Who can rip 20 pages? 25? 30? More? Sure, you have to clean up the pieces. But the behavior harms no one. Note how anger dissipates as sheets of paper are added. The raw emotion of anger morphs into the challenge of who can rip the most.

Explore other positive, physically expressive ways to convey anger. We've seen that anger is like a magic dragon. It is like a powerful furnace, a powerhouse for making things happen. A variant of the red crayon exercise is to use red, orange, yellow, and black markers to draw a picture of anger as a fiery flame, dragon, or image the teen chooses. Other colors may be used, but the warm tones reflect intense anger. If the counseling department does not have large sheets of paper, the cheapest way to get them is to cut paper grocery bags down the side, cut off the bottom, and so create a large, wide canvas for dramatic expression.

If collaborating with other teachers, the art teacher may assign this task. When an entire class does the project, the art may be displayed up and down the corridors. Imagine students observing "Look! I'm angrier than you." "No, you're not. See. I used more red." "Oh, who did that one? It's smaller than a campfire." "Yeah. That's the kid who creeps down the hallways like a mouse." "He should get mad more." "Yeah." When young people are taught that anger converted to art is perfectly acceptable, it is easier for them to then verbally talk about their angers, too.

Sports for Anger Management

In schools athletics provides a readymade avenue for overt and intensely physical active anger. Sports and exercise in all its forms are our commonly accepted means of expressing intense physical energy. Sports are sublimations of the fight or flight impulse, as may be seen in the following chart.

UPPER BODY FIGHT SPORTS	LOWER BODY FLIGHT SPORTS
Depend on	Depend on
Chest-shoulder-arm Power	Hip-leg-foot Power
Sports that primarily involve hitting and/or eye-hand coordination	Sports that primarily involve running and/or dexterity with the legs

Many sports involve both upper and lower body. When considering a sport or activity, center on the primary body emphasis. Tennis, for example, does involve running around the court, but hitting the ball is the primary focus of the game. To run a marathon is clearly lower body, as is soccer. Swimming is both.

If teens differ on where they wish to place a sport, they may vote for the placement. The most important thing is not a precise listing but that teens see that we use sports to sublimate our fight and flight impulses.

Continue the personal application in a teen's AMP by asking, "When you get really, really angry, what do you do? Do you slam doors, throw things, or hit? Or do you run away by going for a walk or a drive? Or do you hit and then run?" Have teens write in their journals whether their actions are primarily upper-body or lower-body expressions of anger.

If some appear stuck, prompt, "Think of the time in your life you got the angriest. What did you do? Hit? Throw? Kick and stomp? If necessary, think back to what you did as a small child." Some may require time to inquire of parents or relatives, "When I was two years old, what did I do when I got mad?" The inclination to be a hitter-thrower or a stomper-runner begins early.

Share that we place no moral judgment on running away as an expression of anger. Indeed, our genes are probably those of our ancestors, who judiciously ran away from the saber-toothed tiger, not of those who imprudently stayed to swing their arms and throw rocks.

Getting psyched up for a game brings more powerful play. Sports as a whole are one of society's major mass outlets for anger. This does not mean that all athletes as individuals are angry people. However, hockey and soccer games often demonstrate the thin line between appropriate anger release and manifest hostility.

Investigate whether openly hostile teens participate in a sport. If not, guiding them to and supporting them in a sport of their choice is critical. Sports provide a positive, physically intense use of adrenaline and cortisol. Aggression and hostility are anger directed outward, anger acted upon in a harmful manner. But sports and other competitions are socially approved methods of anger expression. It has been said that football is just a modern form of battle. The fight is still for ground but it's called yardage.

Teens who are the most chronically angry would benefit from a program of working out in the school gym daily before classes. Work out, eat breakfast, go to class. Exhaust the adrenaline before it has a chance to build up. Teachers take turns at many tasks such as bus duty and cafeteria duty. Coaches and the resource officers may step into the role of decisive change agents as they share gym duty. If the young person is often hostile in the hallways anyway, tackling the issue on the front end is better than waiting for the behavior to happen and then intervening.

Aggressive play on the ball field and intensity in the gym are okay up to a point. The referee, the coach, the rules of the game decide just what that point is. The rules of a sport not only dictate how to keep score, they ensure safe play. Harming someone is a foul. On or off the court or field, harming someone is a foul.

Finally, personalize the exercise by having teens write in their journals a list of sports they prefer. They may make two lists: those they actually play and those they like to watch. Help teens who say they don't like sports to grasp that when they are intensely angry, they, too, need forceful physical activity. The chosen activity may be a going for a fast walk, riding a bike, cleaning their room or, if very angry, the whole house, or vigorously playing in the backyard with the dog. Shoppers may purposely walk up and down every aisle in the store just to walk off the anger. Playing tag or hide and seek with younger siblings or when babysitting are other vigorous options. Assist teens in choosing their own mode of physical movement for lifelong vitality as well as emotion management.

- **Journaling—Handling It**

Instruct teens to review their anger inventory on Activity Sheet 9.1. Teens choose one example of valid anger and one of invalid anger and apply the Four Steps to state, step by step, how they will handle that anger in the future. Application of the steps may be written in journals. If teens are not ready to work alone, divide them either into small groups or have them work with their anger management partner to collectively apply the Four Steps. This activity may be done repeatedly throughout the school year.

- **Small Group—The What If Game**

Ask each teen to write out a What If situation on a 3 x 5 card. Each What If describes a difficult situation in which anger expression is a challenge.

Think of a time you were angry about something or of a situation in which you might get very angry. Then, write a question describing the situation. Begin the question with the words What if ... ? For example, what if someone called you stupid?

Collect and shuffle the cards. Have teens pull any card but their own. Instruct them that as they respond, they are to follow what they have learned to develop their AMP. Remind them to include a physical activity or exercise as one of the steps to Handle It!

A variation is to play the What If about well-known celebrities. Teens pick names of their favorite singers, actors, or public figures before you tell them why you want the names. This is similar to The Self-Talk of X in Chapter 6, but here the emphasis is on what verbal and physical expressions teens would assign to the celebrity. "How might the celebrity verbalize their anger? What sport or activity should they do?" If teens have clips on their phones of inappropriate demonstrations of the celebrity's anger, all the better. Point out who got hurt and the consequences. "Do you think that celebrity could use an AMP?"

If your teens roar at the idea of their favorite singer running track, know your point is sinking in. Let laughter wash over the room to refocus perspective. Allowing ourselves to see our hostile urges in all their absurdity deflates ego and gives us precious time to shift gears from raw emotion to logical thinking.

Teens often are hesitant to share emotion-laden matters. Just calling this exercise a game will pique their interest. Calling it a game moves the interaction away from the scary adult realm of serious talking to reminiscences of a safer time in childhood. Indeed, when life gets too hard, too frightening, too exasperating, adults, too, often retreat to playing games.

- **Anger Management Plan, Part IV**

Assign teens to complete the last segment of their AMPs. Review their journal entries of the exercises from Chapter 8 in which they personalized their plans. In line with Chapter 9 they completed an anger management matrix and may have shared it with an anger management partner. Now in Chapter 10 it's time to apply the four steps of Handling It.

Thus now guide teens in considering the last part of step four, the nonverbal physical expression of emotion. Teens choose the mode of constructive physical activity they shall use as a safety-valve for explosive anger. The list includes the sports, exercises, and other constructive activities that will be their chief physical means to use up and dispel anger.

Stress the importance of thinking through the possibilities and carefully choosing more than one activity. If a teen says, "I'll take a walk" ask, "Even if the weather is bad?" If another says, "I'll play tennis" ask, "What if you can't find a partner?" Guide teens to be realistic as well as specific. Activities that may be pursued alone such as running or in bad weather walking the mall several times or surprising mom by vigorously scrubbing the tub and shower walls should be included along with activities requiring the participation of others.

• **Sports**

Sometimes athletes directly express anger. Lead teens in a discussion of sports figures who have displayed open anger. Ask teens, "In your judgment, is that a display of upper-body or lower-body anger? Does that anger help or hurt that player's game? If you were that athlete's trainer, how would you coach him or her to Handle It?"

For the most physical students, coaches may be critical change agents who support school-wide EI development by locker room pep talks on just how and when to pour fury over a call by a ref into the play and when to breathe or ask for a timeout. Each coach might give a team a special hand signal known only to that coach and team that means, "Get me out of here, coach, before I slug somebody." Just knowing this safety valve is available will assist players who dearly want to play in modulating their behavior on the court or on the field.

It is not so much the use of the signal that matters. What matters is the giving of the option. Coaches who give the option are saying, "I have faith in you that you are able to control your behavior and that you yourself will know when you need a break and will ask for it." As educators we may stop inappropriate behavior by the main force of our adult authority. Or, we may communicate to our teens that we expect them to learn when to stop themselves.[1]

• **Should Inventory: Shoulds About Me: Activity Sheet 10.1**

Self-image consists of a string of self-statements about what one is and should be. When reality does not correspond with the inner self-talk, an emotional reaction is certain. When experience does not reflect our shoulds, we may feel any combination of guilt, shame, hurt, fear, disappointment, grief, and anger.

Assign the worksheet and discuss the results. Elicit insight into the connection between "shoulding ourselves" in self-judgments and emotions such as anger. This inventory is included here since anger is often the response when we feel others do not act as they *should*. We get mad at ourselves for not doing what we believe we *should*. This is why in AA (Alcoholics Anonymous) there is a saying, "Don't should on yourself." Activity Sheet 10.1 may also be used with Chapter 19.

BULLETIN BOARD MATERIAL

Ruthless inner honesty is
one giant leap in one small step.

Play out your anger
before your anger outplays you.

Hit a ball, never a face.
Zap your gall. Run a race.

Note

1 Coaches who wish their own exclusive coaching on issues such as coach burnout might consult *Emotions in Sport Coaching*, P. Potrac *et al*, eds. New York, NY: Routledge, 2018. Presented as exploratory insights, this short book exemplifies the move away from emotionally toxic coaches who use foul language with athletes and impose silent bus rides home to penalize a losing team.

Name: _____   Date: _____

Activity Sheet 10.1
SHOULD INVENTORY: SHOULDS ABOUT ME

	MY SHOULDS	OTHERS' SHOULDS ABOUT ME
About my face	My face should look	Your face should look
About my body & weight	I should	You should
About my appearance	I should	You should
About my good points	I	You
About my weak points		
About my personality		
About me as female or male		
About my emotions		
About my intelligence		
About my talents and abilities		
About my future		

Unit III

Fear

11 Fear and Its Masquerades

Anger merits our first consideration because it is the motivator of hostility and aggression. In a world of enmity and antagonism, civilization is not civil. Converting hostility, an action, back to anger, an emotion, is the *sine qua non* for anger management. We have seen, however, that it is not possible to probe deeply into anger without understanding anger as a cover for fear.

Anger and fear appear to function as the proverbial two sides of the same coin. Anger is outward, throws the arms and legs away from the body and into action, and has the potential of exploding into aggressively motivated violence. Fear is inward, pulls the arms and legs into the body in the fetal position, and has the potential of imploding into hostility against self. In this way all forms of self-destruction may be seen as expressions of fear. Fear may make us run but the running is retreat. Anger stands its ground and attacks.

Anxiety is a four-syllable word for fear. Understanding fear as an emotion and how it works is essential to not only anger management but to all emotion management. Our distaste for fear is so strong that we have a veritable Pentagon full of defensive weapons against fear. Without knowledge of our key most used defense mechanisms, it is not possible to understand ourselves or to fully appreciate how fear erupts into anger in the wider society.

The defense mechanisms of denial, displacement, projection, intellectualization, and rationalization are frequently used. High school students, in particular, are well placed to learn and absorb the meaning of these terms. Doing so means acquiring a skill that will serve them well their entire lives. They are well placed because their reasoning abilities are expanding beyond the world of childhood. Yet they have not so long been in the world to acquire and solidify what may become their lifelong defense mechanisms. However, by the junior and senior years, the process of acquiring defense mechanisms is well begun.

Thus, if the young person's world is immersed in alcohol and that teen sees no constructive emotion management in the environment, denial expressed in use of alcohol may be learned. What we model for our youngsters, they learn. Model denial and they learn "The real grown-ups handle fear by just denying it and getting drunk. I can do that." Teach and model positive emotion management, explain that denial means denial of emotion, and even in a world awash in alcohol, the teen has a chance to choose another path.

In the pragmatic world of actual counseling sessions, the relationship between anger and fear is readily experienced. Teens, particularly the younger teens, jump back and forth between fear and anger. It may be a veritable see-saw. The challenge for the educator is to hold your balance in the up-down, back and forth movement. The challenge is to be sensitive to the shifts. "Wait a minute! My teen here was just shouting. Now she's sobbing vigorously. Ay! Now she's attacking me. Oh, tears again. (Pause) Now silence." Are you able to read the emotions? Or did you fall off the see-saw?

This distressed teen just declared, "I'm mad! I'm mad because I'm profoundly sad or scared. It's awful; make it stop! Oh, I hurt, I hurt. (Pause) Oh why do I say anything? You, grown-up, you don't understand my emotions at all." The accusation, "You don't understand!" more often than not is teen speak for "You don't understand my emotions at all!"

As educators we must start from the position that the child is right. We do have a lot to learn about emotions. Our intention to learn and then teach this dimension of our humanity called emotions is the link between us and our teens. They desperately need and want to learn, for no one wants to live continuously in pain. Because we love them, their pain hurts us. We embrace our own denial because, if we don't, emotional toxicity just continues getting passed down the generations.

The counselor working with that distressed teen has opportunity to stem the tide of toxicity. "Okay, I hear that you're angry. What happened that you are so mad?" Tears elicit, "I'm so sorry this hurts so much. Take a deep breath. We'll breathe together. Now put words on those tears for me, please." We continue with whatever fits that particular see-saw. "So what you're saying is you are really sad because you're afraid you've lost your friends. Is that what you're feeling?" The key shift is from talking about who did what to whom when and why to centering all attention on the emotion. Once you have heard the teen sigh out and exhale the last of the emotional pain, the who, what, when, and why of the matter may be addressed.

Toxic Emotionality

Sometimes called toxic masculinity, toxic emotionality is the broader category. Assigning gender to the emotive style of entire cultures is not helpful. It is true that there are differences between men and women on how they have internalized the culture's denial of emotions. I have heard the words "I'm just weak. I'm so emotional" from women more than men. Men may think the same words but tend not to speak them. But in my experience men more readily and more quickly than women get down to the nitty-gritty of their emotional exploration. It's as if the male imperative to play in the dirt and just go for it, get it done, actually assists the man once he has rejected his denial.

Women step their big toes in and out of the dirt many times before they get it done. The woman cries, "This is icky. Get me out." The man exclaims, "This is icky. Show me how to get out." Men have to get over their denial and reluctance to ask for help. Women have to get over their denial and reluctance to act on the help they have been given. But behind it all and laced through the fabric of our culture is the societal imperative, "Thou shalt not be emotional. And if you are, there's something wrong with you."

Where did this collective denial of emotion, particularly denial of fear, originate? This is a legitimate question for sociologists. But a few observations jump out at a vintage social studies teacher. The British directive during World War II, "Keep calm and carry on," really meant "Don't be emotional. Just do your duty." Right. Bombs are falling on your head but don't be emotional. It would have been more helpful to admit "So we're all afraid. Do your duty anyway." That's courage. That is what our grandparents and great-grandparents did in fact do. But once the war was over, somehow the denial of emotions was not.

Even for our young people for whom the twentieth century is a muddle of wars, the message to deny fear has been their inheritance. A six-year-old boy once declared, "I'm not afraid of anything!" I advised him, "You don't know this planet, do you?" He smiled, missing, of course, the point. One cannot be on this planet, in this age, and not know fear. Denial begins young.

Educators will find it useful to spot instances of denial of our denial. When we accept that we have been in cultural collusion about our collective denial, we are at the beginning point. That acceptance places us like runners at the starting line. Acceptance does not mean the race is won. It does not even mean we are in the act of running. It means, most critically, that we no longer are going to deny our fear when tangible danger is present. Owning our fear is the beginning of fear management, the start of the race.

Denial of Fear

One way to hook the interest of teens is to throw them a curve. The relationship between teens and adults is much more difficult than it has to be. Apparently, it takes a developing human about 13 to 14 years to learn where the adults are coming from. We are so predictable to them. We go left. They go right. We go up. They go down. Independence is part of individuation. A teen will choose not to do something he really wants to do just because you made the error of telling him to do it. That is neither stubbornness nor irrationality at work. That is a teen advertising, "Listen, grown-up. I'm working overtime on this confusing task of figuring out who I am. It's something I have to do myself; I get that. Do you?"

So getting teens to admit they have fears may, in some ways, be even more difficult than teaching anger management. Anger that was external, even explosive, may bring a teen to your office. Fear is internal. It may be totally hidden. We see the anger so the teen cannot deny it. The trick about fear is to reveal it without the adolescent task of individuation generating an enormous defensive response.

One strategy is to address fear indirectly or in a contrary way. You may inform teens in a mildly teasing tone of voice "You guys need to study about fear, but I don't because I'm not afraid of anything!" We recognize that this claim is frequently heard in movies, on TV, and from the mouths of macho teens. By adopting that same claim, the counselor may effectively draw teens into challenging it.

Playfully accept your teens' responses while yet insisting that "Grown-ups aren't afraid of anything!" Allow the cries of disbelief to wash over the room. Then admit that many adults indeed do have a mistaken belief that fear does not touch their lives. For some, alcohol and drug use mask the emotions to such an extent that the mistaken belief is readily maintained. Invite your teens to describe the world of denial as they know it.

In this way we demonstrate a key principle for working with teens.

Be unpredictable.

By this is not meant the necessary predictability of class schedules and meal times. Predictable schedules yield certainty and security. But if educators are to be in charge, their words and emotional responses will have more power if they are judiciously unpredictable. Being predictable to a teen is to let them have you in the palm of their hands. That is not where they need us to be.

The ferocity of emotion with which the belief is insisted upon marks the intensity of denial of one's fears. Explore this notion with a teen by moving progressively up the ladder of responsibility, authority, and privilege. "Well, what about your parents? Are they ever afraid? What about the principal? Now there's someone who's never afraid of anything! No? Well, how about the mayor? The governor? The president?"

Lead a teen to discover that everyone is afraid of something at some time. Before we may get in touch with our fears, we must first have permission to do so. Talking frequently about fears is the first step in making clear that everyone has them. The health classroom might showcase a fear of the week as in the Validation of Fears activity at the end of the chapter.

Mind Tricks

Confronting our fears requires broader understanding of the mechanics of how fear works. The role of defense mechanisms no longer may be hidden away in textbooks for college courses. By the college years an individual's lifelong defense mechanisms are already seeding in. Society does not say, "Let us wait till college to give our youngsters vaccinations. And in college we'll make all vaccinations optional." But when it comes to vaccinating our young people emotionally, that is precisely what we do.

Understanding the many forms of denial yields tools for emotion management. If no one ever tells you that your mind may drive fear away by just denying that fear, how are you supposed to recognize what you are doing? Some even just flatly believe that "Don't think about it" is indeed the right thing to do with fear. It is not. Denying fear does not reduce fear or make it go away. Denial of fear drives it underground. Then, it comes out sideways just as anger, too, may come out sideways.

Explain to your teens that the underground ways we have of taking care of emotions have names. A **defense mechanism** is a psychological process invented by our minds to attempt to protect us from the **visceral** experience of uncomfortable emotions. A defense mechanism is a mind trick by which we try to fool ourselves that the emotion is not there or, if it is, that it does not mean what in our heart of hearts we know it means.

We have seen that emotions, although they are like water, do not evaporate. Instead, they build up until they are either expressed or expand the flood waters behind the dam. If such dams were perfect, we might be fine, although cut off from the wellspring of our emotions.

Displacement

But such dams inevitably leak. The emotion comes out sideways in a psychological defense mechanism known as **displacement**. Display the list of defense mechanisms.

> **Displacement = emotions coming out sideways**

The classic example is kicking the dog when you're mad at a person. Another well-known example is honking the horn at a stranger on the expressway when you are irritable. Parents, sadly, sometimes yell at their children when the innocents are not at all at the heart of the adults' anger. The displaced emotion may be anger or fear or another strong emotion. Teens need to understand that creating a clique with tight membership rules is a displacement of their own fear of not belonging.

Projection

An oft-used defense mechanism applies to fear as well as anger. Probably one of the most hurtful results of displacement of fear and anger is the further elaboration of the displacement process, **projection**. Quite literally projection creates the bogey man. Literature and movies popular with teens project their fears in images of wizards and witches and vampires and werewolves.

**Projection = applying to another person feelings
and beliefs within oneself**

Develop the understanding that projection is denying one's own emotions by accusing someone else of those very same emotions. It is the defense of two-year-olds. "I didn't do it. He did!" Seen this way, projection is cowardly and juvenile. Projection creates monsters. It is fun to let teens speculate about what fears are expressed in their favorite fantasy monsters. Why in the world do zombies go after brains and not toes? Hmmmm.

Such discussion with teens will help them see that what they hate in others in some way says something about their own fears. Those who are afraid that they are stupid love to use the word. Those who are afraid of standing alone outside the community circle called friends love to put others there. Those who don't know who they are love to tell others who *they* are.

The Biggest, Baddest Bogey Man

The most notable manifestation of projection at work in society is **prejudice**. Social studies teachers may be acute change agents by teaching the emotional underpinnings of prejudice. Prejudice is not a rational decision. Prejudice is an emotional outcome. It is a defense against fear. Whether it is prejudice

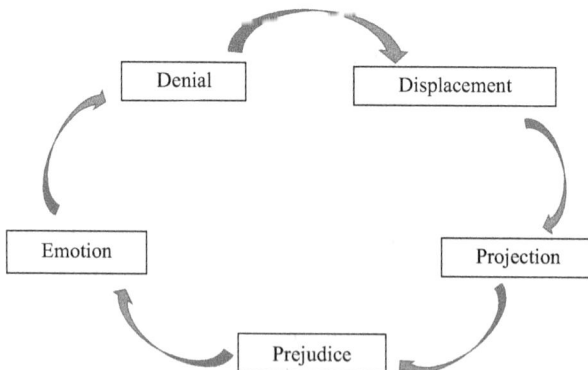

against a certain race or ethnic group or against a clique of peers, the process is the same. One's own fear is projected outward in anger onto an identified group. Prejudice is fear projected outward in anger.

Social studies teachers are well placed to explain that extreme prejudice is called **bigotry**, intolerant zeal for an irrational opinion. The opinion is presented as a stubbornly held, fixed belief. But actually, the belief is thinly disguised emotion masquerading as an idea. In prejudice, self is defined by what one is not. The other, the different one, is what I am not. Healthy self defines self by what one *is*. I am what and who I choose to be. The other, the different one, has nothing to do with that choice. It is evident, then, that prejudice is a sign of the failure of healthy resolution of the tasks of both individuation and community. Defining self by the community that is not-self has led to tragic human suffering.

Bigotry is always an emotional process. It denies and negates reason. Prejudice is a sign of emotions denied, displaced, projected, and generally run rampant. There's no such thing as the bogey man except the ones we ourselves create out of our own fear and anger. History reveals that those have been bogey men enough.

Rationalization and Intellectualization

Rationalization is a big lie used to defend against emotion. Of course, ruthlessly facing the full truth, we admit that all defense mechanisms are lies. A rational explanation gives a simple description of one's position and sensible reasons for it. But rationalization is emotion in the guise of thinking. It is partner to **intellectualization**, the thinking about an emotion in order not to feel that emotion in all its raw power. Prejudice and bigotry are never logical, rational decisions no matter how much logic is used to defend them. Using apparent logic to defend emotional decisions yields the defense mechanism called **rationalization**.

**Rationalization = so-called logical excuse
for an emotion-based decision**

In the display over the words displacement, projection, intellectualization, and rationalization, write in bold letters *Defense Mechanisms*. And this knowledge yields a tip for counseling sessions.

Be mindful of the impact of defense mechanisms.

If we were not afraid of uncomfortable emotions, our minds would never have invented these defenses in the first place. Defenses are not intrinsically bad. Someone in the midst of an immediately life-threatening event needs to deny the terror in order to have the rational capacity to think clearly enough to attempt to survive. Trapped in a tedious faculty meeting if you find yourself getting madder and madder, by all means intellectualize and rationalize away.

• Journaling—Reason and Emotion in History

With little difficulty one could demonstrate that human history is the ages-long war between our collective denial, displacement, projection, and rationalization and the enduring force of human reason to combat those same emotional defenses. If we want teens to know what prejudice is, we must teach what it is. We do not expect knowledge about binomials to just pop into the head. No, we teach a brain-stretching encounter called algebra. In the same manner the specific emotional nature of prejudice and bigotry must be actively taught.

A counselor may use this activity with a student who loves social studies. The health teacher may use this material to teach an expansive view of mental health. Social studies teachers may take care to teach more than cold facts by continuously pointing out the emotions at work in historical events.

Assign teens to find an event from history or current events that demonstrates the interplay of emotion and reason. First, assign work in small groups in class to complete the activity in a short class presentation. Then, ask students to discover another such event and independently write the story in their journals. Stress that for once in history class, dates and names are not as important as the interplay of emotions.

Each version of the exercise should answer questions like: What emotions were at play? In your judgment, what defense mechanisms were being used? Specifically, what was the role of fear? Of anger? Of other emotions? Was displacement used? Were there bogey men? What were the rationalizations? Where was the voice of reason?

Often in history one key person is the voice of reason crying in the wilderness, e.g., Churchill in Britain just before World War II, Lincoln in his "bind up the wounds" speech as the Civil War was ending, Martin Luther King in his "I have a dream" speech, and so on.[1]

• Small Group—Validation of Fears

Distribute five slips of paper to each. Instruct teens to write on each a description of something that frightens them. Concentration should be on personal, daily fears. Teens pull the slips from a shoebox and discuss. After the discussion, pin the slip to the bulletin board. The group arranges and rearranges the slips in order of priority from most frightening to least frightening under a heading, *Our Favorite Fears*.

While learning about fear, teens may pull one to three of these slips per day or per class. In another variant, teens may vote for a *Fear of the Week* or a *Fav Fear*, a specific fear all agree to work together to constructively address during that week. At the end of the week that slip may be posted under the heading *Fears We've Conquered*.

Objectifying fear diffuses it. Calling a fear a favorite uses a terminology teens well know. Fear moves from being foreign and unspeakable to being a familiar topic of discussion. Putting a specific fear into a larger perspective reduces its potency.

This approach uses the adolescent drive to community to reinforce that when it comes to fears, we all have them, we all are working on them, and we all need each other's help in facing those fears. This is strong antidote to the hidden teen fear, a type of fear of fear, with the self-talk, "I'm the only one scared here." This exercise in all its variants may be repeated throughout the school year.

- **List of Fear Words, Activity One: Activity Sheet 11.1**

Assign an essay, poem, or oral presentation entitled *My Pet Anxiety* or *My Favorite Worry*. Distribute the List of Fear Words and instruct teens to use only words from the *first* column. Other columns will be used in future activities. Teens reluctant to talk in counseling sessions may find activities an easier way to communicate about fear.

Ascribing human emotions to objects and animals generates insight, objectivity, and humor. We detoxify fear by making it approachable and silly. Other topics for small groups or for language arts that teens may enjoy are *My Pet's Main Anxiety*, *What an Orange Worries About*, and *Insecurities of a Pen*. Stories are to be written in first person as if the animal or object were telling the story.

BULLETIN BOARD MATERIAL

Everyone's afraid of something some time. And that's okay.

Prejudice is fear projected outward in anger.

Note

1 As on June 4, 1940, Churchill speaks in his own booming voice on the International Churchill Society site at https://winstonchurchill.org/resources/speeches/1940. Lincoln's second inaugural address, March 4, 1865, is at https://ourdocuments.gov. King's August 28, 1963, *I Have a Dream* speech is easily found on YouTube and at the Stanford University MLK site.

Name: _____   Date: _____

Activity Sheet 11.1, p. 1
LIST OF FEAR WORDS

Mild Fear	Moderate Fear	Intense Fear
shy	frightened	paralyzed
concerned	afraid	terrified
sheepish	scared	timid
nervous	anxious	panicky
tremulous	fidgety	shaky
solicitous	apprehensive	wary
shocked	numb with fear	scared to death
insecure	not confident	immobilized
alarmed	aghast	appalled
harrowing	dreadful	horrific
worried	fretful	fearful
startled	spooked	petrified
chicken	timorous	fainthearted
hesitant	reluctant	averse
loathsome	appalling	repulsive
sinister	ghastly	macabre
intimidating	threatening	menacing
foreboding	ominous	perilous
cowering	cringing	browbeaten
flinch	shrink	recoil

Name: _____   Date: _____

Mild Fear	Moderate Fear	Intense Fear
wince	quail	grovel
tremble	quiver	quake
horrified	dishearten	phobia
stupefy	trepidation	panic
dread	terror	suspicion
quaver	falter	tension
traumatic	cowardly	bashful
pusillanimous	lily-livered	defenseless

OTHER FEAR WORDS

_____   _____   _____

_____   _____   _____

_____   _____   _____

_____   _____   _____

12 Normalizing Fear

Fear is the natural and normal human response to danger and the unknown. As for anger, there are valid and invalid fears. As with all emotion, the words we use to describe our emotional encounters are key to positive emotional regulation. With our words we interpret that visceral event called fear. How we name our fears begins the process of expressing the emotion. With words we name that incident and understand or misunderstand the visceral experience. The label given to the experience informs us of the path we are expected to take to express the emotion. Misname the emotion and we don't know what we are feeling. So we don't know what to do with or about that emotion.

At that point the general societal directive to "stuff it" may take over. Denial kicks into gear in one of its many faces. It is as if we are saying, "I don't know what this is. I don't know what to do about it. What I know is it feels awful. I can't stand this! I'm dying. I just want it to stop. Where's that bottle of wine?" A rational being is not able to use reason to fix that which is not named or named incorrectly. A scientist starts by gathering data to explore and define an issue. Science is about precision. But these same scientists may be blasé about precisely identifying their own emotions.

The favorite words of the modern day that are used to say "I'm angry" are also used to say "I'm scared." Can you imagine a scientist confusing bacteria and a virus? "It doesn't matter," pronounces the scientist, "They're both really, really tiny and they both make you sick." Such a purported scientist won't make it out of sophomore biology. Yet when it comes to our emotions, imprecision is not only okay. It is the norm.

No wonder we often say, "I don't know what I'm feeling." We are not lying. We really do not know. Initially, we may not know. So we use the language we have been taught. "I'm upset. I'm under so much pressure. I'm stressed. I'm overwhelmed." This is our perennial way of saying, "I'm feeling something, but I'm not going to name precisely what that is." On the surface none of these words and terms names a specific emotion. What is the nature of your upsetness? Are you scared upset or angry upset? What fears do you name pressure? Is it anger or fear or sadness that is stressing you? What muddle of multiple emotions are you describing with overwhelmed?

In the last chapter we began an understanding of the technique of being unpredictable. In squarely addressing denial of fear with teens, being unpredictable in your words jars the brain into new understanding. "So, let me get this straight. You're saying you are the only one out of the 1,200 students in our school who isn't afraid of what the other kids say about you. Right?" Well, of course, wrong. But when an educator frames words this way, that other teen developmental task, community, is engaged. What teen wants to stand alone against the 1,199? Any teen that seriously claims he does merits intensive intervention.

Yes, as educators we must sometimes use one developmental task to curtail the excesses or misunderstandings of the other developmental task. Teens cannot balance those tasks themselves. That's what they have us for. When assisting frustrated parents, share understanding of the technique of being unpredictable.

Many a parent has found that dropping the tone of voice to just above a whisper is much more effective than yelling at the teen. Even classroom teachers who drop to whispering in the front of the classroom reclaim the eyes that were wandering in the back of the classroom. The trick is to not use any one technique so often that it becomes the new normal and therefore predictable.

Just as anger needs a new vocabulary, so does fear. There is no need to invent words. The vocabulary of fear exists. What will be new is the using of the words. It will be new for us adults, that is. For our teens, teaching them the words and using the language of fear repeatedly with them will be their normal. Our new normal will simply be their normal. One day they will laugh and exclaim, "Grandma! What do you mean you're *stressing*? Stop being so old-fashioned. Are you scared, gram? Or mad? Sad? Tell me about it." They will speak this way to us if we first speak that way to them.

Fear Is Normal and Human

We emphasize that fear is natural and normal because so many believe there is something wrong with them when they are afraid. Those who believe they are not afraid of anything mistakenly believe that they are abnormal, a failure, or a coward when they feel fear.

Popular media has long advanced this belief. What are commonly called action heroes in their many incarnations all support the false belief that the hero does not feel fear. Often the character visibly afraid is depicted as degraded in some way. The message is clearly that if you are afraid, there is something wrong with you. You are something less than a man, even less than human. The something wrong is usually expressed in ugly, derogatory, demeaning language by use of the common slang synonyms for coward like wimp, sissy, wuss, and worse.

It is saddening that in the age of women's empowerment the word sissy is used with no awareness of how demeaning its use is to women. More blatantly, male coaches sometimes call male players girls as a way of saying they have not performed well. They are weak, less than men. This usage is derogatory to both women and men. Its usage reveals the belief that men are necessarily strong and fearless, and women, prone to fear, are necessarily weak.

Use of wimp, sissy, and girl as a derogatory teaches teenage boys that women are less than men and are inherently fear-ruled beings. The truth is adrenaline is adrenaline. Cortisol is cortisol. Men are not exempt from the adrenaline rush called fear. Usage of these words does not advance emotional intelligence.

Similarly, we stress that fear is human. From our observations of animals it appears that they, too, feel fear. We cannot know with absolute assurance that animals experience fear in just the same way humans do. Do animals have a thinking part of fear or only a feeling part? We do know that fearful behavior has been observed in animals. From this we intuit that animals feel fear.

Perhaps because we observe animals sometimes behaving fearfully, we may easily conclude that fear is an animal response and, thus, something less than human. But a trait shared by all humanity in all ages is clearly a human quality. To reinforce that fear is human and not less than human, our definition purposely calls it a human response.

Sources of Our Fears

Danger and the unknown precipitate our fears. Fear is the visceral, physiological response to danger and the unknown. Like all emotions fear has a thinking part and a feeling part. The thinking part consists of the perception of self as diminished, small, and weak. Such a state the brain interprets as a danger. The feeling part consists of uncomfortable visceral or gut-level internal sensations and physiological alterations in the body. The next chapter looks at this part of fear.

Fundamentally, the thinking part is self-talk, conscious or subconscious, which says, "This is dangerous to me." One may be in a situation which objectively is dangerous, even potentially lethal, and not feel fear if one does not interpret the situation as dangerous. For example, a zoologist may be an expert animal handler of big cats. However, the lions' compound is, objectively, very dangerous. When a lion's health necessitates entry, the handler relies on knowledge and skill for safety. A dart judiciously placed immobilizes the lion. Is the handler afraid? Either the experienced lion expert does not feel fear at all or, feeling it, suppresses it to the level of prudent caution until safely out of the compound. The handler manages fear constructively in order to aid the lion and safely exit the compound.

Conversely, one may be in a situation that objectively is not at all dangerous but be very fearful because the situation is construed to be dangerous. Fear of rejection, real or imagined, by a peer group is a danger that is a potent producer of teen anxiety. The fear is a realistic response for a young human working day and night (past when their parents are asleep) on the developmental task of community. Real or perceived rejection is often interpreted by teens as abject failure at one of the major tasks adolescence is all about, namely, learning how to form community groups. If you fail a test, it's disappointing but no biggie. But if you fail in your reason for being, that's terrifying.

The teenage prom is not nearly as dangerous as the lions' compound. But it may be acutely alarming. Who will go with me? Will I look all right? Who will dance with me? What if I trip in the middle of the dance floor? What if my face breaks out the night before the prom? What if my parents don't let me stay out as late as the other kids?

Working with teens, always pose a query for yourself.

Is this teen afraid of a danger, an unknown, or both?

The Great Unknown

We respond with fear to the unknown when we suspect danger in that unknown. Facing the unknown may also generate feelings of expectation, adventure, and delight. As an example, remind teens of what we know about one of the classic explorations of the unknown. Columbus felt expectation and excitement at his great adventure. But as the weeks dragged on, his sailors descended from apprehension to fear to sheer terror. Columbus must have felt moments of fear, not from falling off the world, but from mutiny. But his faith in the correctness of his knowledge and in his own leadership skills enabled him to continuously focus on the adventure of his exploit, not on his fear.

Columbus's example reveals that when the mind views new challenges only as dangerous obstacles and fearful burdens, then fear replaces anticipation. For this reason eliminating the word, problem, and substituting instead words like challenge, obstacle, issue, and concern is advisable. Present this chapter's Activity Sheet 12.1 to teens as a way to zap problems. We have problems because we believe there exists a reality called problems. Teaching this to our young people sets them up for a life of problems.

Reframing our issues as challenges and obstacles and concerns focuses the mind on the excitement and adventure of embracing the unknown. Allowing the heavy weight of what we see as burdensome problems to oppress us guarantees a fear response. The brain, remember, does what we tell it. Tell it you are facing a burden and doubt your ability to face that burden and conquer, and your brain will give you fear. Tell the same brain you have challenging obstacles to overcome and intend to enjoy the adventure, and your brain will give you excitement. Teaching this to our teens sets them up for a life of adventure.

Danger and the unknown produce lack of certainty and the absence of surety. The fear in the state of not feeling secure or safe is called **insecurity**. The absence of assured safety and predictable certainty is very anxiety-provoking. For young people, lack of consistency in parenting and irregular, erratic discipline create intense fearfulness. When the self-talk is "What will happen next, and how will I survive it?" the prospect of both danger and the unknown produces fear that may mount to dread or panic.

Valid and Invalid Fear

Just as sources of anger are valid and invalid, sources of fear also are valid and invalid. A valid danger, one that is objectively real, produces valid fear. Even so, like the lion handler, one may condition oneself to reject or bypass fear. A display may help teens understand.

> **Valid danger　→　Valid fear**
>
> **Invalid danger →　Invalid fear**
>
> **Unknowns　→　Valid fears**

But so-called dangers, things that would not generate fear in most people most of the time, things that are not inherently dangerous, are invalid dangers. They generate real but invalid fear. An entomologist may explain the many scientific reasons not to be afraid of a certain spider. But if you are afraid of spiders, dangerous or not, your fear is real enough. So stress again that such fear, although objectively invalid, is quite real.

With the category of the unknown we cannot make exactly the same equation. Things are either known or unknown. If something is but partially known, one is fearful of that portion that remains unknown. Thus, invalid unknowns cannot exist. If it is not unknown, it must be known. If a known object or situation generates fear, it must be because it is perceived as dangerous.

Consider with teens the legion of their fears of possible unknowns. Their entire life before them is one huge unknown. Who they are as expressed in individuation is partially known but greatly unknown. Their developmental task of community will continue way, way into adulthood. All this constitutes a colossal range of unknowns.

If educators could see teens as Columbus's crew or as pioneering astronauts, we might grasp the depth of the fears all teens face. It was not always this way. In past centuries an adolescent's fate was determined by family and paternal occupation. When we humans changed all that, we opened up a churning sea our young people must sail. Our teens come by their fears honestly. It is our job as counselors and educators to be sometimes lighthouses and sometimes rocket boosters. But let us no longer deny the fear.

•   Journaling—Valid and Invalid Fears

Assign students to make two lists in their journals. One, compose a List of Valid Fears, those that are appropriate responses to valid, real-world dangers. Two, make a List of Invalid Fears, those that are inappropriate responses or overreactions to that which is not objectively dangerous. It is perfectly appropriate if some of these fears are silly, like "I'm afraid the green goop served at lunch is going to crawl off my tray." As much laughter as possible teaches "We don't have to be afraid of fear."

At the beginning of the next class or session have teens share their lists. The process should generate discussion and even debate because of possible differences of opinion about what is and what is not objectively dangerous. The point is not to generate debate to the death over "Is this a valid or invalid fear?" but to inculcate the key concepts. These concepts are that not all fears are valid and that it is perfectly acceptable to experience fear in fear-provoking circumstances.

•   Small Group—Taking The Pledge: Activity Sheet 12.1

Instruct teens to each take out a sheet of paper and their journals. Direct them to use the sheet to write a List of My Problems. The list may be as long or short as time allows.

Then, have teens reframe each designated problem. The task is to rewrite them in terms of a challenge, obstacle, issue, or concern, and synonyms to these words. Your teens' quickest thesaurus search will reveal a minimum of five useful synonyms for each. That's at least 20 words to use instead of "problem." So, "Talking to my parents is my biggest problem" is reframed in the journal as, "Talking to my parents is my greatest challenge." Instruct teens to choose their own unique title for this journal page, like *My Challenges* or *My Issues*. In working with individuals and small groups, always alert to the use of the word problem and coax the teen to reframe it.

Problem? Do you mean challenge or obstacle or issue or concern?

Upon completion of the exercise, invite teens to "throw their problems away" by crumbling or tearing the single sheet titled List of My Problems and discarding it in a trash can. Then, with due ceremony, have each teen Take the Pledge by solemnly reading and signing their own copy of the Pledge, Activity Sheet 12.1. Note that even when we throw away our problems, life's challenges remain.

• **The Sound of Fear**

This activity parallels the *My Song—Anger* activity in Chapter 9. With the aid of the music department, each teen chooses their anthem for fear. Who can forget the classic theme song from Alfred Hitchcock's *The Birds* and from his *Psycho* shower scene? The Beatles gave us fear and self-doubt in *Nowhere Man*. Ominous tones are in passages in *Peter and the Wolf*. Classic opera is replete with emotion, but your teens may appreciate only the briefest arias. Each teen chooses *My Song—Fear*, whether from modern or classical music.

• **List of Fear Words, Activity Two: Activity Sheet 11.1**

Assign teens to use the List of Fear Words, column two, to write or tell a story, *A Scary Day*. Instruct them to mainly use words from column two. A few words may come from column one. Save column three for next chapter's exercise. Instruct students to tell the story of an average day they found frightening. This is not a tale of terror but of an ordinary, everyday fear that, one day, was particularly anxiety-provoking. As with all writing activities, the counselor and all collaborating teachers may participate in discussing fear with teens and in the written and oral activities.

BULLETIN BOARD MATERIAL

I have many challenges and some obstacles, issues,
and concerns—but no problems.

Every life challenge is an exciting discovery.

Name: _____   Date: _____

Activity Sheet 12.1
THE PLEDGE

I hereby state, declare, and affirm that henceforth in my life and for all time to come I shall have

No problems.

However, I reserve the right to have

- Issues to attend to,
- Concerns to handle,
- Obstacles to overcome, and
- Challenges to grapple with.

Duly signed and sealed this day,

_____

[Date]

By:

_____

[Name of no-problem person]

_____

[Name of witness]

13 Detoxifying Fears and Tears

Strategies for addressing fear are both given to us by nature and learned behavior. Our task is to refine what nature has given us and consciously learn helpful strategies. Applying the A, B, Cs of constructive emotional expression is one such strategy. Grasping the significance of our valid and invalid fears is another. Indeed, fully appreciating that a fear is actually something we do not need to be afraid of goes a long way to tamping down the fear. If that fear has been well learned, invalid or not, it will still pop into our consciousness from time to time. At that point recognizing that bogey man for the chimera it is deconstructs it down to a manageable level.

Grasping the fear behind anger presents a model for constructive conflict resolution that does not ignore emotion. Over the decades many protocols for conflict resolution have been invented. Their existence communicates the message that conflict is something that may be resolved, that there is a structure or protocol to follow to do that, and that a positive outcome is anticipated. In this sense it does not matter which protocol is used. However, in a society that denies emotions, it was not to be expected that emotions would be front and center in the process. Rather brainstorming lists, well-verbalized reasons, and above all a superfluity of words revealed the underlying belief that conflict may be resolved by reason.

Has it? Intelligent, reasoning creatures that we are, has our intelligence and reason solved our conflicts? The best and the brightest in the governments of the United Nations labor well to address, reduce, and stop conflict. We in our lives resolve one issue we may label a problem only to see it return in another guise. Whether in the United Nations, in a high school, or in a family, addressing positions, people, events, and reasons while not once even mentioning the emotions behind and infusing those realities yields endless wrangling and alienation.

Our fears are as real as the latitude and longitude of national boundaries. A teen's fears are as real as the basketball she dribbles. A young man's unspoken sorrow is as real as the books he carries. Fears in the hearts of husbands and wives are as real as divorce papers. Living as if the reality of our fears is irrelevant distorts our families, our schools, and our nations.

The twenty-first century begins a long process of inculcating emotional honesty into the way we live. Schools are society's primary change agents for the teaching and sharing of new knowledge about fear. Science teachers are particularly well placed to teach the biology of fear, with its biochemical and neurological underpinnings. Wide-ranging classroom discussion of the impact of fear as pertains to a history lesson is the job of the social studies teacher. Language arts teachers expand characterization and plot by probing what character was afraid of what, when, where, and how. When we teach what fear is and how to handle it, we will, gradually, have less fear-driven lives.

On the personal level, fear of emotions has produced widespread suppression of nature's primary outlet for strong emotion. There is such extensive lack of knowledge about crying that we are now at the point we must teach the meaning and importance of crying as the primary non-verbal means of emotional expression. Think of it. What nature gave us, what came naturally to our ancestors, we must investigate, explore, and define as if we were discovering some new mathematical algorithm. How far we have wandered away from the natural expression of emotion.

The Feeling Part of Fear

The last two chapters focused on the thinking part of fear. This chapter and the next center on the feeling part of fear. This is the part of fear that is most misunderstood. The notion that fear is biological, physiological, in the body is both accepted and simultaneously rejected. We accept it when we recognize a scare gave us an adrenaline rush. Then, next day we deny it as we claim our fear is only a stomach ache from something we ate. Endlessly I have heard people criticize themselves for being afraid. If the individual is open to it, I may reply, "So you don't like being human?" Widening eyes are then willing to hear new information about fear. Fear is human. If you reject the part of you that has the capacity to fear, you are rejecting your full humanity.

Fear is the reason we are all here. Fear and its partner anger were what saved our ancestors long, long before we invented biology and world history and mathematics. Fear protected us so that, in time, our reason could reflect on anatomy and nations and novel characters incised in clay. My hunch is we did much better with fear and anger when our words were fewer. We reacted. We did not yet know we were supposed to define our terms and name and label every minute portion of existence.

In a sense we have gotten too smart for our own good. Modern people almost instantly convert their fear into words in the process of intellectualization. That thinking then, as we say, runs through our heads over and over. "It's driving me crazy! I can't stop thinking about it!" Yes. You cannot, because thinking is not and never will be emotion. Want to stop driving yourself crazy? Consider whether some part of you really wants to cry or scream.

Screaming we cannot easily do because it scares others. But alone in a cabin in the woods or on a vacant seashore, there should be no issue with yelling at the universe. Movies of screaming Vikings and shrieking hordes mesmerize us because we want so badly to scream, to shout, and then to cry. Emotion is visceral.

Once fear is elicited, one may say over and over "I'm not afraid," but the pumping heart, altered breathing, and other physical reactions like a dry throat together loudly proclaim, "You *are* afraid." For good reason we call it gut-level fear. The fear reaction is a complex physiological process which includes the release of hormones into the bloodstream and changes in neurotransmitters in the brain. Once fear has progressed to this point, the statement "It's all in your mind" simply is not true. It's in your body.

Working with teens on their fears means stressing the need to find a physical outlet to express all potent emotion, including fear. An anger management plan targets anger. More broadly, an affect management plan is an AMP that addresses the entire range of challenging affect, in particular the most challenging emotions of fear and grief as well as anger.

Thus, at this point instruct teens with anger management plans to see what portions of the AMP also may apply to other strong emotions. You will find that once you open the door to discussion of anger and procedures for its healthy management, the other emotions underlying or connected to the anger come pouring out. They, too, must be managed.

Allowing and Accepting Fear

The review of the AMP may, in part, anticipate some of the following. Apply the A, B, Cs to fear by expanding the explanation of step A. Select questions for probing fears as your knowledge of your teens and intuition direct. Consider the following:

- How do we know when we're afraid?
- Do we always know when we're afraid?
- If we feel big or inflated when we're mad, how do we feel when we're afraid?
- What kind of self-talk occurs when we're afraid?
- If we fail to *own* the fear, what happens to it?
- Could we express the fear as something else?
- What self-talk might we use to label fear?
- What effect does drinking alcohol and getting high have on step A?
- Tough guys get in fights all the time. Of what are they afraid?

Honest and direct self-talk is best. "I'm afraid. I wish I were not afraid, but I have to admit the truth is I really am scared." Lead teens to see that the first step in handling fear is to name the emotion correctly, to admit that it is what it is, and to claim and accept it as one's own. Our display expands to detail the steps of productive fear expression.

> **A. Allow and accept the fear. Allow it to happen. Claim it. Own it. Name it.**
> **B. Be with the fear. Feel it. Breathe deeply. Breathe through it. Breathe.**
> **C. Choose. Constructively channel the fear. Cry if you want.**

Feeling Fear

Step C will be expanded in the next chapter. As you relate the A, B, Cs specifically to fear, engage in a dialogue about what the steps mean.

- What do we mean when we say be with fear?
- If we run away from our fears, what happens?
- Do they just go away, poof?
- What are some direct ways we may express fear?
- How do alcohol and drugs interfere with step B?
- What happens when the drug wears off or you sober up? Is the emotion still there?

Emphasize that to be with an emotion is to feel it and experience it directly, honestly. When we fail to do so, the emotion comes out sideways in some alternate, usually inappropriate expression. Emotions never just evaporate, poof. They find an outlet whether or not we consciously direct the process.

Being with fear teaches the brain that it does not have to panic when it perceives fear in the body. Being with fear means desensitizing the brain to it. Thus, even our twenty-first-century brains may declare, "Ah, yes. I know this. I've known this feeling from time immemorial. This is fear. I know it well. I can do this. I can be afraid and still be okay." Our Brainy Boos will learn to help us out in this way if we teach them to do so.

The tip to use when working with distraught teens is the reminder to breathe.

Breathe. Breathe with Me. Breathe Deeply. Again.

The Lost Art of Crying

Crying is the natural outlet for all strong emotion, joy as well as anger, sorrow, and fear. But in our day the subject of crying is a sensitive one, more particularly so for boys and men. Modern culture is chock full of "Don't cry!" signals.

Little boys, more often than girls, are told, "Don't cry." A young boy who cries is called a crybaby. A youngster who expresses fear is labeled a scaredy-cat. Rough, tough motion picture heroes are hardly ever seen to cry. The message communicated and internalized as self-talk is "If I am to be a real man, I must not cry."

Garbage thinking does not stop being junk just because it is embraced by mass culture. But by living on top of the garbage dump, one does get used to the smell. Thus, it takes stepping back and applying ruthless inner honesty and critical thinking to reject the garbage thinking advocated by society. In a society that degrades crying, a real man is the man who dares to cry. It takes no courage to follow the crowd. Daring to go it alone by expressing your true feelings takes intrepid valor.

Laughing Through Tears

Exaggeration and teasing are good techniques to diffuse fears of a sensitive subject. Instruction about crying is another opportunity for educators to use laughter to instill new information. For teens that are highly resistant to hearing the message "It's okay to cry," point to each facial feature one by one and ask its purpose.

Follow an outline similar to the one below. Above all, do not tell your teens in advance that this instruction is about crying. This exercise demonstrates that our organs are meant to be used and that society's declaration that the lacrimal glands are not to be used is as ridiculous as green ears.

- Point to your mouth. "What do we do with this?" (We eat. We talk.) "Is it okay to eat and talk?" (Yes.) "Then, it's not unmanly or childish to sometimes eat and sometimes talk?" (No.) "It doesn't make me a little kid if I eat and talk with the same mouth?" (No. One teen is sure to comment, "Not at the same time.")
- Point to your nose. "What is this thing that sticks out of your face for?" (To smell, to breathe.) "Is it okay to smell and breathe?" (Of course.) "So, a strong person does not have to hold his or her breath to prove that strength?" (No.)
- Point to your eyes. "What are these two blue or brown or green things for?" (To see.) Close your eyes. "Suppose someone tells me a real man or a real woman walks around with his or her eyes shut like this. Then do I have to close my eyes all the time to be real?" (No.) "No! Why not? You have to admit it would take a really tough person to do that. So why not?" (Eyes are to be used.)
- Lightly pull your earlobes. "What are these floppy things for?" (To help us hear.) "Well, what if a bunch of people decide to paint their earlobes green and then claim 'You're not grown up until your ears

are green.' Would you paint your ears?" (Various responses are to be expected.) "Why or why not?"

- Pass around a small mirror. "Okay, I want all of you to check your faces. Is anyone missing a mouth? Nose? Eyes? Ears? Now examine the inside corner of your lower eyelids carefully. Does anyone *not* have the tiny holes that are the openings of the lacrimal glands? Are they present in only the girls?"
- "What are they for?" (Crying.) "Are they for anything else?" (To wash the eyes, as when the eyes water.) "Well, your nose is for two things, too, smelling and breathing. Suppose that an evil witch put a spell on you so that from now on you could only do *one* of those. Which one would it be? Your mouth is for two things, too, eating and talking. But that busy witch says you have to choose one. What is your choice? How much fun would life be without talking and the sense of smell?"
- "So, here we have holes in our lower eyelids that are meant for two things. But some of us listen to that stingy ole witch who says we may only use them for *one* thing. Our lacrimal ducts are for crying when we hurt emotionally, so is it okay to use them?"

Naturally, if there is a handicapped individual present, modify the above exercise as sensitivity and decorum suggest. At the last question note who joined in the chorus "Yes!" and who remained silent. Make a particular mental note of any teens that looked away. Find a reason to get those teens into the counselor's office. There is a reason crying is just too sensitive a subject for them to face. Alternatively, any teen who starts crying at so mild an invitation also needs compassionate adult intervention .

Teens enjoy this mini drama because it appears to them that the adult walking them through it is crazy. Being unpredictable means not letting our dear teens know where we are coming from. Engage them, then surprise them. Ending where they did not know you were going is like dancing your teens through an astonishing maze unknown to them. The excitement and surprise you elicit will forcefully imprint the lesson on their brains. You have made crying normal, as natural as a nose. You have not just communicated but demonstrated that there is no need to fear our lacrimal glands. You have detoxified crying.

- **Small Group—A Nightmare on [Your Street]**

Assign teens to work together in small groups to invent a nightmare. First, they compose the scripts. Then, they act them out as mini plays. Alternatively, short essays may be written by small groups of three or four and then shared.

However, unlike in the usual blood and gore horror movie, these plays or stories are to be blood-free—no guns, knives, or chain saws. Rather, teens must concoct *Something Terrible* that is not murderously violent. *My Dog and the Monster Flea* is an example. Others are *My Algebra Book Attacks Me*, *My Social Media Page Autocorrects All My Words into Swahili*, and *My Hair Is Alive*. Dialogue of characters should include words from Activity Sheet 11.1, all three columns. Counselors may save their creative teens' most ludicrous and inventive titles for groups that engage with all the enthusiasm of upturned cafeteria chairs.

- **List of Fear Words, Activity Three: Activity Sheet 11.1**

Instruct teens, "Invent a fantasy story about an imagined day of terror that is horrifically funny. Call it something like *The Silliest Day of Terror*." Direct them to use as many words as possible from column three of the List of Fear Words. Use of similes and metaphors may be encouraged. "I was as scared as a mouse running from an eagle" or "My fear was a torrent of black pitch choking my breath away."

Encourage your teens also to use exaggeration and absurdity. This fantasy is not to be a copy of movie and television horror scripts. It may be a satire, a mock and silly imitation of one such plot. Or it may be entirely original.

Humor diffuses anxiety. Humor reduces the dangerous to manageable proportions. Humor mocks our fear of the unknown by creating something, if only a thread, we may handle. When we turn ignorance to humor, the familiarity of that humor comforts us and dissipates the fear.

- **Mystic Dewdrops**

Instruct teens, "Write a poem about magical, mystical, enchanted tears that are as precious as diamonds and pearls. Whose tears are they? Why are they magic? What wonderful feats of wizardry do they work?"

For another project about crying, see Chapter 18 for the Tissues for Your Issues activity. Especially if done in health class and to be graded as part of class participation, this project involving the use of tissue boxes might be begun before the final unit is presented. This allows ample time for all teens to put their hearts into a creative, comprehensive project.

- **Win–Win Conflict Resolution with Emotion: Activity Sheets 13.1–15.2**

When negotiators cannot agree on the shape of the negotiating table, it is not logic but emotion that is primary. When emotion is ignored, non-issues are treated as if they were substantive. Attention is deflected from true issues.

Only after hours of verbalizing and venting have relieved the emotion do negotiators get down to business. But detailed, multi-page documents are poor substitutes for direct, constructive anxiety and anger expression.

Activity Sheets 13.1–15.2 offer a protocol for negotiating based on affective as well as cognitive input.

While sharing Activity Sheet 13.2 Worksheet One, stress that a Negotiator speaks directly to the Diplomat while the opposing Negotiator is silent. If the two negotiators could constructively speak directly to one another, no diplomat would be needed.

BULLETIN BOARD MATERIAL

It's okay to be afraid.

No emotions are bad. Some actions are.

When you're afraid, find a friend.

… In the night, in solitude, tears;
On the white shore dripping, dripping, sucked in by the
sand ….
Tears. Walt Whitman[1]

Notes

1 One of the leaves Whitman (1819–1892) blessed us with is his poem, *Tears.* Whitman's works are history lesson, great literature, and the epitome of grief transformed into lasting beauty. Should a sorrowful event strike your school system, social studies and language arts teachers may assist school psychologists and counselors by helping grieving students to emulate Whitman by converting sorrow and pain into their own great poems. For social studies class, Whitman's original *Drum-Taps* (online at www.gutenberg.org/files/8801/8801-h/8801-h.htm ebook release September, 2005) composed during his service as a nurse in the Civil War is both bitter history lesson and grief as poetry. For language arts, his *Tears.* in his paean to America, *Leaves of Grass*, honors the deep sorrow of weeping. Should your school system have reason to weep, the emotionally intelligent can do no better than weep with Walt Whitman. *Tears.* is in *Leaves of Grass* in the collection, *Poems by Walt Whitman* (W.M. Rossetti, Ed., 1867), ebook release June, 2005, online at www.guten berg.org/cache/epub/8388/pg8388-images.html

Name: _____   Date: _____

Activity Sheet 13.1
WIN-WIN CONFLICT RESOLUTION WITH EMOTION

BEGINNING

To begin, each disputant agrees to become a **Negotiator**. A neutral third party accepts the role of **Diplomat**, a referee.

DUTIES OF THE TWO NEGOTIATORS	DUTIES OF THE DIPLOMAT
• To be honest and open • To listen • To talk about emotions as well as ideas • To give a little, to bend • To commit to a win-win solution	• To be fair and impartial • To listen • To clarify emotions by reflecting what both negotiators say • To guide the conflict to a win-win solution

Specific time limits are agreed upon for each of the steps.

STEP ONE   Time limit: _____ minutes

In Step One the Diplomat directs each Negotiator to "Describe the matter as you see it." Negotiators do this by giving answers to the items on Worksheet One, Activity Sheet 13.2.

Negotiators share their worksheets for the specific, prearranged time limit. In this step each Negotiator speaks directly to the Diplomat while the opposing Negotiator *listens in silence*.

Name: _____   Date: _____

Activity Sheet 13.2

WIN-WIN CONFLICT RESOLUTION WITH EMOTION, WORKSHEET ONE

• In reference to this matter my emotions are …

_____

_____

• In reference to this matter I want …

_____

_____

• In reference to this matter I need …

_____

_____

• In reference to this matter I would like …

_____

_____

• In reference to this matter I wish …

_____

_____

• Additionally, I want to say …

_____

_____

_____

_____

_____

14 Fruitful Fear

In the last chapter we applied steps A and B to fear. From there we apply step C, Choose and Channel. See the chart in Chapter 13, p. 165, for the steps. As with all emotion we may express fear in two major ways: verbally and nonverbally. Talk it out! is the first and foremost way to verbally express fear. Besides crying, nonverbal expressions include art, music, and physical exercise that work off the physiological emotional discharge.

All toddlers demonstrate our most primal nonverbal expressions, crying and screaming. It is our job to gently move our little ones from these displays into the verbal talk it out mode. Similarly for teens who parallel the impulses of our toddlers, it is our work to move them gently from weeping and yelling and from stuffing or internalizing tears and shouts to a consistent mode of talking out their emotions.

All emotions are energy to be used to make things happen. Fear is a prod to action. That energy must be directed to constructive purposes. Even fear, as uncomfortable as it is, may be channeled into productive ends.

Like anger, fear may be a powerful motivator. Thus, if you are afraid you are going to fail, you just might study harder. If you are scared no one will like you, you might try harder to be polite and kind. If you are afraid the police are going to catch you, you might not drink and drive. Mild fear is an important prod to action. In fact, many daily actions are motivated by a moderate level of fear. Even "I better not do that; the principal will fuss" shows the power of mild fear.

As each category of constructive channeling is discussed, add it to the display. The list on p. 173 is not meant to be all-inclusive. Invite teens to add their own ideas to the list.

Step C. Choose. Constructively channel the fear. Cry if you want.

- Talk it out!

- Change your self-talk.

- Seek new knowledge.

- Ask a person for help.

- Ask for a hug.

- Take constructive action.

- Practice courage.

Change Self-talk

Emotional intelligence is fostered by constantly framing issues and their resultant emotions from the perspective of self-talk. In order to do a good job of handling the feeling part of fear, changing the thinking part is vital. Once hormones are in the bloodstream, they cannot be wished away. However, we may always choose to change our thinking. But if a teen does not even know there is such a thing as self-talk, reframing it is most challenging. The reframing approach must almost be stumbled upon by accident instead of purposely chosen.

Engage teens in a discussion about the new forms of self-talk they may use when the original self-talk means "This is scary for me." A white board in your office or classroom may be used to list teens' suggestions that you accumulate over time. Some new self-talk might be "It's scary, but I can handle it," and "It's as exciting as it is scary," and "It's not so scary when I think, 'I can do it. Other people have. So can I.'"

Stress often to your teens the critical role of self-talk.

What is the self-talk that goes with that fear?

Leaving such a white board or display out all the time allows all teens who see it to learn two things. One, "Here's a positive thing I may say to myself when afraid. I had not thought about that." Two, "Oh, so I see. Lots of kids are afraid; it's not just me." What a blessing to all teens in a school to learn that fear is normal and surmountable. Fear is not a hoard of walking zombies intent on devouring brains. But, interestingly, it could be said that unbridled fear does swamp the brain and devour it. We are our own zombies.

Seek New Knowledge

When fear is the fear of the unknown, the obvious solution is to eliminate the unknown factor. New information may come from reading, from talking to others, from watching a pertinent video or film, and from experience. To learn not to be afraid of something means to see that something in a new, non-dangerous light.

Share with teens that fears require intent self-reflection. To address fear we must first know why we are afraid. Skip this step and we are off and running while not even knowing why we are running. Questions to ask include "Am I scared because I'm seeing this as new, strange, uncertain, or unknown? Is it something I've never dealt with?" If so, then the next question is "Where or to whom may I turn to get the information I need to help me deal with this?"

In this age when we hold entire libraries in our hands, teens must know that new information about a legion of their unknowns is available on their phones. Although obvious to adults, teens who see their phones as primarily the malt shop of their era may not view the internet as a source of new information for managing fears. Encourage your teens to play with their phones by Googling specific questions about the ordinary fears of adolescence, like "How many teens are afraid their friends might not like them?" and "What do teens fear most of all?" They'll love the exercise and soon be having fun with their own inventive questions.

Alas, you may have to explain what a malt shop was. But just as with anger, laughter detoxifies fear. Laughing, Brainy Boo bathed in comfortable neuro-chemicals sighs, "Ah, I see. Fear is not something for me to be afraid of. I got this."

Ask a Person for Help

Many people have the mistaken idea that needing help with something, with anything, means that they are weak or unmanly or less than perfect. All human beings are growing. Therefore, all are imperfect. To objectively view a situation and decide that one is over one's head takes courage. But if we do not explicitly teach "It's okay to ask for help," how is a developing mind supposed to know that?

To the contrary, when we do not explicitly give the permission, the teen may conclude, "This is confusing. I don't know what to do. But I'm supposed to know. Other kids look like they know. It feels so horrible not knowing. I feel so alone. Where's that joint?" Pulled in on ourselves, shrunken fast into a mental fetal position, we do not see that our aloneness is isolation that magnifies fear.

To ask for help, therefore, is an act of wisdom that demonstrates true strength of character. By failing to ask for help when reason suggests we need help, we often scare ourselves far beyond what the situation warrants.

We perpetuate and deepen the pain and anxiety. Share with teens that there is nothing shameful in admitting that something we see as dangerous or frightening or new is scaring us.

Self-help and 12-step groups such as Alateen have expanded the helping principle to the organizational level. When common challenges are shared, the fear, too, is shared and thereby reduced. Fear thrives in secrecy and silence.

Ask for a Hug

When fear is very strong, seeking knowledge and practicing new self-talk and all such rational approaches are very difficult. They are difficult, not impossible. If one has a belief that one should be exempt from doing hard things, these options may *feel* impossible. Today many have a belief that life "should" be easy and that, if it is not, something is wrong.

Lack of resiliency among teens stems from this key misunderstanding. Assist teens in grasping that life is supposed to be hard. It is not meant to be overwhelming or impossible, just hard. In every decade our lives should be just hard enough to keep us reaching, to keep us trying, to keep us growing. But teens who have had much done for them in their young lives may come to believe that when life is hard and a little scary, there is something drastically wrong. This may be further internalized to "There is something drastically wrong *with me*."

Work with teens on how to turn around this self-talk. New self-talk may include "Nothing is wrong. This is hard and a little scary for me. That's all. I can still be okay when things are hard and scary. I need some hugs, and I'm going to ask for them."

When fear is prominent, nurturance has no substitute. Everyone has had the experience of seeing a fearful child calm down in the arms of a loving parent. When fear refuses to give way to reason, the human touch works miracles. Nurturance, if not a cure, is a sure treatment for fear. Educators may always share with teens soft, consoling words and an earnest, compassionate gaze.

The challenges of our age do not change the fact that we are primates. Primates touch one another. Once born, we crave the human touch. Just concerns about inappropriate touching should not push us to attempt to ignore our nature. Every time we try to be human in ways that go against human nature, it just boomerangs in our faces. Some school systems have an absolute commandment "Thou shalt not hug."

But it is human to hug. Giving up a portion of our humanity because some humans have lost theirs is not the way. There is another way. School systems may enact common sense rules about hugging and touching children. These may vary from district to district but the framework must specify that system's guiding principles.

I offer two core principles. One, the integrity of the youngster is to be respected at all times. Two, any physical contact is to happen in public. To those two add what works for your school system.

The first principle is in this day even unclear to some adults. The first boundary of the castle of self is the physical body. Yet many adults touch others without any permission to do so. Sexual assault is a horrific expression of failure to internalize the sacredness of the integrity of another's body. Thus, let schools require that permission to touch be explicitly asked and explicitly given. "May I hug you?" and "Yes" must precede the act. "I want to support you with a hand on your shoulder. May I?" with a yes precedes the act.

Second, acts of physical nurturance are given in public. Schools rightly have a concern about what may happen behind closed doors. The answer to what will happen behind closed doors is nothing, nothing ever. Verbal counseling may occur with the counselor's door closed. But if at the end of the session, the teen wants a hug, the door is opened and both step out into the corridor. If tutoring one teen in an empty classroom at the end of the school day leads to the need for nurturing support, open the classroom door and go out into the hallway to give the hug. At first such requirements may feel stiff but over time both teens and teachers will experience the approach as a new, freeing normal.

Students as well as educators must know the rules. If a teen only wants to be hugged in private, that in and of itself must be explored. Regardless, the school's rule is firm: "No, I can't do that. Go find me three of your friends and we'll have a hug fest in the classroom. We could do that!" Teens will tease, "Oh, I forgot to say may I!" This is good. Spending four years in high school learning that touching another's person happens only after that other person's explicit permission is foundational to a lifetime of full respect for others.

This applies to all physical nurturance, to hugs, to kisses on the cheek, to arms around shoulders, to pats of the hand. "Even a pat on the hand?" some may cry. Yes. Let's make the rules clear. A touch is a touch. If the adult world itself fully grasped this, we would not need laws that define assault and battery. Battery means what the word says. It is to batter, to hit, to physically inflict grievous harm. Assault is the threat of harm which may include touching someone without their permission. Grabbing someone by the wrist to pull them somewhere is assault. But there are adults who think that because the person is not harmed, such grabbing is okay. The law says it is not. Let us begin in our high schools to teach what our laws support. Give hugs freely. Ask for permission to hug often.

Model the behavior you wish to teach.

Would you like a hug?

Nurturance is a sure treatment for fear. When we touch, we acknowledge our connectedness. Without connectedness there is no community. When individual teens feel in no way connected to the community that is their high school, they may rebel and act out against it. Without connectedness we are left alone to stew and bake and erupt in our own fears. Fear explodes in society as hostile rage.

Take Constructive Action and Practice Courage

Changing self-talk, seeking knowledge, and asking for help or a hug are all forms of constructive action. However, other forms of action may be helpful or necessary. For example, if the source of fear is objective danger, the solution is to remove or avoid the danger. If one is afraid of the dark, light is the simplest solution. If one is afraid of an abusive boyfriend or girlfriend, the time may have come to dissolve the relationship.

Fear leads us to waffle in our decision-making. It is helpful for teens to understand that not deciding *is* deciding. To allow ourselves to be paralyzed by fear is to choose to sink deeper and deeper into that fear. Sometimes it is best to do something rather than nothing. When we have asked for help and obtained all the information we may, it is time to fish or cut bait. Act. Do something, but act.

In situations in which immediate action would not be productive, an indirect action that expresses the fear is helpful. Art, music, and constructive physical activity all serve to channel fear. Selections of Wagner's music and Picasso's art incarnate fear in sound, form, and color. Share with your teens that the final strategy for handling fear is something called courage. Courage is so important it is a chapter unto itself.

- **Journaling—What I Will Do**

Direct teens to write in their journals a list of their fears, valid and invalid. After each fear, they should skip three or four lines. Once the lists are made, instruct teens to go back and under each fear write the things they intend to do in the future when they experience that fear. As with other exercises, if teens find it very difficult to work alone, have them complete the activity in small groups.

- **List of Fear Words, Activity Four: Activity Sheet 11.1**

Instruct teens to use whatever words they choose from all three columns of Activity Sheet 11.1 to describe something in their lives they find or once found frightening. This is a serious essay to be titled something like *What Scares Me* or *What Scared Me*. By now teens should be familiar with the range of intensity expressed in the three columns. The purpose of this activity is to choose their words carefully to express just the exact quality of fear that best describes their feelings.

Teens may write a paragraph or story as you or the language arts teacher direct. Advise as to whether the writings will be read in class as this may influence the choice of topic.

- **A Real Nightmare**

Encourage teens to write or tell an actual nightmare dreamed either recently or when younger. The intent of this activity is not to play amateur psychologist but to give teens' new knowledge about fear ample field for expression.

A nightmare, by definition, is a frightening dream. Teens will enjoy trying to decipher the specific nature of the fear in a given dream. In this exercise phones may once again come in handy. Apps and websites abound with information about dream symbolism.[1] Teens will come away from the exercise understanding that the long-held belief that "it's only a dream" is not a sufficient explanation in the twenty-first century. If it's a nightmare, it is fear, too.

- **Win-Win Conflict Resolution With Emotion: Activity Sheet 14.1**

Continue with the conflict resolution exercise. Use Activity Sheet 14.1 to clarify the points on which the negotiating parties agree and disagree. In this step negotiators move into direct discussion with each other with the diplomat acting as moderator. The activity sheets at the end of the next chapter detail the final steps.

The conflict resolution protocol may be presented as a unit unto itself. Emotions, however, must be primary. As long as we pretend our conflicts are about borders and things and people and events and that our emotions have no role, we will be arguing eternally. If your teens maintain they have no conflicts to resolve, let them make up something silly like sneakers vs. high heels or plaid vs. stripes just to have the experience of resolving a dispute.

BULLETIN BOARD MATERIAL

Life is sometimes hard. But I can handle it.

When I'm afraid, I will: Talk it out! Change my self-talk. Seek knowledge.

Ask for help and a hug. Take constructive action. Practice courage.

Note

1 To evaluate dream dictionaries, check the meaning given for flying and water. Nineteenth-century dictionaries were reprinted far into the twentieth century. Flying before the invention of the airplane cannot mean the same as it does today. Today it means freedom, movement, and perhaps escape. Water is the great dream metaphor for emotions. The condition of the water is the condition of the emotions. Calm waters signify balance. Dreaming of drowning means you fear you're over your head in some way. So heeding your dreams about water is a useful emotion management tool. Googling dream interpretation first brings up *Dream Moods A-Z Dream Dictionary* at www.dreammoods. com This is also an app your teens may enjoy investigating.

Name: _____   Date: _____

Activity Sheet 14.1
Win-Win Conflict Resolution With Emotion, Worksheet Two

Time limit: _____ minutes

The Diplomat assists the Negotiators in writing out an Agree-Disagree List. Don't forget to include in the listing emotions shared in common, like "We're both angry" and "We're both afraid." Negotiators may now speak directly to each other as well as directly to the Diplomat.

POINTS ON WHICH WE AGREE   **POINTS ON WHICH WE DISAGREE**

1._____   1._____
  _____   _____
  _____   _____

2._____   2._____
  _____   _____
  _____   _____

4._____   4._____
  _____   _____
  _____   _____

5._____   5._____
  _____   _____
  _____   _____

6._____   6._____
  _____   _____
  _____   _____

7._____   7._____
  _____   _____
  _____   _____

15 Courage in Action

As an additional strategy for handling fear, a new definition of courage may be communicated. A mild level of fear may prod us to action. A moderate level of fear may be dissipated by applying any of the several constructive ways to channel fear presented in Chapter 14. But even after applying multiple positive strategies, there will still be times when only courage will move us out of fear.

Greatly misunderstood, courage is one of those qualities often mistaken for a feeling. We may hear our teens say, "I don't feel very brave" and "I don't feel I have the courage to do that." Working with the military, I have learned to see courage through their eyes. Though many service people do not see courage in themselves, they nonetheless live it. For courage is not a feeling. There is no emotion named courage.

Courage is a decision. It is a thinking thing, not a feeling thing. **Courage** is the decision to act bravely in the face of fear. Courage does not diminish fear. It acts in spite of it. What diminishes fear for service people are the same strategies presented in Chapter 14. When Coast Guard members repel down from helicopters time and again in training, they are entraining neuronal pathways to act in spite of the danger in order to save those on a sinking boat. If some measure of fear is lessened, it is because they know what they are doing. Any remaining fear must be addressed with courage.

Courage Is More than Intestinal Fortitude

Fear is an opportunity to develop strength and courage. Since we are all born as babies, we are all crybabies. Crying is one of our first acts as independent human beings. Crying comes first, and courage follows close behind. The crawling child, of course, does not have the capacity to reason. But if it is not reason, it must be that nature itself pushes us to face our fears and move forward. If it were not so, we would all resume crawling the first time our toddling feet tripped us up, and we painfully crashed our heads to a stone floor. Something inside of us drives us repeatedly to courage. When a teen says, "I'm not brave," see that as a sign that the inner warrior is exhausted and confused. Reply with "That's okay. Sometimes I'm not brave either. Let's learn how to be brave together."

As a decision, courage is an aspect or function of the drive to individuation. The ego, the healthy sense of self, must learn to say, "I can. I will. It's hard but I can. It hurts but I will." Without internalizing self-talk like this, the self may come to believe "I am nothing but a bundle of fears." If simultaneously the individual learns "It is shameful to be afraid," a great wound is created in the inner warrior.

To the contrary we want our teens to grow up knowing fear is natural. Doubting self is normal. Reading, writing, and arithmetic must be learned and so must courage. If the Coast Guard does not teach you how to jump out of a helicopter to save people, I doubt you are going to learn that on your own. In the same way there are fears that we, quite simply, need someone else's help to face with courage. This in no way means we are weak or a wimp. If the Coast Guard has not taught you how to jump out of a helicopter, do you think yourself weak because you don't do that for a living?

Yet when no one teaches us how to be brave, we do condemn ourselves. If teens may learn only one thing in high school about their emotions, let it be that courage is a decision, one that they are fully capable of. No one grows up without repeatedly facing fearful situations and learning to handle them. Facing fear teaches us that it is not so bad as we feared. We can handle it. What frightens us most may be just the experience we need in order to learn that we are strong enough to face our worst fears.

Courage Is Action

It may be helpful to display the definition of courage.

> **Step C. Choose. Channel the fear. Practice courage.**
> **Courage is being afraid of taking constructive**
> **action and doing so anyway.**

There are two dimensions to courage. First comes the thinking part of courage, the decision to act bravely in the face of fear. Next comes the action part. One may be mentally brave, brave in one's thoughts. That is called fantasy or daydreaming. No amount of that will rescue you in a roiling sea. What will help is an angel from the sky acting expressly to pull you up from the sinking boat. Courage is action.

Courage is not the absence of fear. Repeated training helps the individual tame the adrenaline that pushes the brain to scream, "Hey! I can't fly out of a helicopter!" Courage is feeling fear and acting in spite of that fear. It is a grave mistake to assume that brave people do not feel afraid. A prevalent, popular misunderstanding of the meaning of courage is that it means to be fearless, that is, to be without fear.

But not to be afraid in an objectively fear-provoking situation is either foolish or superhuman. As we have seen, it is helpful to be mildly fearful. This is the fear that without thinking causes the service member to check gear one more time. None of us are superhuman. Folly does nothing to maximize human potential. Ignoring all fear leads to reckless action and tragedy. Fearless means reckless. Fear must be honored and accepted as the natural and normal human response to danger and the unknown.

Share with teens the understanding that fear does not make one a coward. Lack of action does. Courage is being afraid of doing what you know you must and doing it anyway. Courage is the decision to act and then acting. Courage seldom feels good when you are in the act of practicing it. The fear does not go away just because you have decided to act in spite of it. In fact it may increase. But later, perhaps many years later, you may look back on the incident with deep satisfaction.

To act with courage and experience yourself as strong enough to face fear produces a feeling of self-competence like no other. Human fulfillment is the fruit of fears successfully faced year after year. If a hero is someone who acts with courage, then we are all heroes.

Everyday Courage

Stress to your fearful teens the many, small acts of courage that fill our days. Begin with the fact that sometimes getting out of bed in the morning is an act of courage. Teens chronically late to school may not have an alarm clock issue. It may not be the playing video games to 1:00 a.m. either. The issue may be courage. Expecting a dismal, unpleasant day at work, don't you pull the covers over your head and take another few minutes?

Just moving the body upright and swinging the feet to the floor may take courage. This is hard to muster when the brain is not yet in wide awake decision-making mode. It helps to memorize a short directive to self, "Get up. Get up. Get up. You can do it. One, two, three, up!" Teaching such self-talk to teens is a must for their beginning the day with courage. Sessions with the teen have the goal of discovering and remedying just why the prospect of school is so fearful.

Talking politely to someone you fear does not like you takes pluck. Smiling at someone who never smiles back is an act of valor. Trying to do, again, something you have failed at before takes bold resolve. Working to change a habitual behavior that you know is in your best interest to change takes true grit.

Bringing up a topic communicates that the topic is important enough to speak about. Never bringing up a topic communicates that it is unrelated to everyday life. Never speaking about courage communicates that it is irrelevant. Teens have no idea about how courageous they may be until we explicitly invite them to be brave. Many stumble across courage by reading of it in books or seeing it in movies and concluding, "Maybe I should do that, too." But storybook courage is not everyday courage. Such a powerful antidote to fear deserves more than a passing nod and a stumble. Inquire often about courage.

Tell me how you were brave this week.

Elicit from your teens their view of what requires their courage. In your discussions share the following synonyms for courage: bravery, valor, mettle, pluck, spunk, and gumption. Add synonyms for the adjectival form: courageous, dauntless, intrepid, bold, valiant, stalwart, and stouthearted. Invite your teens to choose their favorite synonym to describe their own acts of courage. Adding popular slang equivalents for courage and its opposite is at your option. Language evolves. Be aware of teen slang for both brave and fearful which may or may not be popular in your district.

Americans of Courage

Americans like to think of themselves as fearless. We mistake fearlessness for courage. In fact, as the preceding word play may have revealed, some dictionaries list fearless as a synonym for courage. But since strictly speaking "fear-less" means "without fear," it cannot also mean courageous. Courage is *not* foolhardiness, fearlessness, and daring, which are the reckless, brazen acts of the daredevil.

History and literature offer a legion of examples of fear, recklessness, and bold courage. Your language arts curriculum may include works of Mark Twain. With just some refocusing, the lesson plans for these and for many works of literature may be fashioned to include an emphasis on the role of fear vs. courage.

Twain was an American of great courage. Today we take his faith in the equality of all persons for granted. Staunchly, he wrote his beliefs into his works, thereby shocking prim society and getting *The Adventures of Huckleberry Finn* (1884) banned in Boston.[1]

Twain understood the difference between mock fearlessness and true courage. In little-known passages he delineated the difference between courage and recklessness. It is fascinating that the author began his jewel of an exposition on courage by observing that courage begins with observing and reflecting. So, he tells us, courage is pausing and thinking. This thinking is a deep analysis that appraises the whole situation and weighs and measures the costs. Only after such scrutiny is the mind made up to act with determination. To the contrary, recklessness, Twain advises us, does not ponder or analyze but rushes right in with the hurrah of self-congratulation.

The costs of the risks are ignored.[2] How beautiful it is to see that Twain understood that courage is a rational decision to put self aside for the sake of another, but recklessness is just egoism *disguised* as courage.

Twain's breakdown may be a starting point for explaining the difference between genuine courage and the fearlessness and recklessness teens mistake for courage. The synonyms previously discussed for courage may be displayed. The discussion may include examples that include "How are you brave? Have you ever been reckless? Was getting up this morning an act of courage?" Compare and contrast interpretations and examples.

A full exploration of courage in public life is Kennedy's *Profiles in Courage*.[3] The book may be used whenever classroom, small group, or individual emphasis on courage is a beneficial focus. Finding a hero upon which one may model one's own struggle with courage is in and of itself uplifting and heartening. Courage is originally from the Latin *cor*, heart. We still say "take heart" when encouraging or en-*heart*ening others.

Profiles in Courage and many other books about brave souls embolden our hearts to share the ethos of courage with the self-talk, "If they could do it, so can I." When tackling fear is a goal of the AMP—and for those who are bullied, it must be—searching for a Courage Mentor in history, in books, and in life today may be a most valuable element of that AMP. Assist your bullied teens in choosing a hero to be their personal Courage Mentor.

When adults fail to repeatedly invite teens to practice courage, there is no reason to believe they should magically know what courage is. Nor will they necessarily grasp that they, too, are called to practice courage. Having a personal Courage Mentor concretely imparts to teens "Courage is not just about heroes in books. Courage is about *me*. I, too, must be courageous." Thus, the self-talk "I am brave" is internalized as part of the process of individuation. Failing to explicitly learn this leads teens to conclude that the churning sea of fear within is their overriding reality. For some, that reality remains well into adult life.

Kennedy urged us to make high self-regard the bedrock of our personal route to courage. When one individual establishes this core, all benefit. It is when courses of action are unpopular, he states, that courageous devotion to principle is foundational to true democracy. Citizens show courage in embracing their responsibility to be the "boss" that elects sometimes good, sometimes bad leadership. In a prescient sentence Kennedy sees the bravery of a last moment as no more magnificent than the courage of life. The getting up in the morning courage is one kind of courage of life. Kennedy calls us to practice courage by setting aside personal consequences, embracing and overcoming obstacles, and not allowing danger to deter us. Such action, he advises us, is the foundation of all human morality.

Kennedy like Twain understood courage. His *Profiles in Courage* may be used as a ready reference in the search for a Courage Mentor. Invite all your teens to design their own *Courage Profile* with items from books and historical sources and from their lives. Since the brain learns with its tools of words and images, the profile, similar to a vision board, consists of words and pictures about how the teen relates to their Courage Mentor. In line with Kennedy's words, profiles may show what consequences, obstacles, and dangers teens mean to confront with courage.

The words include the teen's chosen self-talk and may be as simple as "I am brave." Pictures may include photographs of people or any image that conveys *Courage!* to that teen. An image of a cat, back raised, confronting a dog three times its size and of a single candle flame in pitch-black darkness are examples. Art students may draw or paint their images. They may further enjoy using strong lights to cast shadows upon a wall to show the silhouette of their profile. The traced black and white image then becomes the background for their *Courage Profile*.

- **Journaling—Popular Sayings**

Direct teens to explain in their journals what the following sayings mean:

- Discretion is the better part of valor.[4]
- The only thing we have to fear is fear itself.[5]
- … to boldly go where no one has gone before.[6]

- **List of Fear Words, Activity Five: Activity Sheet 11.1**

Instruct teens to refer to the List of Fear Words as they write an essay on *The Bravest Thing I Ever Did*. The assignment is to be choosy about just the precise words used to describe the fear and just the right synonyms for courage. If your group is reluctant to be serious, see that itself as a defense against admitting fear.

Shift immediately to fantasy tales like *My Phone's Stouthearted App* about an app that instantly makes one brave and *My Little Brother's Brave Morning Battle with his Cereal Bowl*. In any context, practice with using the vocabulary of fear and courage internalizes the usage of the words. Once internalized they may then be used freely and often in life itself.

- **Literary Adventures**

Direct teens to answer questions similar to these about *The Adventures of Huckleberry Finn*. Who do you think is the most courageous character in the book? Taking Mark Twain's own definition of courage, show point by point how that character was courageous. Was that character ever reckless? Show how that character was or was not reckless.

Alternatively, instruct teens to read a chapter from *Profiles in Courage* wherein each chapter is about a different person. Display the names or assign small groups to work together on one of the profiles. Other biographies may also be chosen. Using Twain's and Kennedy's definitions and teens' own ideas, teens show why they think that person was courageous in either a jointly written essay or in a classroom presentation.

These activities are more than literature and history lessons. The task is to personalize each teen's understanding of fear. The goal is to identify courage as each teen's unique response to fear. The issue is not which politician or book character was or was not bold. The issue for our teens is how to be bold in one's own life. Whose courage will I emulate? Standing side by side even in one's imagination with those who demonstrated courage makes the personal decision to be courageous less fearful.

- **Win-Win Conflict Resolution with Emotion: Activity Sheets 15.1 and 15.2**

Continue and conclude the exercise by working through steps three and four. This series of worksheets describes one process for resolution of issues. Teens may be encouraged to present their own creative protocols for conflict resolution. The protocol does not matter. The outcome matters. Peace and the alleviation of anger and any other uncomfortable emotions are the goals. If the protocol for truly and permanently achieving these goals were for everyone to stand on their heads for five minutes, that would be a fantastic conflict resolution protocol.

When the goal is to involve many students in the process, the negotiations may be extended to include more participants. Each Negotiator may have a Deputy Negotiator or two to serve as helpers. When Negotiators switch chairs, so do their Deputies. The Diplomat may have one or more Aides to assist in referee duties. A number of Observers may be appointed to listen in silence and afterwards evaluate how well each participant accomplished each role.

The focus for the adult moderator, counselor, or teacher is to cue Diplomats to always bring attention back to the emotions involved with comments like "Such passionate debate. So who's mad about what?" It may be helpful for Diplomats to have a cheat sheet in front of them with questions like "Who's mad about what? Who is afraid of what? Is someone sad about something? Is another emotion involved?" Heaven knows how much work the UN would get done if those questions were asked and answered first.

BULLETIN BOARD MATERIAL

Courage is being afraid of taking constructive action and doing so anyway.

The hero is he who is unmovably centered.
Ralph Waldo Emerson[7]

Notes

1 The Norton Critical Edition, 5th ed., (T. Cooley, Ed.) has the history of the censoring of the book. New York, NY: Norton & Co., 1998.
2 Twain, M. (1907). *Christian Science*. New York, NY: Harper & Brothers. See page 154. Twain's (1835–1910) gems are hidden in his lesser-known works.
3 Kennedy, J.F. (1st pub. 1955). *Profiles in Courage*. My summary parallels Kennedy's (1917–1963) passages on pages 259 and 264–6 of the 1964 Memorial Edition. New York, NY: Harper & Row.
4 Falstaff said it to King Hal in Part One of Shakespeare's *Henry IV*. A teen-friendly explanation is at www.shmoop.com/shakespeare-quotes/better-part-of-valor/meaning-now.html
5 Roosevelt, F.D. (1882–1945). *First Inaugural Address*, March 4, 1933. Online with portions in Roosevelt's own resounding voice at http://historymatters.gmu.edu/d/5057/
6 For the surprising origin and fascinating evolution of the phrase see https://wikivividly.com/wiki/Where_no_man_has_gone_before
7 Retrieved from Emerson's 1871 *The Conduct of Life* (*op. cit.*). The quote is from section VII, *Considerations by the Way*, paragraph 26. Online at www.gutenberg.org/license

Name:_____ Date:_____

Activity Sheet 15.1
WIN–WIN CONFLICT RESOLUTION
WITH EMOTION

STEP THREE   Time limit: _____ minutes

The Diplomat assists the Negotiators in writing out a list of all solutions that may apply. Freely list all solutions on Worksheet Three, List of Possible Solutions, 15.2.

Phase One. Negotiators offer solutions from their own points of view.

Phase Two. The Diplomat directs each Negotiator to switch chairs. Now each Negotiator must pretend to be the other person and offer solutions from that person's point of view.

In talking about solutions consider the consequences, the impact of each potential solution, and the emotions involved.

STEP FOUR   Time limit: _____ minutes

The Diplomat directs each Negotiator to speak directly to each other as they use a process of elimination to come up with the chosen solution. Negotiators work as follows:

- Negotiators *mutually agree* on eliminating from the list the two potential solutions that are most unacceptable to both.
- Negotiators *mutually agree* on eliminating the next two least acceptable solutions.
- Negotiators continue in this manner until a solution acceptable to both is reached.

The Diplomat's job here is to remind Negotiators to speak directly to one another and to continue to talk about emotions. After a solution is reached, the Diplomat concludes negotiations by summarizing the agreement and asking each Negotiator, "What are your emotions upon reaching this solution?" Negotiators may sign a contract affirming the agreement.

Name:_____ Date:_____

Activity Sheet 15.2

WIN-WIN CONFLICT RESOLUTION WITH EMOTION, WORKSHEET THREE

List of Possible Solutions

Use the reverse side to list additional solutions.

1. _____

_____

_____

2. _____

_____

_____

3. _____

_____

_____

4. _____

_____

_____

5. _____

_____

_____

6. _____

_____

_____

Unit IV
Grief and Guilt

16 The Mists of Grief

Grief is sadness. Grief is the particular type of sorrow that comes from loss. Usually we understand grief to mean the sadness we feel when someone dies. But we grieve small losses, too. We grieve when we don't get the job we wanted, when we don't reach a cherished goal, and when we think we have lost our great-grandfather's watch or great-grandmother's ring. In today's age the sadness that comes with loss is often called depression. Sadness is not depression. The sorrow of grief is normal. The state called depression is not.

To the contrary, it is not grieving that may cast us into depression. To understand the difference we must understand the nature of attachment, loss, and valid and invalid grief. Our classic understanding of the stages of grief comes from Dr. Eliabeth Kubler-Ross (1926–2004), who elucidated the mechanics of grief.[1]

When the Sunshine Dies

The process of creating and severing bonds is the cycle of life. If emotions in general are like water, grief is like a mist. Sometimes it may be like a soft morning mist that shrouds the landscape at dawn. But frequently, it is like a thick fog that envelops all things. Often it feels like a heavy mantle that makes the simplest movement an act of enormous courage.

Yet grief is our natural and normal response to loss. With society's elimination of mourning rituals, many people do not know the cycle of grief. Like all emotions, grief comes in a flow that peaks and recedes in crests and troughs. The pain of grief alternates with quieter moments. As time passes, the peaks of the crests become less high. The length of time in the ebb stage increases.

With the passing years the length of time in the ebb stage exceeds that of the crests of pain. Yet when attachment has been great, the pain felt on the anniversary of a death may mirror the original. Fear, anger, and guilt are emotions that may be completely worked through and released. But grief for the loss of a great love may be carried until one's own death.

Grief is sorrowful sadness that results from the severing of a bond of attachment. We cannot lose that to which we are not attached. Thus, for grief to be felt a process of **identification** must first occur. One's self-identity must be viewed as tied into the other person, place, or thing. This is a normal part of the process of individuation. In identification we say, "I choose this person outside of me to be a part of me." Identification is the borderland where the task of individuation meets the task of community.

Immersed as they are in their developmental tasks, our teens are always making and breaking bonds of attachment. Thus the most unidentified, underestimated emotion for teens is sadness. Walking the corridors of high schools, I have seen it on their faces broadcasting as loudly as an audible wail, "I'm so sad! I want to cry." But algebra is the next class and our teens know there's no crying in algebra.

One of the most vital roles school counselors and health teachers may serve is to be ever vigilant monitors of a school's collective grief. If the basketball team went to state for the first time in 15 years and lost by one point in a buzzer beater, the next day at school need not be school as usual. When adults keep everything the same after a loss, and more particularly after a great loss, that choice advertises to the student body "The way to get over loss is just to ignore it." From there teens internalize "My sadness does not matter. Just stuff it. Get drunk this weekend." The process puts them well on their way to a lifetime of emulating the adults in denying their grief, sadness, and disappointment.

So what do you do with the team's loss? Celebrate their great achievement in making it to state while acknowledging their disappointment. When adults own "We're disappointed, too," it allows teens to own their own sadness. The lesson is that when we lose we acknowledge the loss, we cry if we want, we celebrate what was positive, and we move on. When we do not learn this lesson with adult support in high school, life itself will teach it to us. But life is not always as empathetic as the average high school teacher.

Attachment and Loss

Many types of loss exist. The object of potential loss may be a person, a family member, friend, or loved one. Loss may even be of oneself in the form of loss of self-esteem or of a habitual form of self-expression. Loss of self, even when the habits given up are self-destructive, may produce profound grief. The object also may be a loved pet, a favorite object, a popular celebrity, or a cherished place like a home.

Even as anger pertains to individuation, loss pertains to community. And as with other emotions, grief may be valid or invalid. Valid loss produces valid grief. In valid grief the object of the loss was first appropriately or reasonably identified with ego. In the drive to establish community the object was defined or seen as a part of self and also as a separate individual. Healthy attachment respects the other person and accepts that person as a fully separate individual. The key to healthy attachment is balance, proportion, and maturity based on genuine respect for the other's independence.

In the borderland between individuation and community, détente occurs only with much trial and error. In history the borderlands were often a place of conflict or a no man's land that was not mine but not yours either. Our teens are sometimes the walking wounded of this battle as they daily work to define the "me-not me." Balancing that dynamic with the "I need people-I don't need people" dynamic yields frequent miscalculations. Errors often lead to unhealthy attachment and deep woundedness.

Unhealthy attachment sees the other only as an extension of self. Seeing the choices of the other person only or primarily in reference to self produces dependency, not valid relationship. Emotional enmeshment, not love, results when two people expect each other to meet all their emotional needs. Modern people in democracies understand political independence. Few understand emotional independence.

Forms of Invalid Grief

Invalid grief, then, is genuine and real but invalid because it is based on invalid premises. Invalid loss produces invalid grief. Invalid grief is based on misidentification, namely, something is identified as a "loss" that one never possessed in the first place. Jealousy and dependent attachment are manifestations of real but invalid sorrow sometimes called grief.

Jealousy is a form of fear, not love. Possessiveness is motivated by fear of one's own loss, not by regard for the other person. When one over-identifies with another person, loss of that other is felt as a loss of self. What happens to produce jealousy is that in building our castle walls, we not only steal someone else's bricks, we actually build that person into our wall. We made a thing, a rampart, a defensive barrier out to them. If they say, "I'm leaving you," we most certainly are going to cry, "You can't do that!" or "I can't live without you!" The fact that we believe it when we say it is shown in the suicides that follow broken relationships.

The emotion is real. The jealousy is real. But it is not a sign of love. Jealousy is a sign of fear. Because of our well-established habit of turning fear into anger, possessiveness produces jealous rages. If teens are not taught the structure of this process, they may be well into their thirties or forties before it occurs to them that jealousy is not love.

Similarly, invalid expectations also may produce invalid grief. This process occurs when we expect the attachment to do something that attachments by nature cannot do. The attachment does not live up to our erroneous beliefs. As a result, we grieve. The lyrics of popular songs often reflect our many collective, mistaken expectations about relationships. For example, one old song sweetly moans about being saved by another's love. The song has it backward. If anything saves us, it is the process of loving—of love freely given.

Mature attachment, then, is based on acceptance of the essential alone-ness of the human condition. We begin in high school as it hits us we must be a self, solitary and independent, separate from our family of origin. We grasp that building our castle walls is our responsibility, not mom's or dad's or teacher's. Hard at work on the task of community, we learn to respect others. We do if we are taught to value the independence, feelings, and choices of the other. Reminders help.

Behind anger is fear. Behind fear may be sadness.

With a solid foundation of individuality and at least an incipient grasp of how community works, we move on to create love from two separate selves. From childhood to adolescence to adulthood we grow in under-standing the meaning of mature attachment. Then, when we grieve, it is valid, not invalid, grief.

The Stages of Grief

Dr. Elisabeth Kubler-Ross in her book *On Death and Dying* has described the predictable stages of dying. In so doing she described the stages of grief even before she wrote her book on grieving. Losing anyone or anything is like a small death. Our response is similar, whether to actual death or to symbolic deaths. Grief is the emotional reaction to whatever the mind interprets as loss.

Every health curriculum that hopes to foster emotional intelligence must include Dr. Kubler-Ross's masterful analysis. We would not dream of teaching biology and omitting the cardiovascular system from the chapters on anatomy. In the same way, Dr. Kubler-Ross's fundamental understandings should in some way be part of every high school curricu-lum. For a full explanation see her own works. In classroom and small group presentations display the names of the stages and key words as you describe the stages.

The first stage of grief is denial and isolation. "Oh, no, it can't be!" we lament. We deny that the loss has happened. Denial takes many forms, including "I don't care," which really means "It hurts too much to care." It is a denial of pain, not genuine apathy. The retreat into isolation is an attempt to escape in order to avoid pain.

That retreat also is due to the press of healthy ego that drives us through the process of loss and detachment to discover our inner strength. Loss is like an attack. We retreat within our castle walls for protection. This experience of detachment is necessary to shape valid individuality. For most people detachment is imposed by external events that produce loss.

First we retreat, then we attack. So anger is the second stage. Seeing anger as part of grief and not as something separate from it was one of Dr. Kubler-Ross's most brilliant gifts. She dared speak of anger decades before there was widespread talk of anger management and emotional intelligence. Now her pioneering work is foundational to the development of emotional intelligence.

As we have seen, when ego has identified some object with self, having it taken away is most threatening. The experience may be as threatening as any attack on self. Since anger is the natural and normal reaction to threat, anger at the loss is inevitable. This is true whether or not the loss was in any way voluntary. When loss is sudden and imposed from without, the anger of grief is often rageful.

Astute observation led Dr. Kubler-Ross to define the third stage as that of bargaining. She described this stage as some sort of agreement with God to postpone the inevitable. It consists of a promise of some type of good behavior in exchange for some favor. The favor may be more time or time to witness some special event, such as a child's wedding or graduation. It usually includes a deadline (the wedding or graduation) and a promise that the person will not ask for more if the wish is granted. The wish is usually kept secret.

The emotion here is guilt, asking for one more chance to make up for past missed opportunities. Although this stage more clearly applies to those who know they are dying, we may find parallels in other types of loss. For example, the alcoholic promises to stop drinking in exchange for reconciliation with a spouse. The girlfriend or boyfriend promises to attend to the absent loved one's every need if only the couple reunite. The small child promises God "I'll be good" if the lost, cherished toy is found. Ball teams promise amazing things for victory. We bargain, promise, and haggle, so great is our fear of loss. So bargaining is propelled by fear.

Sooner or later the bargaining stops and the anger fades. We are left then with the heart of grief, the profound desolation of stage four. Sorrow, weeping, and feelings of emptiness and purposelessness predominate. Appropriate and openly experienced expression of these feelings is known as mourning.

But inappropriate, excessive, and prolonged sadness may produce depression. Mourning is an acceptable and necessary part of the human condition. Depression is not. Designated a leading mental illness, the phenomenon of depression is explored in Chapter 17.

From denial, grief moves to anger. From anger, it moves to fear and guilt. All three stages are attempts to avoid the fourth. Experiencing the sadness is the only way to move on to the last stage, acceptance. If we continue to resist feeling the sorrow, we delay acceptance and genuine moving on.

Acceptance and Why Understanding the Stages Matters

Thus the final stage, acceptance, follows mourning. Acceptance is the release of the strong emotions that supported the attachment. Not just a mental recognition that what is lost is irretrievable, acceptance is an actual emotional and cognitive shift. Usually, making the shift requires a cognitive reinterpretation of the loss, such as "Yes, he's dead, but that does not mean I'll never see him again. I'll see him in heaven." Or, "Yes, the relationship is over, but that does not mean my life is over. I'll love again."

We often refuse to let go because it feels as if letting go of the emotions is the final letting go of the person or lost object. Refusal to let go results when we have overidentified with the object of loss. Letting go is internally experienced as the release of such an essential part of oneself that the choice is seen as impossible. True release lets go of the attachment and the identification or reinterprets that identification on another level in order to move on.

When we know the stages of grief, we know grief will lead us to the stage of acceptance. It is common to say "Everyone grieves in his own way." This is a glib reaction to the confusion of emotions that grief brings. Rather let us talk openly with one another about which stage of grief we are in. In a world in which mass shootings and bombings are too frequent, we cannot wait for deaths to happen and then cry, "What do we do now?" These stages are a guide to figuring out what to do when horrors happen.

First, don't deny or diminish what happened. Expect denial to happen in some teens, but be part of the truth-telling, not part of the denial. Second, expect anger. Provide healthy outlets for anger. If the violence is terrifying, find, create, invent very physical ways to vent visceral anger. I envision mats and pillows spread out over the entire gym floor for pounding and kicking and crying the anger out. Allow it with voluntary participation and see how many take you up on it. If the unit on anger has already been presented, you may be surprised as to who wants to pound pillows.

The gym and bleachers are the only places students are regularly encouraged to scream. Connect that association with the need to cry and shout out the pain in a safe environment well supervised by adults. If the sorrow is horrific, adults also may cry. The difference is, as adults must set the tempo, we must make it clear crying and shouting has a beginning, a middle, and an end, and will be modulated and moderated by teachers as all leave the gym. All the strategies for directing emotion presented in these units starting with the A, B, Cs are tools for addressing horrific emotion as well as everyday emotion.

Bargaining may be converted into plans to honor and remember those who were lost. We can't bring them back, but by commemorating them we internalize what they meant to us. When we put them in our hearts, we do not lose them completely and finally. Mourning must be allowed. Tenderly but explicitly correct those who apologize for crying. Apologizing for crying in grief is apologizing for being human. Acceptance may include plans to convert the emotional energy of grief and most particularly of its anger into righteous anger for action that changes society.

If a school system has not been actively developing emotional intelligence and some horror happens anyway, educators are deluged with the imperative need to provide their student bodies with a crash course in emotions all in one day or one week. That's teaching about emotions the hard way.

- **Journaling—A Letter to Me**

An exploration of the epidemic of teen suicide today reveals the sad fact that breaking up with a boyfriend or girlfriend may precipitate suicide, self-destructive behavior, or suicidal ideation. Puppy love is no longer taken in stride as part of the inevitable ups and downs of adolescence. Society's failure to teach the young how to grieve is highlighted when teens overreact to loss with violent, self-destructive, and other hostile behavior.

Direct teens to write a letter to themselves in their journals about a relationship that produced loss and grief. Teens are to pretend they are their own best friend, writing to give consolation and advice on how to handle the loss. Direct them to use what they now know about loss and attachment as they explore the meaning of the relationship in their lives.

Common losses they may write about include the loss of a pet, the loss of friends after moving to another school, the loss of a close friend after an argument, the loss of a girlfriend or boyfriend, the loss of a parent's presence in the home due to divorce, and the loss of a grandparent who died.

- **A Poem on Grief**

Direct teens to write a poem of five stanzas on the five stages of grief. Each stanza is to describe one of the five stages. Encourage those who have experienced a personal loss of a close relative by death or divorce to use that experience as the theme of the poem. Others may use a lesser personal loss or another topic such as the death of a popular celebrity or public figure. Teens may work in small groups of twos and threes to compose only one stanza about one stage. Then those five stanzas are read as one poem.

- **List of Feeling Words Activity: Activity Sheet 16.1 and 16.2**

Distribute the lists of synonyms for grief, guilt, shame, and other uncomfortable emotions. Direct teens to use the first column on grief to relate the story of *A Disappointment*. Stories may be oral or written.

BULLETIN BOARD MATERIAL

Grief is denial, anger, bargaining, mourning, and acceptance.

Jealousy is fear of loss, not love.

Give sorrow words. The grief that does not speak
Whispers the o'fraught heart, and bids it break.

Shakespeare, *Macbeth*[2]

Notes

1 See her breakthrough work *On Death & Dying: What the Dying Have to Teach Doctors, Nurses, Clergy and Their Own Families* (New York, NY: Scribner, reprint ed., 2014). *On Grief & Grieving* with co-author David Kessler is her gift to the bereaved (New York, NY: Scribner, reprint ed., 2014).
2 In Act IV, Scene 3 Malcolm makes the comment as Macduff learns of the killing of his family. Teaching *Macbeth* is an excellent opportunity to have teens ponder an incarnadine array of anger and greed, grief and guilt, delusion and fear. Make the play personal by having teens relate one emotion and one character to their own life and times. It is a pity that Shakespeare's (1564–1616) sixteenth-century language is so torturous, as *Macbeth* is an exquisite literary expression of why anger, fear, grief, and guilt mandate our own emotional literacy. See your favorite copy of *Macbeth* or online at www.gutenberg.org/cache/epub/1795/pg1795-images.html

Name:_____ Date:_____

Activity Sheet 16.1
LIST OF FEELING WORDS: GRIEF

GRIEF

Mild Grief	Moderate Grief	Intense Grief
disappointed	dejected	disillusioned
saddened	distraught	bereft
dismal	melancholic	sorrowful
gloomy	unhappy	cheerless
discouraged	disheartened	dispirited
downcast	heartsick	crestfallen
morose	woeful	desolate
blue	glum	dolorous
somber	mournful	pining
downhearted	despondent	disconsolate
grieving	lamenting	languishing
discontented	miserable	heartbroken
displeased	dissatisfied	disgruntled

Name: _____ Date: _____

Activity Sheet 16.2
ADDITIONAL CHALLENGING EMOTIONS

GUILT and SHAME		OTHER CHALLENGING EMOTIONS	
Mild	**Strong**	**Mild**	**Strong**
culpable	guilty	possessive	jealous
sorrowful	contrite	covetous	envious
apologetic	repentant	suspicious	paranoid
sorry	penitent	smug	haughty
regretful	remorseful	proud	arrogant
ashamed	abashed	conceited	vain
chagrined	embarrassed	indifferent	apathetic
humiliated	mortified	detached	impervious
belittled	shamed	unconcerned	nonchalant
		sickening	revolting
		offended	repelled
		disgusted	nauseated

17 Grief and Anger Turned Inward

Use of the word depression is common. Its usage has led to the general belief "Everyone's depressed sometime." It is most unfortunate that our longstanding cultural denial of emotion has led to a place where a state of being that is not normal, depression, is widely viewed as a normal state. Depression exists. But depression is not grief. And depression does not have to be expected as an ordinary and usual mode of life.

Teaching teens what depression is and what it is not is a critical element in nurturing emotional intelligence. Many young people I have worked with have called ordinary sadness depression. "I failed my exam. I'm so depressed." "My boyfriend broke up with me. I'm so depressed." "My dog died. I'm so depressed. Do you think I need medicine?" In my mind's eye I can still see the relief on their faces as they heard they are normal and not mentally ill.

When teens know the symptoms and types of depression and the factors that foster depression, they will not erroneously mistake ordinary sadness, disappointment, and grief for depression. Education is society's central vehicle for enlightening the next generation about suicide, the meaning of suicidal ideation, and what to do if one ever finds such ideation in one's own head. Suicidal, and for that matter homicidal, ideation is related to depression in that repression and internalization of anger are key to the dynamics of depression.[1]

When teens do not know this connection, they are set up for leaping to many unwarranted and irrational conclusions. In the worst cases, actual suicide is the outcome. If depression is suspected, the counselor may ask parents to come in and recommend psychotherapy. If suicide is accomplished, there is nothing to do but go to the funeral and support the survivors. A young person cutting off all their future possibilities is heartbreaking.

The good news is we may understand how and why teens get to such an extreme point and then we may act in advance. This chapter is not a point by point what to do if one of your teens is suicidal. Prolific and widespread is the literature on suicide and suicide prevention.[2] Rather, making clear the link to emotional intelligence is our focus. Suicide demonstrates the full absence of emotional intelligence. So does homicide. Thus, every chapter of this book may be seen as suicide prevention.

Depression is hard for us because depression is tricky. Depression lies. It is like an evil sorcerer. It uses surface appearances to mask what is within. This dark sorcerer transforms light into darkness, freedom into imprisonment, and joy into sorrow. The sorcerer seems to have great power. The power of that darkness creates more darkness until at last it seems there is no hope. Teens with their penchant for fantasy will appreciate your using the imagery of the sorcerer to educate them about depression. What teens normally gravitate to are like doorways for adults to enter into the teen mind in meaningful and permanent ways.

So depression is an evil sorcerer because its power is an illusion, a trick. It is a very sly trick, but it is a trick. It is a trick because the dark sorcerer steals all that power from *you*. The way to defeat the sorcerer is to take the power back. The way to win the battle of depression and never go down the road to suicide is not to let yourself be fooled. The central message for teens is that *you* have the power to banish the dark sorcerer from your life.

Symptoms of Depression

The difference between mourning and depression is vast. Openly mourning a valid loss is acceptable. Brooding endlessly in depression is not. Depression is not a fated or inevitable condition. Even when a marked physiological component may be present, the individual still has choices that may be made.

In my work with depressed teens I have observed symptoms like the following:

- withdrawal and isolation
- prolonged and frequent crying
- self-medicating with alcohol or drugs
- poor attention and indecisiveness
- sleep disturbances: insomnia or hypersomnia
- expressions of hopelessness
- suicidal self-talk.[3]

These I have seen in just about that order. It's the first, the isolating, that makes parents take note, as in "He lives in his room." In school it's the kid who always, always sits by herself in the top corner of the bleachers who needs to hear a counselor or teacher say, "I need you to help me carry some books" to initiate connectedness that will lead to further contact and then to community inclusion.

I have not observed as much anhedonia and chronic fatigue in depression in teens as in adults. Alcohol use, frequent crying, withdrawal, and a chronic distracted look are serious signs. My experience with teens is they leave mentally long before they try to leave physically. This gives us hope for it means there is time to intervene.

Suicidal ideation means suicidal self-talk. Teens need to know that the emotions of fear, anger, and guilt may interfere with the ability to think logically. In the confusion the teen temporarily cannot figure out a sensible way to meet the challenge. Suicidal self-talk is determined by feelings, not reason. Not knowing what to do about their fears, stuffing and internalizing anger, mistaking guilty self-talk for absolute fact all combine to push the teen's brain into searching for a way out.

It is a normal for our brains to want to get us out of pain. But when we don't have a clue about how our emotions work, we certainly cannot grasp the meaning of our escapist self-talk. A mental tool helps us focus thinking on facts and truth. Such a mental tool is the explanation of the warning bell. To make the verbal explanation as strong as possible, display actual images of bells and alarms and sirens. Words plus images engage the whole brain in learning.

A Warning Bell

For emotional intelligence to have life-transforming impact all teens must know that suicidal self-talk is like a bell going off in the head. Too many adults mistake suicidal self-talk for facts or see it as a sign of mental illness. In extreme form it may be. We have already seen the role of intellectualization and rationalization in burying and transforming emotion. That foundational understanding is crucial to grasping the full meaning of suicidal self-talk. Suicidal self-talk is an elaborate form of intellectualizing the emotional pain behind the suicidal inclinations. Simply put, suicidal ideation is about emotions, not facts or philosophies, or mental illness. We *think* our emotions in order not to feel their full force.

Self-care about suicidal self-talk is as important as the self-care of eating wholesome nutrition that is taught in health class. Yet adults today come from a world in which no one told us anything about what to do if we find suicidal thoughts in our heads. Enough are the dead from such ignorance. Emotional acumen is intelligence for the living to embrace the emotional self in such a way that there is no need to seek any escapist maneuver.

The mental tool that applies beautifully to suicidal self-talk is that of a bell or alarm. The bell clamors, "It's getting too hot for me to handle. Go get help. Go get help *now*." Suicidal self-talk does not mean the person is crazy. It means they need help they are not seeking. Teens will readily grasp the analogy when you explain that suicidal self-talk may be likened to a smoke alarm going off. Process with your teens the proper steps to respond to an actual fire alarm going off, not just at school but at home when they may be alone. Relate responses to the proper way to respond to suicidal self-talk.

Teens will quickly see the parallels. The first thing to do is not ignore the alarm. It may be a false alarm. However, the reasonable thing to do is to check it out and see if there is a source of smoke. If the source of the smoke is extinguished at an early stage, the house need not burn down. The same is true with suicidal self-talk.

With actual fires the thing to do is call the fire department. Teens, loving to be oppositional, may insist they could put a real fire out themselves. Stress fire is nothing to fool around with and only the professionals may determine if sparks are lurking in the walls. Stress that the thing to do is to hear suicidal self-talk as the warning it is. Teens may think they could put the fire out with a garden hose. Inform them that calling the professionals precedes self-help with the garden hose. Just as we call the fire department when there is fire, we seek professional help when we hear suicidal self-talk in our head. In working with teens frequently consider this.

What alarm bells are ringing that I must hear?

To create generations of young people with new understandings, we must insist our teens learn that if suicidal thoughts are frequent and persistent, it's like a fire in your house. If you can't put it out by yourself, go get help. That is what you are *supposed* to do. That is the okay thing to do, the normal thing to do, the new thing-that-everybody-does. Teens may talk to parents or pastor or a counselor. The talking continues until the teen comes up with another, acceptable way out of the difficulty. The goal of the talking is to achieve the same goal as for the alarm. That goal is safety, security, protection, escape from harm. Thus, we keep talking with the suicidal person until the situation is settled and the suicidal self-talk stops.

The brain is economical. It does not do what it does for no reason. It also does not continue to send out alarms when it perceives the dissipation of painful emotions. When it perceives we have already escaped, it does not keep telling us to escape. Suicide reveals how ignorance about emotions makes traps of those emotions. There is always another solution the emotion-blinded brain cannot see. It's often said that suicide is a permanent solution to a temporary problem. As such, it is the most tragic choice anyone may make.

Types of Depression

Most depression does not get so bad that it gets to the point of suicidal self-talk. Health teachers may aid their teens in educating them to the types of depression and mourning. Counselors must be aware of the types and be able to distinguish depression from ordinary teen emotions like sadness, disappointment, and grief.

When we know a loss is coming, we may experience it ahead of time in preparatory depression. Reactive depression comes after the event has happened. Most depression is caused by the repression of uncomfortable emotions. **Repression** is a psychological defense in which the mind conveniently forgets uncomfortable emotions in order to push them away. In healthy mourning we do not repress the emotions but mourn the loss.

Mourning is normal grieving and the word depression should not be used as a synonym. We mourn because we are human. Depression we create. The brain supports it only because the brain supports everything we do until we are dead. That does not make depression normal. It is simply not true that "everyone is depressed about something sometime."

With teens continue the analogy of the sorcerer. The sorcerer uses tricks and lies to create depression. Repression is the dark sorcerer's main trick. Repression says, "If I just don't think about this, I'll be okay. If I pretend it isn't there, it'll go away." The sorcerer whispers:

> You're not really angry, a fine teen like you! Besides, you have nothing to be guilty or ashamed about. It was all the fault of those other people, you know that. You're not sad! Have a drink! Spend five hours on social media. Smoke a joint! You deserve to feel only good feelings.

With lies like this, the sorcerer pulls us away from our true feelings of fear, anger, guilt, shame, and sadness. These feelings are neither good nor bad. We feel what we feel. We have a right to feel what we feel. To develop any measure of emotional intelligence teens must know that experiencing uncomfortable emotions is part of being human, pure and simple.

The way to beat the dark sorcerer is to reclaim our true feelings, no matter how painful. Claiming emotions is the route out of depression. The way out is to take our real emotions back and refuse to believe that we are not feeling what our hearts know we are feeling.

Depression Drama

Demonstrate for your teens how to talk back to the dark sorcerer. If you're the health teacher or are working with a group, step out a moment and don a Halloween long black cloak and hood. Standing on one side of the classroom, speak as the sorcerer. See the paragraph above with the sorcerer's "You're not really angry" monologue. To this add "You know you're no good. No one likes you. You're ugly. You're stupid. You're a bad friend. You're awful, a terrible, horrible person. And there's no way out!" Add words you have heard from distraught teens.

Fling off the robe. As it drops to the floor, quickly step to the other side of the classroom. Melodramatically turn and talk back with:

> I know you, dark sorcerer! You can't fool me. I'm mad and I know I am. And I wish I didn't, but I feel guilty, too. I feel lonely and scared and, take that, dark sorcerer, that's the way I feel! I know you, but you don't know *me*. Nothing you say is true. You're nothing but my anger and fear talking. I know who you are. You're *not me*.

Marching over to the robe on the floor, dramatically stomp on it three times as you loudly proclaim, "You lie. You lie! You lie!!"

The drama club or theater class may take this simple script and concoct a drama for school assembly. Three teens take the roles: one for dark sorcerer and one teen boy and one teen girl together to speak the talking-back dialog. The talking-back teens, dressed in everyday clothes, may each wield a wand, a symbol of the power of mind to transform itself and its external reality. Or, if you have a very brave principal or vice-principal, one may play the role of dark sorcerer using the best possible "double double toil and trouble" cackling intonations. In this case, chasing the sorcerer off the stage as the cloak is pulled off and then stomped on is a must.

Your teens will howl. Two decades later at their twentieth class reunion they will remember and laugh. But they will all be at their twentieth class reunion. They'll be there, alive. That's the ultimate victory for brave principals, vice-principals, and all educators.[4]

The Critical Role of Anger

I have seen thousands of people in psychotherapy and never met one depressed person who was not angry. Some are fiercely angry, faces frozen into irate, glowering grimaces. Of all the uncomfortable emotions used by the dark sorcerer, anger stands out foremost. Depression may be the effect of repressed fear, guilt, and sadness. But in suicidal and other intense depression, anger is the key emotion. In a trick more amazing than any sleight of hand, the sorcerer turns anger, a force intended to motivate us to self-protection and constructive defense, destructively against us.

The castle walls that are supposed to protect us fall in on us. If the bricks keep falling, yes, it could kill you. We do not realize it, but we are literally hitting ourselves over the head with our own bricks. Then we wonder why we feel like we're walking around with a load of bricks on our backs. The brain is a terrible thing. It is a terrible, wondrous, amazing, frightful instrument that puts the bricks where we tell it. The brain puts the anger where you direct, whether anger in or anger out.

Nature means anger as a force to protect us. But force is force. In depression we allow our own anger to act against us. Teens need to know that all hostile, destructive acts are acts of anger no matter how cool one feels while engaged in them.

Depression is anger turned inward.

Display the statement in the health classroom or, indeed, in the main corridor. Generations of people believe depression is a fated, biological state that has nothing to do with anger. If this were true, depression would not abate when all the layers of anger are expelled. Today's teens have a chance to learn differently. The sooner one learns to connect fleeting feelings of depression with anger, the sooner that brain learns to stop attempting to mask the anger, and so gets right to the main event, "I'm mad as hell."

Suicide, too, is an act of anger. Suicide is the ultimate act of anger turned inward. Whether the hostility is against others or against self, it is still anger being acted out. Many factors lead to and foster suicidal depression. Help your teens personalize the following list.

- Fear of and denial of emotions. Refusal to feel what we know we are indeed feeling.
- False beliefs.
  "Be strong." (This is a highly deceptive injunction that really means "Don't feel. Don't have or express emotions.")
  "Don't cry."
  "I can't live without you."
  "I can't take it."
  "Things are never going to change."
  "Missing someone is a sign you love them." Missing someone is a sign you are attached to them. It may or may not mean you love them.
- Ignorance about what emotions are normal and natural.
- Refusal to accept pain as part of the human condition.
- Drugs and alcohol. Alcohol is a short-term stimulant but soon after, a depressant. Drugs interfere with the natural biochemical cycles of emotion.
- Physiological effects of disturbances in sleep. Many teens do not get enough sleep.
- Other physiological changes in body chemistry. Severe, intractable depression may require medical intervention.
- Elimination of rituals for mourning in society as a whole. Black clothing, arm bands, wreaths on the door, and anniversary religious rituals belong to times past.

•   **Small Group—Role Play**

Allow teens to talk out loud about suicidal self-talk and practice how to respond. Divide teens into groups of three to invent a scenario in which one teen plays someone who is experiencing suicidal self-talk. Other roles are friend and a professional. The analogy may be drawn with first aid before the ambulance arrives. How does a friend help? The quickest, most direct answer is "Talk about the anger."

Stress that friend talking to friend is only first aid, like pressing on a bleeding wound or performing CPR. Such aid must proceed on to professional help. This may be teacher, counselor, pastor, psychologist, or other professional. The one in the friend role steers the person to a professional, perhaps with words like "I'll go with you to the counselor's office." We want teens to accept that not talking or burying the pain is not the way.

•   **The Sound of Sadness**

Since popular songs are often about love and relationships, sadness, disappointment, and loss are frequent themes. Whether it's Mozart's *Lacrymosa* in his *Requiem* or Trisha Yearwood's *How Do I Live*, grief weeps in lyrics, tone, and instrumentation. From the Beatles are their classics *Yesterday* and *Misery*. And is there any sad song that excels Roy Orbison's *Crying*? Challenge your teens to discover one in a song they like.

The music assignment is the choosing of a personal anthem for sadness. Each teen picks one song or piece of music that is *My Song—Sadness*. If teens want to choose music that portrays and expresses emotions other than anger, fear, and grief, invite them to do so.

Lists of Feeling Words: Activity Sheets 5.1, 11.1, 16.1, 16.2

Support your teens in completing a self-analysis of sad emotions. Direct them to use all the lists of feeling words along with what they have now learned about depression to write an essay *My Sadness, My Grief,* or *My Disappointment*. Indeed, at this point your teens should know enough about emotions to pick just precisely the right words to name just precisely the emotion that applies. If a teen chooses to write on *My Disconsolate Blues*, that would be excellent evidence of lessons learned about emotional expression by a typical emotive teen. In all essays, teens describe their self-talk and Help Talk in quotation marks as well as their emotions and behavior.

Displaying the following may prove helpful.

> **When you are depressed:**
>
> - **What is your self-talk? Use quotation marks.**
> - **How do you feel physically?**
> - **What are your emotions?**
> - **What do you do? How do you act?**
> - **How do you use alcohol and drugs or other escapist behavior?**
> - **How do you get yourself out of that emotion?**

- **Sad Sacks: Activity Sheet 16.1**

Divide teens into pairs. Distribute crayons, small slips of paper, and one brown paper bag per pair. Each first talks for three minutes, or longer, about why they are sometimes sad. Use the list of grief words, Activity Sheet 16.1, as a guide. As one person talks, the other writes on a strip of paper what makes them sad. On another slip put one word from the grief list that precisely names that sadness.

After six minutes, both together draw and color a face on the bag. That's the Sad Sack. It must be made sad enough to fit all the words the two have chosen from the list. Teens then get up by twos and alternate to choose slips and talk about the Sad Sack's sad feelings. One person wears the mask. The other speaks. It helps to not advise teens in advance that the mask will be used in this way so that they do not restrict the words chosen from the list.

The above format is designed to develop the social skills of cooperation, teamwork, and empathy. Alternatively, each teen may design an individual Sad Sack. Either way, the laughter the activity elicits helps teens tangibly feel that sadness is nothing to be afraid of, that it exists in many varieties, and that all sadness is only an expression of self, a mask, and not the core of one's being.

BULLETIN BOARD MATERIAL

Depression is anger turned inward.

Suppressed grief suffocates. It rages within the breast,
and is forced to multiply its strength.

Ovid[5]

Notes

1 According to research at Harvard Medical School, suicides for 15–24-year-olds are at nearly 29 a year. All our fine education dies for 29 per 100,000 souls before they are 25. Gonsalves, S. (2019, August/September). Research: Number of suicides continues to rise. *New England Psychologist*, p. 8.
2 The Centers for Disease Control website at www.cdc.gov/violencepresention/ suicide is a great starting point for links to resources on suicide prevention. The ASCA at www.counseling.org/ and NASP at www.nasponline.org/ both point to resources for suicide prevention and awareness.
3 For a formal listing of diagnostic criteria see www.psycom.net/depression-definition-dsm-5-diagnostic-criteria/
4 Turn your Depression Drama school assembly into a jubilation by playing and screening Zach Williams' 2018 song *Fear Is a Liar*. YouTube has many versions, but the Official Lyric Video and Official Video both display striking visuals appropriate for public education sensitivities. Enlist your music, choral, and band teachers to lead your teens in singing while the official videos play. If there may be an anthem for suicide prevention, this is my pick. Released 2018, lyrics by Zach Williams, J. Ingram, J. Smith, and E. Pollock. Available from Word Entertainment, 25 Music Square West, Nashville, TN.
5 Ovid (43 BC–17 AD) did not use the word depression, but his word choice shows he understood the danger of suppressing emotions. Retrieved from Wikiquotes under *Grief* at https://en.wikiquote.org/wiki/Grief and from the original, *Ovidi Nasonis Tristium Liber Quintus*, vol. V, section 1, lines 63–4, *Fifth Book of Sorrows by Ovid Naso* found at www.thelatinlibrary.com/ovid/ovid. tristia5.shtml *Tristium* is Latin for sadness. Translated as suffocates, *strangulat* was Ovid's powerful verb. The translation I offer is: Imprisoned grief strangles and rages within, forced to multiply itself. I particularly appreciate Ovid's observation that suppressed emotion *is forced to* increase. Clinical depression does strangle the entire emotional self in self-enforced rage.

18 Good Grief

Just as skills may be learned to beneficially direct fear and anger, proficiencies may be acquired to manage grief. Knowing what to do to handle grief is an art and a skill that was gradually lost as the twentieth century moved from decade to decade. Now funerals make us uncomfortable, not only because we may fear death but because we literally do not know what to do. Where do we stand, what are we supposed to do, and what are we to say fill us with angst. Society let go of the elaborate Victorian mourning rituals and replaced those rituals with a vacuum.

This places us in the position of inventing new rituals and guidelines for what to do. Ritual structures emotion. Mourning rituals structured the grief of our ancestors. In the structures they knew well from childhood, they were able to grieve openly and fully. There is no evidence in history that our ancestors often fell into clinical depression as they transformed simple mourning into complicated grief. But today it is not unusual for ordinary grief to morph into clinical depression. Robbing ourselves of all rituals of mourning, grief turns inward. All the stages of grief—including, most critically, anger—invert and suffocate us.

There was a purpose for black dresses and black armbands and black-ribboned wreaths on the door. We do not have to go back to wearing lockets with the lost loved one's hair. But we must evolve new rituals that work for us. If ritual is too noxious a word, consider its synonyms. A ritual is a ceremony, a formality, a custom, or convention. Ritual is a convention that structures grief so that everyone knows where to stand, what to do, and what to say. This structure does not make the grief hurt less, but it assures that unnecessary anxiety and annoyance are eliminated. A routine that all expect consoles the grief-stricken as they may leave the cemetery knowing they have done all that was expected of them.

School systems confronted from time to time with the deaths of their teens would do well to evolve their own unique ceremonial conventions. Plan the structure before it is needed. Keep the core of the structure to use time and again. The day will come when seniors have been exposed to four years of the same practices. This produces certainty and support. Official structures for grieving communicate "It's okay to grieve. We're all grieving. We adults support each other and our teens in grieving."

Such support begins the process of healing grief. That is, it will if in advance you have educated your teens about grief. Waiting for deaths to happen and then launching a crash course in grief management overwhelms the adults and mystifies and confuses the teens. One would think that we adults would know by now that death happens. Our historic denial of emotion has meant denial of grief, too.

There are natural processes in grief that may be incorporated into grief management structures. Key among these is the process of identification. In grief our minds naturally lead us to identification. So knowing what nature is driving us to do anyway and going with the process is most helpful. Seeing a value in loss by reframing its meaning is also most valuable in positively governing mourning. Both processes may be built into a school system's mourning rituals.

The Value of Loss

Educating teens about the causes of depression must include emphasis on the difference between mourning and depression. It is not beneficial for teens to mistake mourning for depression. Thus, instruction about mourning must follow instruction about depression so that all clearly distinguish the difference. Support grieving teens by encouraging them to say, "I'm so sad" instead of "I'm depressed." Not making this distinction sets teens up for a lifetime of attempting to avoid grieving their losses in order, as they may think, to avoid depression. We avoid grief-induced depression by fully grieving. Foolishly trying to squash grief may create the depression we want to avoid.

In mourning we openly express and allow ourselves to feel the uncomfortable feelings. But in depression we repress the emotions, that is, we shove them underground. The words allow for a little word play. In mourning we usually feel a little better in the morning. But when we *re*press, we get *de*pressed. In mourning we still have the ability to say, "Tomorrow is another day." In depression the dark sorcerer whispers, "There is no tomorrow." Embrace that understanding as a guideline for yourself and your grieving teens.

Release mourning in the morning. Then grieve.

Both mourning and depression provide us with opportunities to develop our inner resources. Loss may lead us to discover inner strength. From loss comes detachment. Detached and alone, we must seek individuality and independence. In this way grief supports the process of individuation. Romantic ballads would have us believe we cannot live without a special loved one. The truth is we stand on two feet only and honor those we have lost best when we stand tall in the fullness of the person we are becoming.

Display the following diagram.

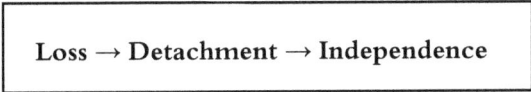

> **Loss → Detachment → Independence**

Several valuable qualities seem to require the experience of profound grief. Grief is good grief because it creates empathy, compassion, and constructive social and personal action. Add the following to the display.

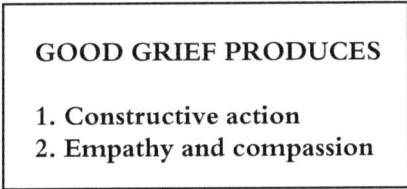

> **GOOD GRIEF PRODUCES**
>
> **1. Constructive action**
> **2. Empathy and compassion**

Share with teens that grief may motivate us to live for the best qualities which the lost loved one represented. A natural healing process whereby we incorporate the loss into self comes from the same process we saw in Chapter 16, identification. That identification makes us one with our loss and thus negates it. We make what we have lost a part of ourselves to magically undo the loss.

For example, Bob Kennedy wore his brother's jacket after the President died. Eleanor Roosevelt devoted herself to the social and political issues that had concerned her husband. Similarly, Coretta Scott King devoted herself to human rights. More common examples also are evident as when a young girl wears her brother's sunglasses right after his funeral.

But the identification that proceeds from grief may be destructive as well as constructive. It is constructive when it results in constructive activities that are in line with the valid desires of self. Identification is destructive when it results in destructive activities and is not congruent with who one really is. Forcing oneself to live forever in the shadow of a dead loved one is unhealthy. Queen Victoria, always in black, mourned for decades after her husband Albert's death.

The most serious consequence of such misplaced loyalty is survivor guilt. In fact, the inability to separate one's identity from that of the dead loved one seems to hasten one's own death. At times we see a spouse die a few years after the death of a beloved husband or wife. One determines whether identification is positive or negative by the activities it produces and by the measure of happiness brought or denied. If one is happy and content with a constructive life brought about by the identification, then grief is transformed into good grief.

In their mourning ritual, school systems may incorporate structures for allowing positive identification to happen. The simplest way we demonstrate identification is by naming things after our dead. We say we do so to honor them, but we are also assuaging our need to keep a part of them with us. The Washington Monument in all its abstract, looming presence broadcasts that what Washington did and what that means is very much alive.

A simple monument at the school, a garden, or a tree planted all could commemorate those lost. Knowing losses will occur over the years, a memorial garden may be designed to account for expansion. Another possibility is naming corridors or even classrooms after those lost. The ceremony of installing the plaque is huge and meaningful for the teen survivors. But the adults will know that in four years the incoming freshmen may not know why biology is in Cindy's Classroom.

School system guidelines for ceremonies with flowers and candles must be spelled out in advance. Candles without flame may be required. Balloons, once released to the heavens, are now a no-no as the whales do not appreciate our balloons. Who speaks at the ceremonies, what poems or literary pieces read, and the role of the school chorus or band all must be specified in advance. Adults design the overall structure. When the day comes that the structure is needed, teens follow the guidelines to know their contribution and role.

The ceremony may be a Celebration of Life. In it the dead are honored with words, songs, and pictures of gratitude and respect. A large board with collages of photos may be particularly meaningful for teens. Such formalities structure the saying of good-bye with decorum and graciousness. Ceremonies that end on a high note with an uplifting song or the triumphant cry of trumpets console and aid in the drying of tears.

The Two Paths of Grief

Another facet of good grief is the empathy, love, and compassion it produces. Since the experience of loss is universal, grief may induce profound empathy for our common humanity. Grief takes the air out of the most inflated egos. No one may prevent all loss from touching their lives. No one is above or below the experience of death.

How to channel the energy from grief into positive action whether personal or social may also be structured into allowable school system rituals. Remembering a dead teen may center on admired qualities. "She was friendly to everyone" may translate into *Be Everyone's Friend Week* at school. Poems, music, and artwork may all center on the positive qualities of those lost so that the living may celebrate and emulate them.

Such ceremonial remembrances create good grief. Other experiences may produce empathy, but grief must be actively channeled into good grief to do so. The alternative may be bitterness and emptiness. Display the following diagram.

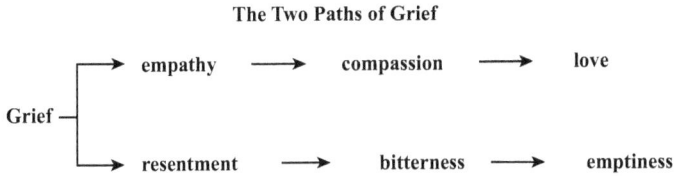

The Two Paths of Grief

```
              ┌──→  empathy  ───→  compassion  ───→  love
Grief  ───────┤
              └──→  resentment  ───→  bitterness  ───→  emptiness
```

Explain to teens that empathy is mostly feeling, not thinking. **Empathy** is emotional sensitivity to another's feelings. Empathy is feeling with the other. **Sympathy** is mental commiseration for the other, feeling for them, pity. Empathy is 80 percent emotion and 20 percent thinking. Sympathy is the reverse. Expressions of empathy, compassion, and love in their honor are the highest forms of commemorating dead loved ones.

Genuine empathy produces compassion. **Compassion** is the active part of empathy. Empathy is feeling. Compassion is acting. Compassion is shown in acts of goodwill, charity, and mercy. Compassion is the feeling, the empathy, with the expression.

Empathy and compassion must be taught and modeled if this is what we expect young people to learn. Should death visit your school, shift focus from despair to the most positive of our human qualities. In crisis and on ordinary days, guiding teens means consciously guiding ourselves into compassion.

In every interaction model compassion.

Grief is sorrow, a valid human emotion. When experienced, grief does lessen with time. Depression may not. Grief, like all emotions, comes in waves. One may learn to go with the flow. But depression is like a flood surge that ever remains at high tide. Grief ebbs and recedes. Depression suffocates. We may learn to convert grief into empathy and compassion. It is very difficult to find a positive purpose for depression.

A display of the following may be of aid to those grieving.

A. Allow and accept the grief.
   Recognize and admit your feelings.
B. Be with the grief. Breathe.
   Feel the sadness and other emotions.
C. Channel the grief.
   Choose constructive action.

- **Journaling—A Letter to Your Son or Daughter**

Direct teens to write a letter in their journals. Instruct them to:

> Pretend it is many, many years from now. You have a wonderful
> spouse and children. You have lived many fruitful, happy years.
> Write a letter to be delivered to your son, daughter, or children after
> your death. Write words to help them heal from their grief and to
> understand the value of loss. You may make it a letter written before
> you died or a letter from heaven, as you prefer.

- **Journaling—Composite Emotions: Activity Sheet 18.1**

As society progresses, old usages of words are modified. New words are
invented to reflect new understandings. New words also may reflect
consensually shared misunderstandings. This is especially true of the
words used to describe emotions.

Share Activity Sheet 18.1 with teens. Lead a discussion on the many
words that are disguises for and elaborations of our simple, raw
emotions of fear, anger, grief, and guilt. Then, have teens write in
their journals which of the composite emotions apply most personally
to them and why.

- **Small Group—The Two Brothers or Sisters**

Focus teens on the two paths of grief, destructive and constructive
identification. Direct them to tell the tale of *The Two Brothers* or *The
Two Sisters* in which one sibling takes one path and the other takes the
opposite path.

Stories may be written or oral. If oral, let teens one by one add
a sentence to the story. One may begin, "Once there were two people
in the same family who took very opposite paths after a loved one
died."

- **A Letter or Poem to a Friend or Relative**

Direct teens to write a letter or poem to a friend or relative who is
grieving. Instruct them to include in the writing what they have learned
about good grief that may be of help to the bereaved.

Teens whose families have experienced recent, actual losses may
write real letters or poems. Others may invent a loss and write what
they imagine they would say. Alternatively, they may choose a recently
departed celebrity with whom they had a particular attachment and
write what they imagine they would like to say to a surviving
loved one.

• **List of Feeling Words: Activity Sheet 16.1**

Invite teens to compose a poem or essay entitled *Desolation* about the time they felt most desolate. Direct them to use words from the third column of Activity Sheet 16.1.

• **Tissues for Your Issues**

By happy coincidence a box of tissues has a top, bottom, and four sides. As a project to be completed at home or in school, decorate a tissue box to celebrate our emotions. Each of the four sides bears one emotion as title: anger, fear, grief, guilt. On the bottom is placed, "Emotions I hide." On the top is placed, "Emotions I show." On these two panels one or more emotions may be chosen. Decoration is with construction paper, pictures, words cut from magazine titles or downloaded, and personal artwork.

The finished result is six mini-collages. This may be a quickly done project with a few words and one or two pictures on each side. But if done for health class, it may be a serious project that is graded as part of the class grade given for participation. Carefully done, creative boxes reflect more time and effort and therefore greater participation.

It is expected that teens will share observations on each other's boxes. This we want. When all participate, the overriding life lesson is that we all have these four fundamental uncomfortable emotions. We all have them. We show some of them. We hide others. We cry. We dry our tears. For teens who hesitate to name their hidden emotions even on the bottom of the box lest another teen turn the box over, they may present their hidden emotions in pictures only or, indeed, by color and shape only. When completed, each teen will own a tool which says, "When any emotion is very strong and painful, it's okay to cry. Have a tissue."

Happy Emotions: Activity Sheet 18.2

The Happy Emotions activity sheets may be used in parallel fashion to the other lists of feelings. See previous activities.

BULLETIN BOARD MATERIAL

Grief develops strength, empathy, and compassion.

Let morning bring you out of mourning for a while.

We thought to weep, but sing for joy instead …
For nothing but the weary dust is dead.
Louisa May Alcott[1]

Note

1 Known for her inspired book, *Little Women* (Boston, MA: Roberts Brothers, 1868), Louisa May Alcott (1832–1888) also published poetry, often under another name. The passage is in her poem of grief for her mother, *Transfiguration*, in *Louisa May Alcott: Her Life, Letters, and Journals*, E.D. Cheney (Ed.), in verse ten, pp. 263–4. Boston, MA: Little Brown & Co., 1898. Retrieved from www.gutenberg.org/files/38049/38049-h/38049-h.htm

Name: _____   Date: _____

Activity Sheet 18.1
DEFINITIONS OF COMPOSITE EMOTIONS

Upset   Often anger. Frequently fear and grief as well.
                "I feel upset" = "I feel emotion, but I don't want to tell myself what precisely it is I'm feeling."

Depressed   Anger turned inward. Grief. Fear and guilt. Severe depression is grief and guilt mixed with anger and fear.
                "It's too depressing" = "I am depressed."

Confused   Presence of more than one emotion at one time. Ask yourself, "What am I afraid about? Angry about? Sad about? Guilty about?"

Bad   Bad is not a feeling. "I feel bad" is used to indicate many emotions, like guilt, sadness, fear, anger as well as to refer to physical illness and fatigue.

Hurt   Anger, resentment, and grief turned inward. Some fear also may be present.

Distressed Anxiety or embarrassment or grief or irritation in combination. Also, a rough synonym for upset.

Sullen   Anger plus sadness.

Frustrated Anger plus the belief that one is unable to act.

Lonely   Fear, hurt, and sadness experienced in isolation. Frequently, grief and anger, too.

Dismay   Anxiety, fear, and disappointment.

Self-pity   Wallowing in anger over disappointment, guilt, and sadness.

Moody   Tendency to demonstrate emotions and to allow them to determine external behavior. Moody usually combines sadness with another emotion.

Pressured   A modern usage meaning fear and urgency.
                "I'm under so much pressure" = "I'm afraid I cannot meet what I perceive as urgent demands."

Stressed   Usually anger primarily and fear secondarily. May also indicate grief and guilt. Stressed out and stressing are modern synonyms for upset. Neither usage gives any information on the truth of what one is really feeling.

Attitude   Angry arrogance. Anger combined with aloof pride.
                A protective position to hide fear and hurt.

Name: _____ Date: _____

Activity Sheet 18.2, p. 1
HAPPY EMOTIONS

Mild	Moderate	Intense
cheerful	sunny	excited
courageous	brave	bold
animated	spirited	vivacious
happy	merry	bright
festive	joyous	ecstatic
curious	fascinated	engrossed
hardy	strong	robust
tender	affectionate	devoted
touching	poignant	stirring
exultant	overjoyed	euphoric
safe	secure	self-possessed
content	blithe	happy-go-lucky
grateful	appreciative	obliged
intent	avid	keen
assured	soothed	tranquil
interested	concerned	intrigued
earnest	determined	resolute
proud	magnificent	glorious
longing	sentimental	nostalgic
jolly	mirthful	jovial
glad	contented	complacent
hopeful	encouraged	eager
calm	composed	serene
silly	giddy	ridiculous
splendid	wonderful	fantastic
playful	frisky	jaunty
free	independent	self-reliant
fine	splendid	sublime
romantic	amorous	passionate
fanciful	flighty	frivolous
quiet	peaceful	placid

Name: _____   Date: _____

Activity Sheet 18.2, p. 2
HAPPY EMOTIONS

Mild	Moderate	Intense
pleasant	comfortable	cozy
reassured	comforted	forgiving
earnest	fervent	vehement
warm	cheery	lighthearted
excited	electrified	delirious
motivated	heartened	inspired
firm	steady	unwavering
emotional	mushy	maudlin
delighted	enthralled	blissful
merry	buoyant	jovial
elated	exuberant	jubilant
aghast	astonished	stunned
friendly	genial	affable
pleased	satisfied	fulfilled
close	affectionate	loving
kind	tender	compassionate
sensual	sexy	erotic
playful	whimsical	capricious
joyful	elated	delighted
trusting	confident	certain
ardent	enthusiastic	zealous
lively	energetic	high-spirited
raving	effervescing	gushing
invigorated	exhilarated	rejuvenated
thrilled	enchanted	rapturous
startled	surprised	shocked

19 Guilt, the Unappreciated Emotion

Whereas anger, fear, and grief are wired fast and hard into our brains, guilt is something we learn. We learn the specifics of what to be angry or scared or sad about, but the raw, visceral emotional underpinnings we are born with. Guilt is different. If it were not, there never would have been any such thing as a serial killer or school shooter. Grieving, we wish these murderers would have learned to feel guilty and ashamed. They did not.

A discussion of guilt necessarily tiptoes into the territory of values. When we fail to live up to a chosen value, we feel guilty. Values education, however, is a separate parallel field and possibly a separate curriculum. But an explication of guilt must necessarily consider values.

Guilt is an internal reaction to failed expectations. What we learn to say "should" to ourselves about underlies our guilt. Thus, *should* self-talk has a central role in the felt experience of guilt. A tool to teach constructive guilt management is making and using a should list.

Guilt is certainly a peculiar emotion. Guilt is our invention. We invented it long ago when we invented the word "should" and came into collective agreement about the meaning of the word. Guilt is felt when one does not live up to the expectations of one's moral code as one *should*. We know our expectations by our self-talk, as in "I should do this. I should not do that."

Display the following diagram.

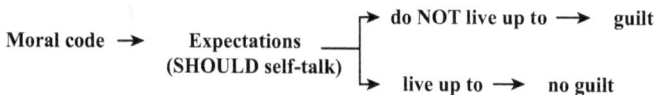

```
                                      ┌─→  do NOT live up to  ─→   guilt
  Moral code  ─→    Expectations  ────┤
                    (SHOULD self-talk) └─→  live up to  ─→   no guilt
```

The validity of one's guilt, then, stems ultimately from the validity of one's moral code. Defining an appropriate moral code is beyond our present scope. We have been debating just what an appropriate moral code is since at least the time of Hammurabi, probably much earlier.[1] Here we simply examine our collective beliefs about "shoulds" and "should nots" and how values are learned.

Valid guilt derives from the recognition that one has failed to live up to one's own, freely chosen code. Though valid guilt cannot be imposed from outside, what to feel guilty about must be taught and internalized. Valid guilt is keen disappointment in oneself for not being true to a code one has chosen and believes in. Valid guilt is healthy guilt. It is a plausible drop in self-esteem due to a mistake, an error in judgment, a temporary failing, even though a serious mistake.

Healthy guilt is the mother of humility. No one is perfect. No one lives up to their moral code 100 percent of the time. Valid, healthy guilt spurs us to resolve to do better in the future. Healthy guilt is temporary and far from paralyzing. Valid guilt is the response of a healthy ego that does not come undone by disappointment in self.

But of all the qualities that mark healthy guilt and distinguish it from invalid guilt, the most singular is self-forgiveness. In healthy guilt we forgive ourselves and move on. In unhealthy, invalid guilt we do not. Unhealthy guilt feeds on secret pride. We can't believe we did what we did. How could our actions have been so bad? Our pride, our self-esteem, is crushed.

	Valid Guilt	Invalid Guilt
Moral Code	Freely chosen and internalized	Imposed by authority and uncritically accepted
Expectations	Reasonable	Unreasonable
Should means	Is constructive Is profitable Is helpful	An unconditional, absolute MUST
Disappointment	In a mistake	In a terrible moral failure
Drop in self-esteem	Plausible and temporary	Paralyzing and enduring
Ego	Healthy	Unhealthy
Self-forgiveness	Yes	No
Moral quality	Humility	Pride
Outcome	A better human being	An emotional shell Drug/alcohol abuse

The very act of forgiving ourselves is felt as an admission that we are less than we would like to believe. When self-identity is uniquely tied to the belief one is a good person, then recognition of bad behavior is a devastating blow to ego. Then invalid guilt may paralyze us with disappointment.

What becomes clear from the listing on p. 225 is that true, valid guilt has little in common with invalid guilt except for the name. Invalid guilt is a tragic distortion of healthy guilt, even as cancer is a distortion of the normal process of cell growth.

Guilt may be addressed in the same manner as all emotions. It may be relieved by following the three basic steps of constructive emotional expression. Display the following.

> **A. Allow the guilt. Admit and accept it.**
> **B. Be with the guilt. Feel it. Breathe.**
> **C. Channel the guilt. Take action. Choose.**

Internalization of Expectations

In the case of unreasonable guilt, the action to be taken usually must include some type of revision of expectations. Sometimes an individual is able to do this alone. But often when expectations are tied into a rigid moral code learned in childhood, talking with parents, teachers, and friends is necessary to sort things out. For some, counseling with a member of the clergy may prove helpful. Add the following to the A, B, C diagram.

> **C. Channel the guilt. Take action.**
> **Explore and change expectations.**
> **Change behavior.**
> **Above all forgive yourself.**

Expectations have a central role in the formation of guilt. In fact, expectation is just another way of talking about what we should or ought to do. "I expect you to do your homework" conveys "You should do your homework."

Somewhere along the line in the twentieth century guilt got a bad name. The connection between expectations and guilt was either not understood or was ignored. Guilt as a process of the human mind is not inherently bad. Yet, "You said that just to make me feel guilty" became a sharp accusation. You may have also heard someone say, "I don't go to church. They just want to make you feel guilty." Failure to comprehend the positive function of guilt has led to tragic consequences. In working with teens who seem sad or sullen, always consider the possibility that some guilt may be weighing on their minds.

Guilt may be a burden that will not be disclosed unless you ask.

Guilt is the necessary inner prod to correcting inappropriate behavior. Guilt is a type of sorrow over loss of one's good self. Its purpose is to prod us to correct the behavior. Its purpose is to drive us to be our best self. Healthy guilt is not feeling bad about ourselves just to feel bad. Healthy guilt is feeling just bad enough to actively change the behavior about which we are guilty.

Expectations are meaningful when they are clear and forcefully stated. The tragedy of the present day is that too many are being raised with little or no expectations of what is and what is not appropriate behavior. When teens have heard few shoulds that define appropriate behavior, they have nothing to internalize. There will be no guilt because nothing has been internalized.

Many values may be used as examples, but I'll center on ones about which I believe we may all agree. From before the time of the Code of Hammurabi, an injunction came into Western civilization. It has come down to us expressed simply in four words, "Thou shalt not kill."

In modern translation this is "You will not kill." Traditionally, we first heard someone say, "Thou shalt not kill." We heard you will not kill. Do not kill. It was a simple, direct, explicit, forceful message.

Whoever first gave the message understood something about human psychology that many today do not. First we hear a message from the outside. We hear it with the pronoun you, you should or you should not. Then over time the brain itself flips the pronoun. You becomes I. What I heard as "you should not," I now say in my head as "I will not." I heard "You will not kill" often enough to internalize "I will not kill."

This is called the formation of a conscience. It is a natural process as old as the ancients before Hammurabi. It is a process that depends on guilt for it to work. The process begins with the messages given. Do not kill. Do not hurt others. Do be kind. Do not lie. Tell the truth. Give to others. Do not steal.

Notice that each injunction is short, to the point. Such short statements the brain easily internalizes. The brain takes time to digest books and chapters and verses. But it readily digests short, definitive injunctions. It does so because of its ability to flip the pronoun that begins the sentence.

How many teens in your school system have internalized the injunction, "You will not kill"? If one has not, there is no guilt upon which you may rely to serve as a check on that teen's violent behavior. If after a school shooting that teen acts like they've done nothing wrong, adults must understand that inside that teen's head is no "I will not kill" self-talk. When those explicit words are not internalized, guilt cannot exist.

In my experience with parents and educators, many adults either fail to give clear and strong injunctions to the next generation or do so with mild words. Perhaps we feel we are preventing our youngsters from feeling the painful guilt we may have suffered. For example, the directive to the toddler "It's not nice to hit" substitutes for "Do not hit!" This conveys to the brain "On any given day of your life that you want to be nice, don't hit. On the other hand, if you're not feeling nice, hit." The child's brain internalizes what the adults say.

High school is not too late to communicate uncompromising values with uncompromising speech. Let "You will not!" be heard in school corridors more and more. The bully must hear an uncompromising "*You will not* speak to another student that way" instead of "It's not kind to talk to people like that."

The teen you know who has a history of lying needs to hear "You will not lie to me." Yes, their next sentence may be another lie, but that is not the point. The point is you have four years to nurture their brain into internalizing "I will not lie." A forceful "You will not lie to me" conveys "I have faith in you that you have the ability to tell the truth." If a teen feels or even remotely senses this faith and still lies, guilt and perhaps sadness will follow. Maybe not that day, maybe not the next time that teen is in your office, maybe years later when high school is a memory, a nagging voice in the head that sounds suspiciously like the vice-principal's will whisper, "I will not lie." And the truth will follow. What is absolutely certain is that if the teen never hears the firm, direct, uncompromising directive "Do not lie," they have a poor chance of internalizing that value.

The same is true about "Do not hit" and "Do not harm others." Whether spoken to a toddler or a teenager, the method must support what the brain does naturally. If the words are yelled, if the look on the shouter's face is a frightening scowl, then all the youngster hears is the anger. The visage that fills their field of vision frightens them, perhaps markedly so. The brain will be too busy processing these emotions to complete the internalization process.

Rather, words spoken in a tone just below conversational in a clear, declarative manner have the most chance of being internalized. With an assured but compassionate look on your face, speak the directive slowly as you pause ever so slightly between words. As you continue to deliver the same message with the same exact words after each transgression, move closer to the youngster, ask for eye contact, and whether or not you get it, drop your tone of voice to just above a whisper. Repeat the same words. Don't confuse the brain with a sermon or lecture. Get clear in your own mind about what value you wish to impart, choose the words to teach it, and repeat those words frequently. If all toddlers and children were raised this way, the behavior of our teens would reflect their internalization of the values so taught.

High school offers four years of intensive remedial inculcation of values for those who need it. Teach your young people that feeling guilty about doing the wrong thing is a good thing. Recognizing the guilt is the first step in moving on through the A, B, C steps. In this case, that last step means changing the unacceptable behavior.

- **Journaling—Should List**

Direct teens, "At the top of a page in your journal write the title *Should List*. Write out a list of your should self-talk. For example, 'I should do my homework,' 'People should like me,' and 'No one should hurt another person.'" If necessary, have teens verbally share items on their lists in order to help others get ideas.

Next direct teens to number each should. Then, using the same numbers but on a separate page in the notebook, teens write the translation of the should.

At the top of that page is the title, *Translation of Shoulds*. Number by number, change the wording of each should statement to make clear what the should is really saying. So, "I should do my homework" means "It would be constructive for me to do my homework." "People should like me" becomes "It would be helpful and nice if people liked me." "No one should hurt another person" is acceptable as is for it reflects consensual values.

Most shoulds may be translated with variations of "is constructive," "is profitable," "is helpful," and synonyms thereof. Explain that if no constructive translation readily comes to mind, one must then rethink the item. Is it genuinely advantageous? Is it a should one should have? To get teens to think, offer exaggerations like "Everyone should like me" and "I should only get As."

The list on p. 230 may be displayed.

- **Incomplete Sentences Using Activity Sheet 16.2**

Direct teens to refer to the columns of guilt words on Activity Sheet 16.2 for this exercise. Teens write ten sentences that begin "I feel _____ when …" with the blank filled in with one of the guilt words. Each sentence is to use a different guilt word, e.g., I feel sorry when …, I feel ashamed when …, I feel humiliated when …. Sentences may be shared in class or in small groups as appropriate.

Synonyms for Constructive Shoulding		
The word *should* should mean:		
Is constructive	**Is profitable**	**Is helpful**
effective	fruitful	supportive
practical	gainful	useful
productive	lucrative	beneficial
advantageous	favorable	conducive to
valuable	rewarding	worthwhile

• **How I'll Handle Guilt**

Decide before beginning the activity whether or not it will be shared. The activity may be done twice, the first time for sharing in class, the second time for sharing only with the health teacher or a school counselor. Doing the incomplete sentences activity, above, before this one may be helpful. Just raising the subject of guilt silently invites teens who need help to self-refer themselves to the counselor's office.

Instruct teens to think of something they feel guilty about. If some have nothing they now feel guilty about, they are to think about something they have felt guilty about in the past and pretend they're still feeling guilty. If a group of older teens is resistant, coax them with "Well, what about when you were a little kid? You must have done something you felt guilty about!" Apply the elements of step C, channel the guilt. Present the following questions to focus helpful responses.

Handling Guilt
• **What constructive action will you take?**
• **What expectations will you change?**
• **What self-talk will you change?**
• **What new self-talk will you use? List it.**
• **By what actions will you *show* you forgive yourself?**

• **Decisions, Not Emotions: Activity Sheets 19.1 and 19.2**

Teens' fund of knowledge about emotions is now at a maximum. They may enjoy discussing and debating Activity Sheets 19.1 and 19.2. Modern language allows for a very careless mixing and meshing of *affective* and *cognitive* concepts. Such language usage leads us to confuse emotions, the feeling process, with decisions, a mental process.

BULLETIN BOARD MATERIAL

What shoulds should you do?

Guilt is a prod to constructive action.

I have learned that success is to be measured
not so much by the position that one has reached in life
as by the obstacles which he has overcome while trying to succeed.

Booker T. Washington[2]

Notes

1 Hammurabi ruled circa 1750 BC. A succinct summary of his Code is at http://chnm.gmu.edu/worldhistorysources/d/267/whm.html If you want to see how the Babylonians handled their rebellious teens, see laws 168 and 169 in the translation at http://avalon.law.yale.edu/ancient/hamframe.asp
2 Retrieved from *Up From Slavery: An Autobiography* (first published as a serial, 1900–1901) online at www.gutenberg.org/files/2376/2376-h/2376-h.htm Release date October 20, 2008. In this short book, Washington (1856–1915) dispassionately describes his life from slavery to freedom to leadership. His compassionate life is direct confutation to any angry "I can't help it. He made me mad. It's his fault" oppositional teen who after instruction in authentic emotionality still insists that circumstances cause emotion. Whether assigned by school psychologist or counselor or by social studies teacher, the reading of this book, its conveniently sectioned parts perhaps discussed in small groups, is both counseling and history lesson that irrefutably affirms that we are indeed not disturbed by events but by the view we take of them.

Activity Sheet 19.1
DECISIONS, NOT EMOTIONS

Unaccceptable Decisions

Despair:	The belief that the situation is hopeless coupled with the decision not to try to improve things.
	"I'm tired of trying" = "I've allowed my uncomfortable emotions to so overwhelm me that I have little energy to think and act constructively."
Stubbornness:	The decision to protect one's ego interests at all costs. The inflation of ego.
Hatred:	The decision to project anger outward in actual hostile acts.
	"I hate you!" = "I'm furious!"
Revenge:	The decision to act on hatred and anger over some wrong or hurt, real or imagined. Aggression.
Prejudice:	The decision to project fear outward in anger.
Worthlessness:	The decision to believe that one is worth nothing.
	"I can't do anything right" = "I have a belief that I can't do anything right, and I feel sad, scared, and angry about it."
Boredom:	The decision to believe that other people or external things are responsible for one's entertainment and stimulation. Life is not boring. Ask any two-year-old. "You're boring" = "Don't you know that on this planet you're supposed to entertain me?"
	"It's boring" = "My judgment is that this does not interest or stimulate me."
Loneliness:	The belief that one is disconnected from people. Lonely is a sad feeling, but continued loneliness is a choice, a decision.
Apathy:	The decision to hold onto hurt and anger because others, in your judgment, are not interested in you.
	"I don't care" = "It hurts too much to care."
	"It doesn't matter" = "I have a belief that I don't matter, and since I don't, nothing else does."
Greed:	The decision to interpret external things such as money, position, and people as necessary extensions of ego. Easy, convenient ego inflation is a denial of and defense against fear.

Name: _____ Date: _____

Activity Sheet 19.2
DECISIONS, NOT EMOTIONS
Constructive Decisions

Understood:	The belief that someone else has heard, listened to, and given compassionate empathy for one's emotions.
Empathy:	The decision to feel with another and to understand their emotions. Feeling another's emotions as they do. Apathy and noninvolvement are opposites.
Forgiveness:	The decision to release hurt and anger. "I forgive you, but I won't forget" = "Intellectually, I pardon you, but I'm hanging onto my hurt and anger." The opposite of forgiveness is resentment.
Faith:	The decision to trust what cannot be seen or felt. The decision to suspend judgment long enough to allow oneself to experience that which is believed. For example, to believe in a person is to suspend judgment long enough to allow oneself to experience that person as trustworthy and worthwhile. Faith is given. Trust is earned. The opposite of faith is passing judgment.
Hope:	The decision to live with expectation and anticipation. The choice and conviction that life is worth living. Opposites: hopelessness, despair.
Trust:	The decision to believe that another person is reliable and honest. Opposite: suspicion.

LOVE

Compassion:	The decision to act to allay someone else's hurt or pain. Compassion is love in action.
Tolerance:	The decision to suspend judgment and value others as worthy human beings. Tolerance may take faith.
Humility:	The decision to accept all as interdependent and equal with none higher or lower than the rest.
Vs. Egoism:	The decision expressed in words and deeds to value the thoughts and feelings of others as highly as one's own.
Vs. Apathy:	The decision to express affectionate concern or devotion. Genuine love cannot be uninvolved.
Vs. Hostility:	The decision to act with empathy, benevolence, fairness, goodness, kindness, and helpfulness.

Conclusion
Cries of Joy

Moving away from old but common misunderstandings about emotions will be a decades-long process. Old beliefs die hard. The difficulty is more with us, the adults, than with our teens. Being children, for we know that they are, they are much closer to their emotions than adults well practiced in the denial of emotion. It is to be expected that it will be literally easier to teach our teens emotional openness than to learn it ourselves.

When a teen you love or care about comes back at you with "Oh, you're in denial" and your heart breaks because you know they have spoken the truth, rejoice. Rejoice and answer, "I'll think about that" and not the ancient, "No, I'm not!" Rejoice because if you have taught them about emotions, they will speak their feelings with you and brook no opposition in attacking *your* denial, rationalization, intellectualization, displacement, and projection. Get ready. Be ready for teens with refined emotional intelligence to unleash that intelligence on you.

For they will not operate from the position that the truths we have taught them about emotions apply only to them. Oh, no. They will reflect those truths back to us with abandon and probably with cutting accuracy. Let us make up our minds in advance that we are big enough to take it. When the day comes when we experience teens as living examples of emotional authenticity, let us rejoice. Let us then high-five each other in our minds and relish the feeling of victory.

When you are moody or mired in depression, be ready for some teen to remind you that emotions flow like water in a wavelike flux of ebb and flow. Prepare, as they will proceed to walk you through the A, B, Cs of constructive emotional expression and helpfully inquire, "What are you angry about?" When they so engage, your answers best be more than "Leave me alone" and "I don't want to talk."

The mysterious, fascinating, and puzzling dimension of emotions is about to get a makeover. In the modern age we may no longer allow ourselves to be ignorant of emotions and how they work inside us. If we teach our young people to accurately name and constructively express our most challenging emotions of anger, fear, grief, and guilt, then we ourselves must prepare to do the same.

As we enter the age of emotional literacy, our already well-programmed adult brains will resist. So here's a hint. Stay in step B. Breathe. Stay in step B much longer than your teens will need to do. Breathe, meditate or learn yoga, walk, exercise. Brains fixed in old habits need time to learn new ones. Expect your brain to fight you as you strive to learn these principles yourself. Consider your age. How many decades have you been practicing telling your brain not to inform you of your emotions? How many times in your life have you used the words upset, stressed, pressured, overwhelmed, depressed?

Consider the dilemma we are presenting our brains. "Listen, human, for decades you've been telling me you didn't want to know. You have purposely used vague and global language that tells me nothing about your genuine emotions. And now, now you want me to reverse all this?" Yes, I'm afraid Brainy Boo is going to be mad at us for a while. The neurons won't know when to fire and where to fire. Expect this.

Expect it and admit it to your teens. "I'm learning, too. You guys will learn this much faster than my old brain." It's true. Foster your own progress by using our special adult Help Talk like "I can do this. If my 14-year-olds are learning to do this, I can do it." Be with the emotion. Feel it. Breathe. Commiserate with your brain. "Listen, Brainy Boo, you know the pain I put you through. I'm commanding you now. Denial is over. Over, over, over. If kids can learn to be emotionally authentic, you, Brainy, can, too."

Dance around the classroom with a long line of teens trailing behind as you chant "I'm celebrating my emotions, my emotions, my emotions." Spin and twirl as you loudly chant "I'm mad!" with a fist jabbing at the heavens. Then with one hand partially covering your face, croon "I'm scared!" Whirl again and in low tones whisper "I'm sad, I'm sad, I'm so sad" as one finger flicks imaginary tears from your face. Fingertips lightly over your guilty lips turn to the person behind you and murmur "I'm sorry." Dare to be so expressive and your teens will soon be leading you. Equally as important, with every step and cry you will be advising your own brain "This is the way now. Get with the program, Brainy Boo, because we're not going back." Part of channeling emotion is informing your brain of your decision to do so and insisting that your brain comply.

Retrain your own brain the same way you teach. Build your own emotional literacy with words and images. The words are the new self-talk you choose. With those words pair visuals. Draw a picture for your poor, beleaguered brain. Those images are whatever visuals have meaning for you. Choose your verbal and nonverbal modes of emotional expression. When stuck, observe your teens. They will show you that emotional expression comes naturally.

Only with much practice do we learn to stifle the development of our emotional intelligence. If you have been practicing doing so for many decades, you have probably gotten quite good at it. You are also probably in a great deal of pain. Relief from emotional pain is in the pain. Reverse course. It is never too late to let the brain operate as it was intended to function. If you have been practicing emotional repression for less than four decades, you are most fortunate. Your brain will have less rewiring to do. If you are among the fortunate few whose parents understood emotions and were ahead of their time, say your prayer of gratitude and resolve to share your good fortune with all the teens you touch.

In my experience, adults fail to help themselves by making the transition into emotional authenticity overly complex. I call this complexifying. Educated people whose brains are chock full of three- and four-syllable words most dearly insist on using those words to describe and define and detail their emotions. This is **complexifying**, a special adult branch of intellectualization teens have not yet learned. Complexify and you'll be 90 before you know your emotions, if then.

Alcoholics Anonymous has gifted us with many brilliant sayings, like One Day At A Time. For combating complexifying, nothing beats Keep It Simple. Do not punish yourself by committing yourself to a three-day retreat or workshop to, as we adults love to say, "figure out my emotions." You will only complexify yourself into misery.

Keep it simple. Ask yourself four questions. What am I mad about? What scares me? What am I sad about? What am I guilty about? You may answer those four questions for yourself in a half hour sitting in the corner of a coffee shop. Then elaborate if you must. To gain more clarity, stare at the Decisions, Not Emotions lists on Activity sheets 19.1 and 19.2. Be honest with yourself about what decisions have led you into which emotions. That's another half hour. Emotional honesty is worth one hour of your life.

Be gentle and firm with yourself at the same time. Be gentle in accepting that the age, the century from which you come, did not teach you how to be emotionally authentic. If your self-talk muses on forgiveness, ponder whether ignorance needs forgiveness. How is it possible to forgive those who did not know for not teaching us to know? How is it possible to forgive those who did not know for not teaching us how to know?

But also be firm with yourself. Spend not a moment lamenting that you did not learn about fear or anger when you were 4 or 14. If you are now committed to emotional openness, you have the entire rest of your life to practice it. Working in a high school with our teens, it is your special privilege to join with others to build generations of emotionally honest, emotionally intelligent individuals. So be patient with your Brainy Boo, but at the same time uncompromisingly insistent your brain will embrace the same knowledge you teach your teens.

Think of those teens you teach or counsel or work with. How are you most like them? What do you both have to learn or improve upon? Whatever comes to your mind, pick that to work on first. Let's say it's the emotion anger. As you share with your teens the unit on anger, whether in the classroom or in counseling, rejoice that you are learning about anger, too.

In the wider society, only healthy emotions may provide a check on the excesses and errors of so-called reason. Such invalid reason is the reasoning distorted by anger, fear, and grief that history has repeatedly shown. Most disastrously, the holocaust of World War II reveals the depths to which invalid reasoning may take us. In such horrors, reason operating through a filter of distorted emotions becomes far from reasonable.[1] When we claim our own anger and fear, there is none left to project outside of ourselves onto a designated enemy. We may long have enemies. But the probability we will respond reasonably and rationally is heightened by owning our own anger and fear, not by denying it and projecting it.

Emotions are intrinsic and essential facets of our humanity. We may heal our epidemic ignorance about emotions. High schools are excellent venues for developing emotional literacy. Teens have a reputation for moodiness. Their emotions are often on the surface. They are also curious with brains rapidly developing in reasoning power. This juncture of reason and emotion is the perfect ground for developing emotional intelligence.

Living a life that constructively addresses the full scope of emotional pain releases the full power of positive potential, also. There is no courage without fear. Determination feeds on anger, on just enough anger to move us to endure with tenacity. Righteous anger transforms nations and individuals for the good. Compassion and empathy proceed from grief. Healthy guilt drives us to our knees so that we may stand again as better human beings.

My parting gift for you, for both the adult you and Brainy Boo, is contemplation of our highest human emotions, our peak emotions. May you experience them before you are 90.

BULLETIN BOARD MATERIAL

To love your life, live love.

… to make knowledge valuable,
you must have the cheerfulness of wisdom….
The joy of the spirit indicates its strength.
Emerson[2]

Notes

1 The multisyllabic word that names the absolute opposite of emotional intelligence is *alexithymia*, which may be translated "no words for emotions" or "no words from the heart." And, not to worry, if you've read this far, you don't have it.

2 Emerson, R.W. (1871). *The Conduct of Life* (*op. cit.*). Retrieved from section VII, *Considerations by the Way*, paragraph 15, online at www.gutenberg.org/license

Name: _____ Date: _____

Activity Sheet 20.1
PEAK EMOTIONS

Constructive decisions do not always have comfortable emotions attached. Empathy for someone else's pain hurts. Faith may feel like a fog of darkness. Hope is often purely mental. Trust frequently feels very frightening. Love in action may be devoid of good, sweet feelings.

But in those rare and precious life moments when the thinking and feeling parts of emotion mesh with the spiritual, the highest of human emotions are felt.

Six Peak Emotions	The Emotion Produces Feelings Of
Empathy	Whatever the other is feeling. Full attunement with another. Compassionate love.
Forgiveness	Peace. Relief. Release from hurt and anger.
Faith	Serenity. Absence of fear. Feeling safe and protected.
Hope	Enthusiasm. Eagerness. Pleasure of anticipation. Feeling a future joy in the present.
Trust	Confidence. Assurance. Confident expectation.
Love	Joy. Delight. Warmth. Interest. Attraction. Satisfaction. The pleasure of connection and union.

Glossary

bigotry   intolerant zeal for an irrational opinion. Fear and anger expressed as thinking.

challenging emotions   synonym for the uncomfortable emotions.

comfortable emotions   emotions that feel good, like joy, surprise, and excitement.

community   herein used to name the developmental task that parallels individuation. The building of one's place in and connectedness to social groups. What both obsesses the teen mind and breaks their hearts.

compassion   the active part of empathy shown in acts of love and goodwill.

complexifying   the intellectualization educated people show in profuse use of three- and four-syllable words. Making an inherently simple emotion complex in order to avoid feeling that emotion.

courage   feeling fear but taking constructive action anyway.

defense mechanism   a psychological process whereby the mind attempts to protect the ego from uncomfortable emotions. Denial of the felt experience of emotion.

determination   resolute action of tenacious steadfastness. A decision that uses visceral emotion to positive end. It uses self-talk like "I can. I will. I must. Do it. I can. I will."

diaphragmatic breathing   slow, deep breaths in which the diaphragm pushes down and out so that all three lobes of each lung fill with air.

displacement   the psychological defense mechanism in which emotion comes out sideways. Emotion shown removed from its emotion-generating context.

emotional dysregulation   emotional expressions that are poorly regulated. The use of defense mechanisms to avoid the felt visceral experience of the pain of uncomfortable emotions.

ego   the sense of who one is. Self-identity. The mental self. Herein visualized as castle walls. What teens are working overtime on forming.

emotional quotient   a measure of emotional intelligence, abbreviated EQ.

empathy   emotional sensitivity to another's feelings.

empowerment   self-talk and emotion that support anger constructively used. A function of healthy ego that has learned to convert anger into determination.

feeling part of emotion   the physiological sensations and bodily impact of emotion due to changes in hormones and neurotransmitters.

garbage self-talk   cognitive distortions. A useful term with teens to emphasize errors in thinking replete with highly personalized exaggerations and inaccuracies in reasoning.

hatred   hostile action taken with malice aforethought. Projecting anger outward instead of owning it within self.

Help Talk   purposely chosen self-talk to help you accept, breathe, and positively express uncomfortable emotion. Example: "I'll be okay. I'm feeling strong emotion. Breathe!"

hostility   animosity actively expressed. Anger converted to destruction.

identification   self-identity tied into another person, place, or thing. Also, the healing process in grief whereby the loss is incorporated into self.

I language   a statement, particularly about emotion, that begins with the word, I. Example: "I am angry because…" in place of "You make me mad."

individuation   a central psychological task of adolescence. The building of individual identity. What frightens, excites, and angers teens continuously.

insecurity   the fear created by believing one is not safe or secure.

intellectualization   the thinking about emotion in order not to feel the visceral emotion. Using words to think and think the emotion in an attempt to escape feeling it.

prejudice   fear projected outward in anger.

projection   the psychological defense mechanism of applying to another person feelings and beliefs within oneself.

rationalization   a so-called logical excuse for an emotion-based decision. Using words to deny and deflect the visceral experience, not simple excuse-making.

reframing   changing negative self-talk to more appropriate and helpful self-talk.

repression   defense mechanism in which the mind forgets uncomfortable emotions in order to avoid feeling emotional pain. Repressed emotion drives much dysregulated behavior.

righteous anger   anger directed with determination to create positive, just, and equitable outcomes

self-talk   what you say to yourself in your head about yourself and your world.

sympathy   mental commiseration.

Talk It Out   the process of experiencing emotion and affectively expressing it with words.

thinking part of emotion the cognitive correlate of emotion including the Before Self-talk and the After Self-talk. In a word, self-talk.

uncomfortable emotions primarily anger, fear, grief, guilt.

upsetness a useful word to force us to focus on the failure of the word, upset, to name emotion.

verbal hostility cursing, swearing, name-calling, put-downs. A form of verbal abuse that demonstrates the emotional dysregulation of the abuser.

visceral emotion the raw, direct physiological sensations of emotion driven by hormones and neurotransmitters. What emotional intelligence demands we learn to direct well.

Index

For Product Safety Concerns and Information please contact our EU
representative GPSR@taylorandfrancis.com
Taylor & Francis Verlag GmbH, Kaufingerstraße 24, 80331 München, Germany

www.ingramcontent.com/pod-product-compliance
Lightning Source LLC
Chambersburg PA
CBHW050636280326
41932CB00015B/2673

9 780367 175528